Other books by Mel London

Getting Into Film
Easy Going
Second Spring

With Sheryl London

The Fish-Lovers' Cookbook
Sheryl and Mel London's Creative
    Cooking with Grains and Pasta

The BREAD WINNERS COOKBOOK

Forty-five remarkable bread bakers share 200 of their favorite recipes—all made with natural ingredients.

by Mel London

Editor:

Charles Gerras

Design:

Marvin Simmons and K. A. Schell

Line Drawings:

Donald Breter

Color Photography:

Carl Doney

Additional Photography:

Mitchell T. Mandel

Photography Food Stylist:

Laura Hendry

A Fireside Book
Published by Simon and Schuster
New York

Previously published as *Bread Winners*

Designed by Marvin Simmons and K. A. Schell

Manufactured in the United States of America

1 2 3 4 5 6 7 8 9 10 Pbk.

ISBN: 0-671-47051-5 Pbk.

Edited by Charles Gerras
Line Drawings by Donald Breter
Color Photography by Carl Doney
Additional Photography by Mitchell T. Mandel
Photography Food Stylist: Laura Hendry

To SHERYL

who is the butter on the warm bread of life. . .

and to GEORGE MELUSO

who taught me how to bake my first loaf and started me on a
lifetime of pleasure.

Acknowledgments

My gratitude is, first of all, given to Carol Everingham, who researched, probed, spent long hours on the telephone, discovered new Bread Winners and even tested some of the recipes herself. Her devotion and enthusiasm over this last year have kept a perpetual smile on my face.

To the people of the Rodale Test Kitchens, who tested every bread in the book and, in turn, kept perpetual smiles on the faces of the Rodale staff by offering them a taste of breads fresh from the oven each day: Faye Martin, Anita Hirsch, Beth Correll, Diana Reitnauer, and Susan Hercek.

Our appreciation to La Belle Cuisine Fine Cookware, 36 South 9th Street, Allentown, Pennsylvania 18102, for lending us equipment essential for testing and photographs.

Thanks to Art Director Karen Schell, who cheerfully and efficiently rode herd on the overall graphics of this book.

Proofreaders Dolores Plikaitis and Ann Snyder accepted the challenge of analyzing over 240 recipes from 45 different bakers for any stylistic quirks I might have missed. For their unflagging thoroughness, I am in their debt.

To the friends, old and new, who joined in the search for interesting and unusual Bread Winners: Peg Moore, Owen Hallberg, Eve Gentry, Lois Reamy, Caryl Litzenberger, and Robert Gutter.

And to Barb Venable and the *Alamosa National Valley Courier* in Colorado; Jack Zaleski and the *Devil's Lake Daily Journal* in North Dakota; Jane Schroeder of the Extension Service in Redmond, Oregon; Barbara Gibbs Ostmann and the *St. Louis Post-Dispatch;* Herb Lippert of the Extension Service at Timber Lake, South Dakota; Andrea Diehl and the *Philadelphia Daily News;* Donna Lee and the *Boston Herald American;* Renee Peck and the *New Orleans States-Item;* Glady Nelson of the Baldwin Extension Service at Bay Minett, Alabama; Glenda Duckworth of the Lyon County Cooperative Extension Service in Yerington, Nevada; Ethel Louise Prince of Vincennes, Indiana; Janet Weaver and the

Iron County Record of Cedar City, Utah; Margaret Nofziger of The Farm, as well as the *Columbia Daily Herald* in Tennessee; and Nancy Pappas of the *Louisville Times*.

And most important of all, I have been twice blessed through the writing of two books. My first editor was all that a new author could ask for. The lightning of good fortune struck twice when I met Charles Gerras, my editor for *Bread Winners*. His support, his encouragement, and his delight through every step of the long process have changed a working relationship into a deep and loving friendship. He has my heartfelt thanks.

Contents

**The Saga of
Sourdough**

The Treat of Triticale — 210

By Way of Introduction 1

We live on an island a part of the year. It is our escape, our vacation home, our Christmas through New Year's retreat. In the summer it hums with activity, the beaches filled, the children riding their bikes on the wooden walks, the pines and the dunes glorious under the sun. There are no cars.

In the winter it becomes still and awesomely beautiful. Deer appear on the dune ridges. The snow falls and makes accordion pleats on the walks. The ocean becomes angry and then placid. And there are only 14 families to contrast with summer's booming population.

On the island, time expands to meet the job to be done. There is no hurry. The city has been left far behind. It was here that I began to bake bread. And it was here that an unusual Christmas tradition began.

Each year, on the day before Christmas, I bake 15 breads. Each Christmas morning I wrap them in foil, decorate them with a sprig of island-grown holly and set off on my bike, dragging a wagon, to deliver the home-baked gifts, a small note attached telling the recipient just what kind of bread it is, and how it can be used, warmed or frozen. For years now, these 14 breads have been delivered (one is, of course, kept for us)—and they have become an island tradition, spoken of to the "summer people" and discussed at the village store when it finally opens in early spring.

A few years ago it was an Irish Soda Bread, followed by a Mennonite Pumpkin Bread and a Mexican *Jalapeno* Hot Pepper Corn Bread, and then an Italian Whole Wheat Bread. This past year, walking through the doors of the cozy, decorated homes at Christmastime, I was greeted with, "What is it this year?" And this year it was a Spoonhandle Sourdough Rye (see Index).

Over the years, the interest in bread has developed on our island—just as it has throughout the entire country. People everywhere have begun to tire of the commercial substitute for wholesome, delicious, nourishing breads. Bit by bit, I began to collect a strange and wonderful collection of "students." Would I teach them to bake bread? Does it take much time? Would I telephone the next time I bake so that they might come and watch?

My informal classes have, at one time or another, included a 15-year-old high school student, a psychiatrist, an interior decorator, a pathologist, and an editor of a fashion magazine.

My favorite memory is one of my friend, Mike, all 230 pounds of him, kneeling on the floor and looking into the oven, his butt high in the air as he watched the breads rise through the oven glass. Mike is the president of a wholesale food firm. He, too, is a bread baker.

But the idea for the book flourished when I began to speak to people all over the country. My business trips are many. As a filmmaker I travel almost two hundred thousand miles a year and I have found bread bakers everywhere, in every section of the United States. Bit by bit, I added *their* recipes to my files—from Montana and California, Minnesota, Tennessee, and Colorado. A mountain climber, a sculptor, a housewife—people who live on farms, people who go to work in the city and then bake bread on the weekends.

As the writing of the book progressed, others joined in to share. A client of mine, Owen Hallberg, spotted an article in the *Omaha World-Herald* and dropped me a note telling me that Mrs. Yanney might well be included in the book. She is, of course, one of our bakers (see Index). Other friends in New Mexico and North Carolina told me about friends of theirs who would be perfect—people who were in various professions during the day but who baked bread in their spare time. Not one of them is a professional baker. (Nor is the author.) They will all be found in the pages that follow.

And so, all of them—my students, my friends, my new acquaintances, all of them—have contributed their knowledge and their joy of bread baking to this book. And all of them, like millions of others, have learned to judge bread by the quality of home-baked results rather than accepting the "store-bought" cardboard-and-paste variety with all the nutrition baked out.

They have all learned, as I have over these past years—as you will learn when you bake your first breads—that there need be no mystique about bread baking. For some reason, the imagined secrets of bread baking, the mysterious rising of the dough under cover of a towel, the awesomely gorgeous results, have created a "fear of trying."

I have always tried to teach my students *not* to be afraid of bread, of the properties of the yeast, of the slim chance that the bread will fall. Bread baking is easy—and it's fun. It's sensual, and it's completely absorbing—and the end result is a prize that is hard to equal.

As my house smells of the baking of fresh bread, *your* house will be filled with the aromas of yeast and sourdough starter and rising dough and baking loaves. The pressures and the frustrations of the daily job will be left behind for just a few hours while your hands become coated with flour and your nostrils take in the special perfumes of bread.

With the tasting of the warm, fresh first slice, newly out of the oven, you will no doubt agree with the author that although life, indeed, is not by bread alone—bread sure does help to make living more enjoyable!

2 Before You Begin

Of course, there are some basic requirements for baking your own bread. You must choose some kind of flour or grain, some type of liquid, and the degree of heat. But, other than that, bread baking is surely one of the most flexible of arts. Leavener is used sometimes, and sometimes not used. Flour amounts vary with the humidity and the temperature of your kitchen (something that will come up time and time again in this book). You might bake your first breads on a cookie sheet, in a bread pan, or on the floor of your gas oven. The rising times of dough will vary with the grains used. Baking temperatures are, in fact, variable by as much as a 25°F. setting.

It is this very flexibility of approach which makes bread baking at home an inventive joy—without worry, without complexity. Certainly things can go wrong. I still have not solved all the mysteries and complexities of Salt-Rising Bread (see Index). But, generally, what goes wrong can easily be fixed. All it takes is practice, a small amount of experience, and an attitude that says, "If they can do it, so can I."

Perhaps my own introduction to bread baking was the right one. My teacher, George Meluso (see Index), was easy, loose, unworried. His attitude, in turn, was passed on to me and the craft has never frightened me.

Your kitchen might be a simple alcove in a small city apartment or it might be a complex setup of contemporary design that could put the kitchen of a gourmet restaurant to shame. Plain or fancy, it doesn't really matter. Bread can be baked in clay ovens in a backyard—the Egyptians did it in pits dug into the earth. As long as you have a counter, an oven, and a mixing bowl, you can bake bread along with the rest of us.

As there are, indeed, no hard and fast rules, the important thing is to learn just what your ingredients are capable of doing and how they behave under certain conditions. And then—practice. Soon you will learn just what texture the dough should be in order for it to rise and bake properly. You will know just how much flour above the recipe amount is right for your location on this planet, and what the limits of experimentation are.

Before you begin, read these next few chapters that precede the recipes. I have tried to give all the information necessary to start you off. The types of flour, leavenings, the ways to knead dough and how to get the proper rise—these are all the basics you will need for baking your own bread.

As for the recipes themselves, they belong to the friends who have so generously given of their secret files, their baking tips and their sheer joy at seeing the homemade loaf come from the oven. As they share their shortcuts with me, I pass them on to you, and I also learn in the process. And that's good.

Occasionally, you will find that more than one recipe is given for a specific type of bread (whole wheat, sourdough, corn bread, for example). This is done where the ingredients vary enough to produce a different texture or taste, or where the procedures for making the breads are somewhat different. It gives you some choices. You can experiment until you find the recipe that suits your own taste. Still there are over 240 different recipes in the book—enough to satisfy the most curious and adventurous of bread bakers.

Given all of this, what should you have in your kitchen to begin work on the first masterpiece?

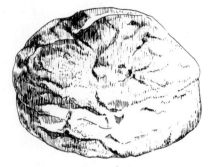

The Equipment You'll Need 3

My wife is a "gadget freak." We have gadgets to remove corks that have dropped into wine bottles, gadgets to take the marrow from bones, to peel, to scrape, to sculpt, and to smooth the ingredients we use in our cooking. Baking bread is, thankfully, simpler. There are only a few things that you'll need in your kitchen in order to bake your own breads. Later on, you'll find, as I do, that each shopping expedition becomes another adventure in discovery, so I have also included some of the other items you may want to buy as you become more adept at this new satisfying hobby. To help some of the readers who might find that the stores in their communities do not carry some of the more unusual items, I have included a list of Mail-Order Resources at the back of the book.

For Starters

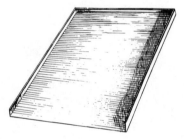

A large bowl, either ceramic or glass, about 13 inches across the top. This size is large enough to let you mix more than one or two breads. I find that I like to bake at least four to eight breads in the oven at one time. It saves energy and makes the freezer bulge.

Measuring cups.

A wooden spoon.

Baking pans.
 Medium - 8½ × 4½ × 2½ inches
 Large (standard) - 9¾ × 5¾ × 2¾ inches

A cookie sheet.

A wire rack on which to cool the breads.

Expanding the Collection

Having tried bread baking, you will no doubt like it, and you (like the rest of us) will then expand your collection of equipment to include most of the items listed below (though probably not *all* of them). These, too, can be ordered by mail if they are not available in your local stores.

A curved plastic scraper to scrape the mixing bowl when turning the dough out for kneading. Some bakers use a rubber spatula.

A metal scraper with a flat edge and a wooden handle. I find that this is one of the handiest tools in my baking kitchen, since it helps to scrape all the dough off the counter prior to rising or shaping.

Pastry brush for glazing the tops of the breads. If you don't have one, try a soft paper towel.

Special pans such as muffin tins, *brioche* pans, cast-iron bread pans (for crustier loaves), bundt pans, two- or five-section French loaf pans. (For the latter, you can also use aluminum foil and bend it into the shape of a French loaf.)

Electric mixers and food processors. Though I personally prefer to do it all by hand, some bakers use a dough hook attachment on the electric mixer for the first part of the kneading process, continuing to the end on a floured board. My feeling is that the machine can never substitute for the pleasure that handling the dough gives me. Too, I find that the average mixer or food processor just does not hold enough dough for more than one or two breads at a time. However, they do save time. It is something you will have to decide for yourself.

Quarry tiles. These are unglazed, clay tiles about 5½ inches square. Lined across the standard oven rack, they give an even, diffused heat during the baking process and a special kind of crustiness to the breads that are baked on them. The tiles can be used instead of a cookie sheet when baking free-form breads. Just dust them with a light coating of cornmeal to keep the dough from sticking.

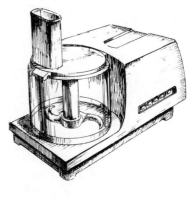

Thermometers. If your oven seems to vary in temperature from setting to setting, if you don't trust your own skin sensitivity to determine "lukewarm" from "cool," thermometers can help. In any case, it's a good idea to have an oven thermometer hanging on a rack so that when you open the door, you can quickly check to see if the temperature is close to the one you want.

Begin with only a basic list. Get to know what you need as you go along. Bit by bit, the closets and drawers will overflow. The day I was ceded my very own closet space for my utensils, I knew I had been accepted as the bread baker of the family.

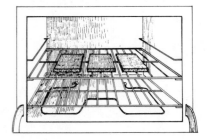

4 The Ingredients You'll Be Using

Since bread is a naturally basic staff of life, I have always instinctively used natural ingredients in my breads and, with just two exceptions, most other bread bakers do too. You will probably find, as you grow more adept, as you experiment with grains, liquids, and seeds, that your bread baking will take you into a world of wonder. It is a world filled with so many new discoveries waiting to be tried: yogurt for sourdough starter, beer as the liquid for a Finnish bread, nuts and seeds to give the breads nutrition as well as texture and crunch, and any number of cereals and whole grains for food value and new taste sensations.

Some time back, in a fit of wild abandon, I even tried Bordeaux wine in my batter. The combination produced an unmitigated disaster, only proving that wine is best drunk out of a glass at dinner time (along with some other kind of fresh, home-baked bread).

The two exceptions to natural ingredients mentioned above are sugar and enriched-bleached-presifted white flour, neither of which you will find in this book. Sugar has been replaced with honey, and the nutritionless prepared and bleached flours have never seen the light of my kitchen in all these years of baking bread. In fact, as you read other books, find other recipes in your local newspapers or favorite magazines, sugar can be replaced easily by honey, either for flavoring or for proofing yeast.

Flours, Grains, and Meals

One of the most common mistakes made by the beginning bread baker is to follow the recipe as gospel, especially when it comes to the amount of flour required. I've stated it before and I'm sure I do so many more times before the end of this book: *The amount of flour given is always approximate.* The reasons are simple. Flour absorbs liquid; it thus absorbs moisture in any humid climate. Depending upon the kind of day, the location, the altitude, the humidity, and the temperature, the amount of flour used may vary by as much as a cup or two! Because of the damp atmosphere on our island, those of us who bake there find the recipes in most books are shy by about one cup of flour. The important thing is to get the *feel* of the dough as you learn to bake, using as much or as little flour as you feel is necessary.

Of course, since many recipes call for mixing dry ingredients first and then adding liquid, another "damp day" solution might be to *decrease the liquid* in order to give the dough its proper texture.

An hour ago, I prepared some sourdough breads, now rising

upstairs in the kitchen. It is wet, rainy, miserable outside, just the kind of day for baking bread. It is, in fact, so damp, that I used the amount of flour given in the recipe but *reduced* the liquid by one whole cup!

Unbleached White Flour: In thumbing through cookbooks and in reading the food columns in your newspaper, you'll discover that most recipes for bread include white flour (bleached or unbleached). Occasionally it is mixed with other grains.

White flour contains a large amount of a substance called *gluten,* an elastic protein that stretches when wet and thus expands to hold the gases given off by the yeast. Basically, it is the gluten that gives the expanded shape or "frame" to a finished loaf and there is no doubt that the texture of breads baked with white flour tends to be lighter and fluffier than that of loaves baked with only whole grain flours. To those of us interested in the *nutrition* of the bread as well as the *texture,* this emphasis on "light and fluffy" seems to have grown out of all proportion. Many whole grain breads are texturally beautiful and, at the same time, they retain the essential elements of good taste and good nutrition.

Long ago there was an unfortunate shift in consumer preference from whole grain flours to finer, less nourishing flours. Basically, there were two reasons for this. As far back as the time of Caesar, it was considered a sign of affluence among the Romans to eat the breads of finer texture made with white flour. Peasants ate the coarse, whole grain breads. The trend toward whiter, finer-textured breads as the ideal continued to grow. Until recent years, when added millions of people began to make their own bread again, we were also the victims of the "whiter-the-better" philosophy.

The second reason for the shift to refined flours is a much more practical one. The wheat kernel—the whole berry—contains an outer layer of bran, an oily germ, and a starchy core called the endosperm. Most of the vitamins, minerals, and other nutrients are contained in the bran and germ, but these two parts of the berry spoil quickly and they also give the flour a darker color and a coarser texture.

On the other hand, the endosperm, which makes up about 75 percent of the total wheat kernel and has few vitamins or minerals, is light colored and quite high in gluten. The commercial millers concentrate on using the endosperm and, anxious to make the white whiter, sometimes use gas to bleach the flour. They also try to put back some of the nutrition by "enriching" the product. Unfortunately, they can't put Humpty-Dumpty back together again, and many important vitamins and minerals are still lost.

Of course, if you want full-nutrition breads, the answer is to use whole grain flours wherever possible. If, however, you must use unbleached white flour (and I will soon explain just where I have used it in this book and why), be certain to use the best of the unbleached white flours available to you—never the prepared, general purpose variety. Where possible, you can also blend it with nutritious ingredients as described in the Cornell formula given below.

Incidentally, the professional baker does not use the same quality of unbleached white flour that we buy in our supermarkets. Generally, the commercial flour is called *hard wheat,* a spring wheat grown in the Midwest and especially in Texas. It is noted for its high gluten and mineral content and it makes a firmer, more elastic bread. However, it also has a tendency to absorb more liquid, so that kneading time may be increased. When I find that I must use unbleached white flour, a small local bakery in my neighborhood will generally sell me a small amount of their supply of hard wheat. I've also found that some natural foods stores and specialty food shops around the country are also beginning to stock hard wheat flour.

Of course, there have been many attempts either to eliminate the use of nutrition-poor white flour in bread baking, or to enrich it so that much of the nutrition is returned, providing at the same time a light-textured bread and a flour that will keep for many months. Some have been eminently successful.

Many years ago, long before so many of us discovered the values in natural foods, Dr. Clive McKay of Cornell University developed the Cornell formula for enriching unbleached white flour:

> *To make one cup of flour, combine one tablespoon of nonfat dry milk solids, one tablespoon of soy flour, one teaspoon of wheat germ. Fill the balance of the cup with unbleached white flour.*

Another suggested formula:

> *Add one-quarter cup wheat germ to one and three-quarter cups of unbleached white flour.*

For many of us, of course, totally eliminating the white flour, while keeping a light and airy texture, becomes the goal. In the April 1978 edition of *Organic Gardening and Farming*® magazine, Kathy Woeltjen of Crestline, California, suggested a method for just such a result.

Separate one egg. Beat the white until stiff and fold it into a small amount of the whole grain flour called for in the recipe before adding the rest. Mix the yolk with oil and salt (if used) and add it to the flour and egg white mixture.

Of course, if you decide to use unbleached white flour in some of the recipes, you will find your own devices and your own balances of flours and grains as you go along. Someone once wrote (and I have not counted) that there are 30,000 variations of flours, grains, meals, and bread additives available in the world today.

As you read the long list of flours, grains, and meals available to you, you'll find an astounding variety of ingredients that can be used in bread baking. The whole wheat and rye will probably be your staples. The others such as triticale, soy, and graham will open a wide potential in this most exciting of kitchen crafts. Just use your imagination.

A logical question has probably been gnawing at you for the past few pages. "Why," you ask, "does he bother to discuss white flour—bleached or unbleached—at all, if whole grains are more nutritious?"

Through the writing of this book, there were many long, hard discussions that dealt with the solution of this problem, for it soon became evident that some white flour might have to be used in specific recipes. Actually, I got to like the discussions, for some were held in publisher Bob Rodale's cozy office in Emmaus, Pennsylvania—and on cold winter days he'd keep the fireplace crackling while the snow threatened outside the window. Right before the manuscript for this book was to be delivered, we set some ground rules and we have followed them throughout the development and the testing of the recipes. Unbleached white flour would appear in a recipe *only* under the following circumstances:

• Where the added gluten it carries was an absolute necessity for creating an acceptable finished product. The use of triticale is a good example. In addition, the high altitude baker *must* have a flour with a high gluten content. Thus you will find that the starters used for breads baked at high altitudes, as in the case of Haven and Margaret Holsapple's recipes (see Index), do use unbleached white flour.

• Where the breads are traditional. The old, familiar, cherished recipes for *Challah, Lefse,* and certain of the holiday breads call for unbleached white flour and we, in turn, have bowed to tradition. This does not mean, of course, that you cannot bake them with other flours. (I have been quite successful in converting certain of these breads, and the information necessary for you to make the conversion, if you would like to try it, is supplied with many of the recipes.) However, the converted version just could not be called traditional bread. In trying to make this book as complete as possible, I have retained the recipes as they were given to me.

• Where the breads, as developed by the baker, call for unbleached white flour for some specific and terribly important reason. The recipes of the Minnesota State Fair ribbon winners are good examples of this exception. The recipes I've passed on to you are the ones that actually won the prizes. Certainly, if you prefer, you can change them to suit your taste and your nutritional requirements.

One other thing came out of our long discussions in Bob Rodale's office. You'll note that one of his recipes is also included in the book. (See Index.)

Whole Wheat Flour: During these past few years, whole wheat flour has been regaining its popularity, and with good reason. The flour is made from the entire wheat kernel—bran, germ, and endosperm. It thus contains a wealth of vitamins and minerals, most of which are milled out in the manufacture of the white wheat flours—B vitamins, vitamin E, protein, magnesium, potassium, and iron. Added to all of that, the flavor of whole wheat breads can only be described as delicious.

Some whole wheat flour is made from soft wheat, some from hard wheat. The latter contains more gluten, making it better for baking bread. When you purchase whole wheat flour from your local supplier, buy only enough to fill your needs for a few weeks, since it tends to become rancid rather quickly. If you can't use it in your breads within a month, store whole wheat flour in the refrigerator or freezer until you are ready to bake.

Some bakers prefer to buy the stone-ground whole wheat flour rather than the flour ground in high-speed mills (a commercial process which tends to leave the germ in small clumps, thus spreading rancidity). However, the stone-ground flours are usually coarser in texture, requiring about twice the amount of yeast in the dough.

Because of the renewed interest in baking with whole wheat flour, commercial whole wheat flours have begun to appear on the supermarket shelves. However, look carefully at the labels since many of them are nothing more than bleached white flour (to make for longer shelf life) with bran added.

You'll find many recipes in this book that use whole wheat flour, either alone or with other flours and grains. You'll find that it makes a marvelous, tasty, and nutritious base for yeast breads, quick breads, and muffins.

Whole Wheat Pastry Flour: This is a more finely milled whole wheat flour normally used for pies and pastries. When used in bread, it gives a finer and lighter texture than regular whole wheat flour.

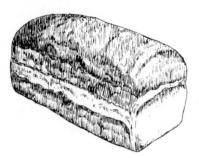

Rye Flour: This is a flour milled from the rye grain—with superb flavor and texture. It is a heavy flour, with a low gluten content, and thus it is used in combination with the higher-gluten wheat flours. You'll also find that it makes a fairly sticky batter and you'll soon get used to having your hands coated with the wet dough as you knead. The breads themselves will probably have a close, moist texture. Rye flour comes in four varieties—white, medium, dark, and pumpernickel. The medium is the most commonly used, though I much prefer the dark rye to give my breads a healthy, substantial homemade look.

Gluten Flour: As mentioned, the gluten is the protein portion of the endosperm. On occasion, you will see a large crock in your store labeled, "Gluten Flour" or "High-Gluten Flour." Though not technically a flour by definition, gluten flour is made from ordinary wheat flour with most of the starch eliminated. It is said to be excellent for people on a diabetic diet.

Soy Flour: Made from ground soybeans, the flour is remarkably high in protein (about 40 percent) with a very low fat content. It has a very strong, almost bitter taste and should be used sparingly because of it. Also, the gluten content of soy flour is nonexistent, so it must be blended with wheat flours.

Graham Flour: This is actually a type of whole wheat flour, ground from hard wheat, with the bran left as a very coarse ingredient. A recipe that calls for whole wheat all purpose flour can take graham flour instead.

Barley Flour: The finely milled kernel of barley, this flour is occasionally used in conjunction with wheat flours. It gives a cakelike texture to bread and it's fairly moist. If you can't find barley flour and you're anxious to know what it's like, you can use rye flour in its place.

Potato Flour: For milling, the potato is cooked and then dried whole. It can then be used in combination with other wheat flours. Look for potato flour in your specialty shop or in the local natural foods store.

Corn Flour: This flour is made from finely ground kernels of corn. If you want a slight corn taste, you can substitute corn flour for a small portion of wheat flour. However, traditional southern recipes call for cornmeal rather than corn flour.

Notice that as we progress with this list of possible flours, grains, and meals, the comments about mixing with other flours keep reappearing. The reason is that very few of these ingredients react to yeast at all. They are, therefore, *used only as additives* to give flavor and texture to the breads. To use them alone would result in something resembling a block of stone that would be both inedible and ugly. Thus, with rare exceptions, they are mixed with high-gluten flours in yeast breads.

Triticale: More and more, as I scour the stores for new bread ingredients, and speak to bakers across the country, I am beginning to find a new name in the vocabulary of bread—triticale. Just recently, I spotted some in Seattle, and a few months before, I found the wrinkled kernels in a natural foods store in New Orleans. Triticale is a hybrid grain that is a cross between rye and wheat, with a much higher protein content than either. It seems to be gaining popularity rather quickly and I predict that the next few years will see more and more recipes including triticale as a staple. The flour has a ryelike flavor, though it's not quite as strong. If you decide to use it, you should measure about half triticale and half wheat flour, since triticale contains very little gluten. I have become so fascinated by triticale, that I've included a separate section about the grain, along with some unusual recipes. (See Index.)

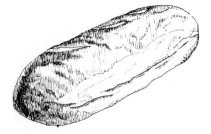

Wheat Germ: Of course, this is not really a flour, but it's made from the vitamin—and mineral—rich kernel of the wheat grain and it makes a marvelous additive, both for flavor and nutrition. Normally, the germ is removed from the flour because it contains fat and has a tendency to turn rancid. Nevertheless, since wheat germ is available in most stores, it can be used to enrich your breads by using only a small amount. However, you must take care of wheat germ just as you do whole wheat flour. Make certain you refrigerate it after the package or jar has been opened.

Cracked Wheat (Bulgur): These coarsely milled whole grains of wheat are generally used in Middle Eastern and Greek cooking. Some bakers have learned to use cracked wheat to add a crunchy texture and a nutty flavor to their breads.

Cornmeal: Unlike finely ground corn flour, cornmeal is coarsely ground dried corn and it's used in the traditional breads of the South—corn bread and spoon bread. It can be yellow or white. You will also find that cornmeal is called for in some recipes to coat the bottom of baking pans to prevent the dough from sticking.

Rolled Oats or Oatmeal: These are the ordinary cereal oats (but not quick-cooking) and they can be added to your breads to give them a heartier flavor and a rougher texture.

Whole Wheat Meal: In making this flour, kernels of wheat are coarsely ground, with rough bits of bran remaining.

Millet Meal: This one takes us back a way, to the ancient Romans. Millet is a cereal grass that is used extensively in Europe and the East. Some old recipes show us that the ancient Romans made a bread of millet meal and wheat flour. However, in the United States it is mostly used as fodder. If you'd like to try millet, add a half cup of it (ground in a blender or food processor) to about five or six cups of wheat flour. It will add crunch to the bread.

Yeast and Other Leaveners

Yeast lives! And, truly it does. Yeast is a living organism and without it much of the magic of baking would disappear leaving us to eat the unleavened bread of the ancient Israelites. It is today, the most common of all bread leaveners.

Though yeast does exist in a natural state, floating in the air and hiding in the soil, it was first produced commercially from the dregs of beer, for it is yeast which gives beer its distinctive taste. As a matter of fact, the bread bakers of grandmother's generation merely went down to the local brewery to get their yeast—or they made their own! One of our baker friends, Suzanne Corbett, sent me a recipe for Milk Yeast that she found in her great-grandmother's cookbook (circa 1880).

Milk Yeast

Take one pint of new milk, one teaspoon of salt, a large spoon of flour and stir together well; set the mixture by the fire and keep it lukewarm. It will be fit for use in an hour. Twice the quantity of common yeast is necessary; it will not keep long. Bread made of this yeast dries soon; but in the summer it is sometimes convenient to make this kind when yeast is needed suddenly. Never keep yeast in a tin vessel. If you find the old yeast sour and have not time to prepare new, put in saleratus (soda), a teaspoon to a pint of yeast when ready to use it. If it foams up lively, it will raise the bread; if it doesn't, never use it.

Today, of course, though it might be fun to visit the local brewer (if there is one in your neighborhood) or to attempt great-grandmother's recipe, yeast is sold at supermarkets and natural foods stores. It comes in two basic forms: dry and compressed (fresh) yeast. The dry yeast is the most readily available and, to a great extent, it has replaced compressed yeast as a leavener.

Dry Yeast: This yeast is produced by removing the moisture in the yeast and is available in one-fourth-ounce packages that measure about one tablespoon. The yeast is inactive, nevertheless the date stamped on the packet is important. Check the dates of expiration and then store the extra packets in the meat-keeper compartment of your refrigerator—they're good to have around in case the urge to bake overwhelms you one rainy morning.

In the natural foods stores, dry yeast is now available in jars, but I find that the jars are not dated and some of the tops have not been put on tightly enough. Unless the store sells enough so that there is always a fresh supply on the shelves, there is a chance that the yeast will die either through age or through contact with the air.

Frankly, my choice is the dated, sealed packets. I always have four or five on hand for an emergency.

Compressed Cake Yeast: It makes no difference, they tell me, whether you use dry yeast or compressed cake yeast. I am considered by my peers to be old-fashioned, rigid, stubborn, narrow, unyielding. I am, in fact, all of these. But I still prefer the compressed yeast. I like the feel of it when I handle it, I prefer its

rising qualities (no matter that I cannot prove it does any better than dry yeast), and I swear that I can taste and smell the difference.

To make the cakes, the yeast is compressed with a small amount of starch. When fresh, it is crumbly and falls apart between your fingers and, since it is an active yeast, it will spoil rather quickly. Even under refrigeration, the life of compressed yeast is only about 10 days to 2 weeks. However, for those of us stubborn enough to still use it, it can be frozen for extended keeping.

A friend of mine taught me a trick about freezing compressed yeast and it works beautifully. Make sure it's wrapped well in recipe-sized packages, then freeze it in a container filled with flour. The bed of flour makes the yeast freeze gradually and it seems to keep as long as three to six months without spoiling. Just thaw the yeast at room temperature when you need it.

I get my compressed yeast in one-pound packages from a local Italian bakery (and they, in turn, get it from a brewery just as grandmother did). However, stores around the country are beginning to carry compressed yeast in one-half-ounce (some are two-thirds-ounce) and two-ounce cakes.

To activate the yeast and release the gases that make the dough rise, it must be fed. A combination of air, food, and moisture will do the trick.

Dry yeast can be dissolved in liquid at temperatures of 100° to 115°F., or slightly above the temperature of the human body. In the past few years, the manufacturers of dry yeast have begun to recommend the "dry" (rapid-mix, no-dissolve) method. The yeast is merely sprinkled over the other ingredients and it becomes active when liquid is added. It is a method that does work and it makes the whole process much simpler. It need not be "proofed" (see below). However, when using dry yeast, I still choose to dissolve it in warm water before adding it to the other ingredients.

For those of us who refuse to bend, compressed yeast takes more time and more effort.

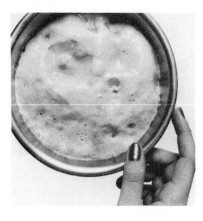

Proofing the Yeast: The yeast is crumbled in a glass or cup (make sure it's at room temperature if you've been refrigerating it), and about one-half cup of liquid is added.The liquid should be at about 80° to 95°F. Though the liquid used is generally water, it can also be milk, potato water, or reconstituted nonfat dry milk. Then we feed it—a small amount of honey or molasses will do. Stir and let it stand. In about 5 to 10 minutes you'll notice that the mixture is bubbling and rising in the glass. The yeast has been "proofed." It is now ready for your dough.

Now, here again, I must comment. I have never used a thermometer to test the temperature of the water, and I have never known my teacher, George Meluso, to do it either. The yeast always proofs. The bread always rises. Adrian Bailey, in his excellent book, just reissued, *The Blessings of Bread* (New York: Paddington Press, Ltd., Two Continents Publishing Group, 1928), states that yeast becomes active at about 78°F. and the action is destroyed at 140°F. So you do have some flexibility.

The important thing to remember is that too much heat will destroy the yeast. Cold will slow the action but will not harm the organism.

Having gone on at considerable length about my preference for compressed yeast, it is now my duty to inform the reader that all recipes in this book have been structured with dry yeast. The simple reason is that I know it is available wherever you might live. Also, dry yeast is (I must admit) easier to work with and to store.

However, if you decide to use cake yeast, one one-fourth-ounce package (one tablespoon) of dry yeast equals about two-thirds ounce of the compressed cake. Here again, the measurement will not affect the bread. If you use one ounce of compressed yeast instead of one package of dry yeast, the gods will not descend upon you and take your baker's hat away.

And, finally, if you do decide to use compressed yeast, reduce the amount of liquid in the recipe by the amount used to proof the dry yeast (about one-half cup).

Sourdough Starters: The history of this marvelous concoction has been written about over and over again. Its very name calls up images of those intrepid men, the Sourdoughs, who traveled to Alaska during the gold rush. Since they could not very well carry fresh yeast with them and still keep it alive, the chuckwagon cooks developed their own leavening agent. I've read stories about how these men ingeniously kept their starter alive and active sometimes by taking it to bed with them under the covers and, on long journeys, carrying it inside their shirts to keep it close to body temperature. Today, of course, sourdough bread is well-known to those who live in, or travel to, San Francisco, but many bakers across the country make and keep their own starters. It gives bread, rolls, and muffins a distinctive, pleasant sour taste. A sourdough starter is easy to make, though sometimes tricky to keep.

Kept in a scalded crock or glass jar, the sourdough starter must be used every few days or else stored in the refrigerator when not in use. When a cup or two is taken from the original starter, you merely "feed" it with equal amounts of new flour and warm water and it continues to provide a most unusual and delicious leavening.

My own current starter has been active now for almost three years. There are several starter recipes in the book (see Index).

Yogurt Sourdough Starter: Some time ago, in California, I discovered an interesting variation for sourdough starter. By using plain yogurt and skim or low-fat milk along with flour, the starter develops in much the same way as the standard formula, but it adds a most unusual pungent flavor to the breads. (See Index.)

Potato Starters and Other Fermentations: The Sourdoughs were certainly inventive and competent bread bakers, but many of our immigrant grandmothers also brought starter recipes with them. Potato water has a leavening quality when properly prepared and aged—sometimes used with cornmeal, as in Salt-Rising Breads (see Index), sometimes used in conjunction with hops, sometimes alone. The combination of hops and potatoes was also known as "farmer's yeast" when it was dried and crumbled into small bits. It was stored and then reconstituted with water when needed, very much like the dry yeast in today's supermarkets.

Baking Powder: Though generally used in baking cakes, baking powder is frequently used alone or combined with baking soda (see below) in what are called "quick breads." These doughs require no rising before they are baked and can be popped into the oven as soon as the batter is mixed. You'll find that most of the baking powder now being sold in the stores is designated as "double acting." That means that the first rising action begins when you add the liquid, the second when the bread hits the heat of the oven. With double-acting baking powder, the bread can be mixed early and then baked later on when it might be more convenient.

During the testing of our breads, we found that most brands of double-acting baking powder are treated with aluminum sulfate, a chemical which can cause harm to the system, and serves no discernible purpose in terms of improving the quality of the final product. Several commercial double-acting baking powders are manufactured without the additive. If you prefer to use the product that is free of that chemical, read the label carefully before you buy. Faye Martin, who did so much of our testing at the

Rodale Test Kitchens, makes her own very successful baking powder:

One-half teaspoon cream of tartar, one-fourth teaspoon sodium bicarbonate and one-fourth teaspoon cornstarch or arrowroot yields one teaspoon of single-acting baking powder. (The cornstarch or arrowroot standardizes the measurement and maintains the leavening factor.)

Baking Soda: It must be used in conjunction with ingredients that are acidic: buttermilk, yogurt, sour milk, sour cream, fruit juices, or molasses.

You will be using various liquids during your baking "career" and the variations are as diverse as the flours and grains that are available (not including my famous Bordeaux wine fiasco). Primarily, the purpose of the liquid is to moisten the dough and then, in yeast breads, to develop the gluten. *Remember to keep the liquid at room temperature,* just as you do with all other ingredients. Frequently, I find that I am ready to bake but have forgotten to take the buttermilk or yeast out of the refrigerator. The process waits while everything warms up.

Water: Of course, this is the most common liquid. Water gives a crisp crust to the breads as well as a fairly dense crumb.

Milk (Including Skim Milk and Nonfat Dry Milk): In addition to giving a softer, thinner texture to your breads, milk also adds protein and calcium. Just as there are opposite camps for the dry-yeast-versus-compressed-yeast schools, so there is a debate over to-scald-or-not-to-scald. Years ago, when milk was not pasteurized, it was essential to scald the milk and then bring it down to room temperature before using. (Scalding takes place when the tiny bubbles appear around the edge of the milk heating in the pan.) The scalding destroys any harmful bacteria that might cause the dough to sour. Others claim that scalding improves the texture of the bread. Having already proved that I am old-fashioned and unyielding, I still scald the milk. Why take chances?

Potato Water: Used as a leavener, it also adds flavor to the bread, gives a smooth crumb and helps the yeast grow.

Buttermilk and Sour Milk: Used in quick breads, the acid content makes either of these perfect for mixing with baking soda as a leavening agent.

Liquids

Beer: Occasionally beer is used in bread, as in the Finnish sour rye, *Hiivaleipa* (see Index) and Gerry Franklin's Beer Wheat Bread (see Index). Other liquids that might be used in bread baking include vegetable broths and even tea.

Eggs

Sometimes eggs are used to give a richness to the bread, or to add a golden color. Actually, eggs are not a necessary ingredient for bread baking, but you may want to add them for their flavor. The egg yolks, mixed with a bit of water and then brushed on top of the bread, will give a golden glaze to the loaf. George Meluso's *Challah* (see Index) is a typical bread that uses this technique.

Fats and Oils

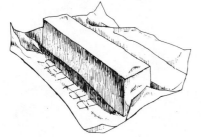

In some breads, the fats act as a sort of lubricant, allowing the loaf to expand easily during the rising process and while baking. They also flavor the breads and help to keep the loaves from drying out during storage. One of the most common uses of butter, for example, is for greasing the pans before baking to allow for easy removal of the finished loaves. Also, butter does not burn as easily during the baking process.

Other fats and oils that appear in recipes include: vegetable oils, lard in a few cases, and you will even find a couple of recipes that call for goose grease and chicken fat. I generally use a polyunsaturated vegetable oil such as peanut oil.

Seeds and Garnishes

One of the things that makes a bread look professional is the way in which it is decorated or garnished. In addition to using seeds such as caraway in the bread itself, a light sprinkling of them over the top of the bread will add to the visual delight. In addition to caraway seeds, I have used black caraway (a startlingly black strong-flavored seed that originated in eastern Europe), sesame seeds, and poppy seeds. Recently, I discovered a new taste sensation that I've been using on my sourdough breads. It's a Japanese roasted sesame seed called *Irigoma* and it gives the bread an individual and unusual flavor.

Nuts, Spices, Herbs, Raisins, ...and More

The list would be endless—almost anything that grows, dries, peels, or crunches can be used in bread without changing the recipe amounts. Walnuts, pecans, currants, cranberries, cloves, dill, nutmeg, onion, cumin, apricots, savory, thyme, sage, peanuts, and more. And much more. If you have an herb garden, you might want to use the fresh, pungent, newly harvested dill in your bread. The combinations and the taste treats are endless.

You might keep one thing in mind—some bakers complain that raisins or nuts sink to the bottom of the batter as they bake. A simple solution: flour them first, before adding them to the batter.

Sweeteners

I like my breads not-too-sweet. The people who work in my office prefer them much-too-sweet, according to my taste. Therefore, every time I bake a bread that doesn't suit my taste buds because of too much sweetness, I take it to the people who work with me and they love it. Sweeteners are really subject to personal taste and you will have to learn just how much to use. I constantly adjust recipes that I pick up in newspapers and magazines. You will, no doubt, do the same with the ones that are printed in this very book.

Sweeteners act as natural preservatives for bread, though too much will inhibit the growth of the yeast and probably cause the bread to burn. The most common sweetener used in natural bread baking is honey. It adds flavor and, perhaps more important, it starts the action of the yeast. Molasses and malt syrup are also used to darken breads like pumpernickel and to add a sweeter flavor.

Salt

Many bakers feel that even a very small amount of salt in breads (as little as a half teaspoon per loaf) contributes to the flavor and acts to control the action of the yeast. Too much salt inhibits the growth of the yeast. The recipes given in *Prevention* magazine no longer contain salt, since there's been much in the way of evidence that salt can cause high blood pressure, fluid retention, and even migraine headaches in susceptible individuals. In response to that sensible policy, you will note that I have marked the amount of salt *optional* in all but certain traditional recipes. In some instances my bread-baker friends have totally eliminated salt. It is all a matter of personal taste and viewpoint. Feel free to cut down on the amount or to eliminate salt completely in any of the breads. As Bob Rodale so nicely put it, "The salt shaker is in your hands."

Table of Non-Measurements

Since bread baking is so flexible an art, the amounts given in recipes will sometimes be approximations. It is the texture of bread that counts, rather than the accurate measurements of ingredients. Ever since my grandmother's day, good cooks have passed on their recipes in a strange kind of shorthand. If, while reading this book, you find the following "measurements," smile, and then use your own judgment. It will be right—you'll see.

A Pinch: Generally this is the amount that can be comfortably held between the fingertips. Since fingers vary in size, so will "a pinch."

A Handful: Again, the hand is a multi-sized appendage and your handful may not be the same as your neighbor's.

Some: Over and over again, bakers told me that they threw in "some" caraway seeds or "some" nuts. Wherever possible, I have tried to pin them down and have asked them to measure. If in doubt, "some" means "not a whole lot," not "a tiny amount"—whatever "some" means to you.

To Taste: They love very sweet breads where I work, but I lean toward less sweet breads. You may prefer molasses. Of course, all recipes will probably be changed eventually to suit *your* taste.

A Bit: This is the same category as "some" or "to taste." The only advice another bread baker can give in a case like this is: if a recipe ever calls for "a bit"—just don't put in "too much."

The Simple Steps in Making, Baking, and Eating a Yeast Bread 5

There is a definite and logical pattern for making most yeast breads. All of them require some kind of flour, a liquid, and of course, yeast. The additions will vary, but the steps in making your own breads will remain pretty much the same. The most important thing to remember is that practice will give you the "feel" of the doughs as they are prepared for the oven. Here are the steps you'll be following. Dig in—don't be afraid to get flour on your clothes, dough on your hands. The little boy in me emerges each time I lay out the ingredients before mixing and baking. My wife, sensing this, occasionally quotes the instructions from a child's cookbook she remembers from years back: "Tie on your apron—wash your hands—have your mother show you how to light the oven. . . ." It is time to mix the ingredients.

Mixing the Ingredients

Make certain all ingredients are at room temperature. I like to have everything laid out in front of me before I begin. Trying to find a scraping tool or the sesame seeds while my hands are covered with dough has an end result of making the cabinets and drawers look like I've been finger painting with flour and water. Check the recipe and have everything on the counter right at the start.

Dissolve the yeast in warm water (about 80° to 95°F. for cake yeast, about 100° to 115°F. for dry yeast). If the recipe does not give separate liquid amounts for proofing the yeast and for mixing the ingredients, remember to deduct the water used in proofing from the total specified.

Some recipes suggest that all dry ingredients go into the mixing bowl first, followed by the wet. Others reverse the process. Don't let this throw you. It makes very little difference, if any, what order you follow. Both work.

Just as there is to-scald-or-not-to-scald controversy when it comes to milk, there is a diversity of opinion on the question of to-sift-or-not-to-sift flour. Most whole grains are added unsifted. When I do use unbleached white flour in an occasional recipe, I still choose to sift, for I sometimes find tiny hard lumps of flour in the bag. I use a regular strainer to do the job. Your breads will work out either way.

As you add the ingredients, stir them in with a wooden spoon, and stir well. This is the first time you will be mixing the ingredients and the more thoroughly you get them blended, the easier it will be to turn out the dough for the next step.

Bit by bit, the texture will change, and mixing will become more difficult. The texture will be soft and biscuitlike. Again, you will learn as you go on just what the texture for each bread will be. You will find that whole grain breads, such as rye, are stickier and much damper. If the batter seems to be too wet, add more flour. Again the humidity of your kitchen, temperature, altitude—all will play a role in determining the amount of flour to use. Finally, the batter will seem completely blended, or as nearly so as you can possibly get it with only a wooden spoon. There might be some crumbs of dough lying on the bottom of the bowl. Don't worry. They'll all be mixed in eventually.

Flour a large board or working space. Put aside some extra flour in a small cup. You may need it to add to the dough as you begin the next step. The dough is now ready to be kneaded.

Kneading

This is another of the parts of bread baking that make it all worthwhile. It is physical. It is sensual. It is sheer magic as the dough changes texture under your hands. The biscuitlike dough which you thought could never possibly become a bread now begins to have potential as a work of art. It is also a time to get rid of any aggressions you might have, for it is not, by any means, a delicate process. You are alone with the newly mixed dough, and minute by ticking minute it will begin to change.

Choose a counter that allows you leverage, for you will be using your arms and shoulders to knead the dough. If the counter is too high, you'll find that you can't "get into it," and it will take you much longer to achieve the final texture.

The surface is dusted with flour. Also dip your hands in flour before you begin. Keep the flour handy nearby, either in the small cup I suggested, or in a small bowl. As you knead, you may find that the dough becomes sticky again. Don't be afraid to add more flour to the dough and to put more on your hands. I find that I constantly dip my hands in flour as I knead, until the dough no longer clings to my fingers. Eventually, you will learn just when the texture is perfect. The dough should have a damp feeling rather than a dry one.

Keep in mind that the reason that you knead bread is to distribute the gas bubbles formed by the yeast fermentation as thoroughly as possible throughout the dough. This, along with the gluten, will cause the bread to rise later on—still more magic to be discovered. Turn the dough out from the bowl onto the floured surface. It is crumbly, to be sure, and it seems to get away from you when you try to push the excess dough into the middle. But all that will change. . . .

With your right hand, pull the rear of the dough into the middle and push down with the heel of your hand. Push down hard! Then, using your left hand, turn the entire dough mass slightly in a clockwise direction. (Left-handed people may reverse the process. It will work. Left-handed breads taste just as good as right-handed breads.)

The secret to good kneading is good rhythm. Right hand pulls the rear into the center. Left hand turns the dough. Then again right hand pulls the rear into the center, left hand turns the batter. Bit by little bit, you will learn to increase the pace and the rhythm will begin to make itself felt. But don't be afraid to push. You can't hurt the dough. I take off my shirt in the kitchen when I knead. A woman I know makes believe that each push is an aggressive release toward someone she doesn't like. Most of my students are much more positive in their attitudes.

If you find the dough sticking to your fingers or if it seems to be getting too damp to handle, dust it with flour and again flour your hands.

In a few minutes, you'll begin to feel the texture of the dough changing. The crumbly mixture will become more elastic and smoother. Somehow it no longer seems ready to fall apart and it bounces back with each turn and push of the hands. The satiny, shiny glow of the dough will begin to make the kneading worthwhile. Don't let up on the rhythm. The dough will change once again—smoother, shinier, bouncing back when you push into it. It will normally take from 8 to 10 minutes of good hard kneading, but the treasure in front of you will have made it all worthwhile. On the counter sits a perfect hillock of shimmering, sensual dough. You have changed it from an ugly duckling into a thing of beauty. I never tire of taking just a moment to look at my handiwork.

The dough is now ready for the first rise.

A Note About Electric Mixers and Food Processors: I have never used them for I love the sensual texture of handling the dough. That does not mean that they can't be used for a part of the mixing and kneading. Some heavy-duty electric mixers come with a bread hook attachment, and hand-crank model bread mixers are also available. The new food processors all come with a plastic blade that can be used for kneading dough. However, you will probably find several disadvantages with all of them. Unless you have a professional model machine, you will have to mix and knead only small amounts, and the dough will probably still have to be turned out onto the counter to complete the kneading process. Of course, some of us do not have the physical strength to do the entire kneading process by hand and, in that case, the electric alternative is a welcome one. You will have to find your own way—and your own method. But before going "electric," why not try it the way that dear old grandmother used to bake bread? Try kneading by hand to start out.

Thoroughly kneaded, the yeasty gas bubbles and the gluten have been well distributed throughout the mixture. Lightly oil a large bowl and put the dough into it. Using a pastry brush, you might also lightly oil the top of the dough so that it does not dry out while it is rising. Then cover the bowl with a light towel or cloth and put the bowl in a warm place in the kitchen until the dough has doubled in size. The time will vary with different breads, so individual instructions are given with each recipe. But, the standard yeast bread generally takes about 45 minutes to 1 hour to double in size.

You can tell when the bread is ready by pushing down into the dough with two fingers. If the indentations remain, it is ready to be punched and shaped.

Now, much has been written about just *where* to put the bowl for the rise. Not every kitchen has a perfect place that measures 85°F. exactly. Here again, the mystique is not worth the trouble. *Any* draft-free place will do. If the temperature is cooler than 85°F., it will just take a little longer. (There are, after all, *brioche* recipes that require that the dough remain overnight in the refrigerator, and they come out perfectly fine.)

Some bakers use a sink half-filled with warm water and they place the bowl either in the water or on a platform above it. Others place the bowl near the pilot light of a gas stove. And still others place the bowl atop a warm radio or television set. (Just remember that the newer solid-state television sets do not give off any heat. And still the dough will rise, never fear.)

As I keep saying, the lovely thing about bread baking is that all the rules we lay down are eventually broken anyway and somehow most of the breads do come out. I read somewhere that you must never place the rising dough on a radiator or out in sunlight—and two weeks later found a book where the author said she *always* puts the bowl on top of her radiator, with an underlayer of flagstone. Still later, I met someone who swore that the only way to make the dough rise was to place the bowl on a rock in a field—directly in the sun, just as her grandmother did!

So find that warm spot in your kitchen, cover the bowl with a towel and go take a walk or read the morning paper.

The First Rise

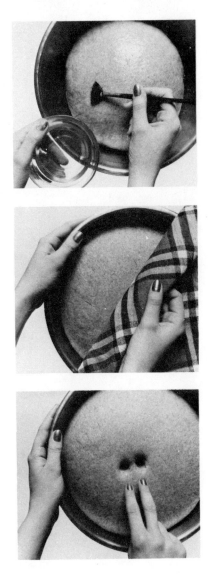

Before the Second Rise

Twenty-five times you have peeked under the towel to watch the dough rise. (A watched dough always rises!) Somehow it seems to be filling the bowl. There are times when it will rise up and begin to push the towel upward in a lush, full mound. It is another part of bread magic.

Take off the towel and admire the dough for a second. Don't forget to test it by pushing in with two fingers. If the indentations remain, it is ready for the next step. Turn it out onto a lightly floured surface, just as you did before. *And hit it!* Yes, hit it—pound it and watch it deflate and just lie there quietly. Let it rest for a minute or two. Unlike the first time you turned it out, when it was crumbly and unshaped, the dough now has a satiny texture and a slight dampness that makes it a pleasure to handle.

Knead it for a few moments. Get the feel of the dough again. Pull in with the right hand, push with the left. Then, pick it up and slam it down on the counter top. Hard!

Do it again, and let the dough begin to form a long, heavy strip while you beat it down again and again to further distribute the gluten and the gas bubbles before the next stage.

Now, where on earth did I ever learn to hit the dough, to pound it down on the counter? One bread-baking day I heard a knock on the downstairs door at my island home. My neighbor, Margaret Peabody (see Index), a superb bread baker, had come to call. Dressed in a bathing suit and wearing a floppy straw hat, she had a huge dollop of dough strung over her shoulder. She, too, had been baking that morning, but she had a question to ask me and saw no reason to interrupt her kneading just because she wanted to visit next door. She merely took the dough with her.

As she came up the stairs, the dough undulated and wiggled. Obviously, it was in the midst of being kneaded prior to the second rise. In the kitchen, Margaret took it in her hands and threw it down on my counter. All the while she kept up a conversation while I watched her in awe. A few words, then SLAM!—down went the dough. Finally, she explained (SLAM!) that it was the best way to guarantee thorough blending (SLAM!)—and that her bread textures were far superior to the ones she had previously baked.

I now do it, too. It works.

Triticale Bread (Mel London) page 212 *33*

34   Cinnamon Twists (Corinne Wastun) page 62

On occasion, you will find a recipe that requires two rises in the bowl, with the final (third) rise taking place when the bread is shaped. The San Francisco Sourdough Loaf recipe given in this book (see Index) is a good example. It is the kneading and the rising that distribute the gases more evenly and eventually give your bread the final texture. Generally, the more times you allow the dough to rise, the finer the texture of the end product. However, most breads take one rise in the bowl and one after being shaped and are then placed in the pans or on the baking surface.

In shaping your loaves, remember that they will rise again before being baked, and then again in the oven, so don't make them too large or fill the pans too completely. The recipes will tell you how many loaves you can expect to get from the dough, so if the shapes look small and puny, don't let it bother you. The surprise is yet to come.

Roll the dough between your hands until it is one smooth ball. Then, with your fingers, pull it apart in equal sections to make the number of loaves called for in the recipe. One shaping technique merely requires that you sculpt each shape between your hands, making certain that it is perfectly smooth all around. Another technique suggests that you shape it like a "jelly roll," smoothing the ends and pressing it firmly together when shaped. All will work, and the second rise and the baking will take care of making everything come out even.

Bread baking offers many opportunities to experiment with shapes. Leonard Silver is a friend of mine who loves the "heel" (the end) from the long French loaves of bread. He will eat no other part. Invited to his house for dinner, I baked a special gift of sourdough bread with *10 heels.* I merely shaped it to resemble a long thin tree with 8 limbs and 2 ends. He was in ecstasy over his gift and even took a picture of the bread before diving in and devouring the crunchy heels.

Bread Pans: The most common method of baking loaf bread is to use the classic pan—the large, standard size (9¾ × 5¾ × 2¾ inches) or the medium size (8½ × 4½ × 2½ inches). I find that for a small family, three medium-size loaves are better than two large ones. If you are using a glass baking utensil rather than a metal one, make certain the temperature of the oven is 25 degrees lower, since glass retains the heat longer than metal.

French Bread Pans: These are designed for the long loaves of French, Italian, or sourdough breads, bringing forth images of bicycle riders in Paris carrying their loaves home from the tiny

Shaping

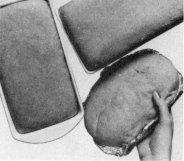

bakeries. They are available in shapes that allow for two breads or five. If, however, you want to attempt a long loaf before buying a special pan, fold a piece of aluminum foil in a long tray shape and place the dough in it for baking.

Free-Form Shaping on Cookie Sheets: Many breads look absolutely glorious when baked on cookie sheets, with no bounds on your imagination as to shape or size. You can bake oval loaves, round loaves, square loaves, long loaves. Breads such as *Challah* or Swiss Lemon Twist (*see* Index) require that you braid them in three- or six-braid breads before you bake them, and though they are sometimes placed in standard bread pans, it is free-form baking that helps them achieve their full beauty.

Special Pans: Some breads, like muffins, rolls, or *brioche,* will require a special pan. Just follow the directions given in the recipe. In addition, some breads can be baked in coffee cans and well-washed clay flowerpots.

When the shapes are made, follow instructions as to buttering the pans or sprinkling with flour or cornmeal to prevent sticking. Then place the shapes in the pans or on the sheets. We are one step closer to the final act!

The Second

Rise

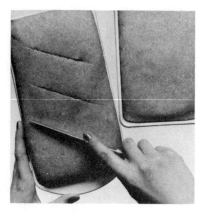

Cover with a towel and put the pans or cookie sheets in a warm spot in the kitchen. The dough will rise again, but be careful this time. Another common mistake made by beginners (next to not using enough flour in damp climates) is allowing the second rise to go too far. Remember that you must leave some room for rising while the loaves bake. If the dough rises too much in the pans, the loaves may well burst and fall when they meet the heat of the oven. The rise should go to about double. Judge it by *eye* and, this time, don't stick your fingers in to see if the indentations remain.

Some recipes will then call for decoration or for the addition of seeds atop the bread before baking. Others will require that you add a glaze or spray them with water. All of these special requirements will be covered in the recipes and all will help to make the bread taste better and to look more professional.

There *is* one technique, however, that never fails to frighten the beginner (and I was no exception). Some recipes require that you slash the bread—either with a knife or a razor blade—before baking. Slash my lovely bread? It's bound to fall! Look at all those gases pumped up in there because of the yeast and gluten!

It will not fall. Slash it as required. It helps the bread expand more evenly in the oven and prevents it from bursting unevenly at some weak seam as it rises. It also makes for a lovely decoration. Some of my breads are slashed with lines, some with crosses, some with stars. Somehow, after they've come out of the oven, these breads look the most picturesque of all.

Finally, in the oven! The aromas will fill the house—essence of yeast—neighbors will walk in and say, "I could smell the bread the minute I came through the door." There are several points to remember about this critical stage:

Baking

Temperature is accurate only to a point. At about 350° to 375°F., the oven is considered "moderate" and above 425°F. it begins to get "hot." I find that a 25-degree variation makes no difference at all. If the temperature is slightly lower, it just takes a few minutes longer.

Remember that the temperature of any oven may vary depending upon where you place your breads—hotter near the top than at the middle. Place your breads so that the air can circulate around the pans and then, during the baking, move them from place to place in the oven, turn them front to back, so that they bake evenly. I have one hot spot in my oven (top, upper right) that requires constant watching so that the upper right bread doesn't burn before I move it.

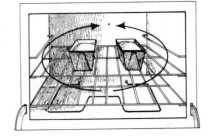

Professional bakers use steam in their ovens to keep the breads moist while baking. For the amateur bread baker, there is an easy way to accomplish the same results. I merely heat a brick atop the stove while I'm preparing the dough and I boil some water in a kettle. When the oven reaches the correct temperature, I pour the water into an oblong deep pan, place the hot brick in the middle and then put the entire thing on the bottom floor of the oven. The steam begins immediately and continues throughout the baking process. (Don't put the brick in first—it may burn your pan.)

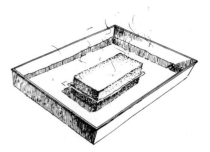

My personal practice in baking bread is to make as many loaves at one time as my oven will hold. It is practical in terms of the labor involved—and it saves a great deal of energy. If I am going to heat my oven to 400°F. and keep it there for the better part of an hour, I want to see a bounty of results.

One way to utilize more oven space is merely to double the recipes as given. I find that the recipes in most books are geared to 1 or 2 breads. Why not double and bake 4? It is really just as easy to bake 4, 6, 8, or 10 breads at one time as it is to bake 2. One can be eaten, the others frozen.

Another method, and one which I like better, is to bake two *different* kinds of breads that require the same oven temperature, such as Sourdough Bread (see Index) and a quick bread like Buttermilk Rye (see Index). While the yeast bread is rising for the last time, I whip up the quick breads and pop them into the oven at the same time.

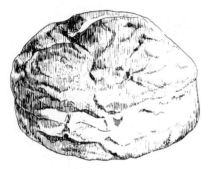

Recently, I came across another suggestion for saving energy—do not preheat the oven. That way the breads go in while the oven is cold and they take about 10 or 15 minutes longer to bake. However, my head keeps telling me that it takes the same amount of energy to bake an additional 10 minutes beginning with a cold oven as it does to bake 10 minutes less by starting with a preheated oven. We have all already agreed that I am old-fashioned. I preheat my oven.

Testing: The breads will brown (evenly, we hope)—and the same anxious looks that were given the rising dough will also accompany this phase of the baking process. If your oven has a glass door and an oven light, the performance is worth watching. The breads will, indeed, rise, and the clicking clock timer will tell you that the moment of truth is approaching. When you think they're done—when they should be done—test them by taking out one loaf (while wearing asbestos gloves or using pot holders, of course). Turn the loaf over into your hand. The bottom should be brown and, when tapped, it should sound hollow. If in doubt, use a cake tester, pushing up from bottom to top and if it comes out clean, the bread is done.

If the bottom of the loaf seems soggy and the tapping does not produce a hollow sound, put it back in the oven, but check it every five minutes or so. On the other hand, if the *top* is brown and seems right, but the bottom is yet undone, cover the top with aluminum foil before you put it back in the oven. This will keep the top from burning while the rest of the bread bakes through.

Cooling

They are out. They are beautiful. Turn the loaves out of the pans or take them off the cookie sheets according to directions and place them one by lovely one on a wire rack in a draft-free place. The reason for the wire rack is that the bottoms will cool evenly as well as the rest of the loaf, preventing moisture from collecting underneath the fresh breads and making them soggy. This is the time to call the family in to see the results—a pleasure only superseded by the next step.

Tasting

The bread should be cool before you cut it—or, at most, slightly warm. Don't cut it while it's piping hot. It needs time to firm up its texture and, besides, my mother used to tell me that it causes stomach aches.

No bread will ever taste as good, and you will never tire of the thrill of cutting into the first piece of bread, fresh from the oven, served dripping with butter. (I am convinced that fresh-baked bread must have butter on it to bring it to its full glory.)

Freezing

Let the breads cool completely and then wrap them in some kind of freezer paper, plastic wrap, or foil. I find that heavy-weight aluminum foil does the best job because it's easier to eliminate all the air inside the package, a prerequisite to good freezing. Make sure you label the new breads before you store them. When you want one, just take it from the freezer, let it thaw at room temperature, and then open the wrapper and put it in a moderate oven for about 10 minutes before serving. This will freshen the bread and also firm up the crust again. Properly wrapped, the bread can remain frozen from 3 to 4 months without losing the flavor.

A Reminder

Wherever possible, whole grain natural flours are used in the recipes. In three specific categories this policy is suspended, and unbleached white flour is given as an ingredient:

- Traditional breads whose authentic appearance, flavor, texture and color all depend upon the use of unbleached white flour.

- Where especially heavy grains, such as triticale, are used and need to be lightened by the high gluten content of unbleached white flour, and for the special rising requirements of high altitude baking.

- Prizewinning recipes that must be presented as they were judged, and special recipes developed by individual bakers where, in their opinion, whole grain flours might mask or alter the delicate flavors.

You can experiment with using all whole grain flours to make even the exceptional breads above. (We have made many of these breads both ways and, where measurements change, we provide measurements for the whole grain version.) Each recipe in the book has been tested by the author or by our marvelous and enthusiastic staff at the Rodale Test Kitchens.

Quick Breads 6

Several times I've mentioned "quick breads" and perhaps a word or two about them is in order before getting to the recipes. Basically, if we were to describe quick breads in a few words, we might just say: "No need to knead!" And that about sums it up. They can be whipped up using combinations of flour and buttermilk, with baking soda and baking powder as leavenings. Once they're thoroughly blended, they can be placed right in the oven for baking by themselves or along with other yeast breads that require the same temperature. You'll find that Irish Soda Bread (see Index) is a delight for breakfast; Buttermilk Rye/Whole Wheat Bread (see Index) is easy to make, and all kinds of fruit breads and nut breads are available for baking right before lunch or dinner.

Although complete kneading is not necessary, just make certain that the dough is well blended in the bowl. Sometimes it helps to turn the dough out onto a floured board just as you do with yeast breads and then blend it more thoroughly with your hands. This will keep the bread from being lumpy—and though what you're doing seems like kneading, it really is just a smoothing out of the batter before shaping.

Since almost all of the quick breads, like the others, use whole grain flour, you'll find that they're on the sticky side. Don't be afraid to add flour to the dough, but don't make it too firm and dry. The dough should be slightly damp when you shape it.

In the oven, make sure the bread is baked through thoroughly. The crust should be brown and firm, and the bottom should sound hollow when you tap it as you do in testing yeast breads. Again, if you're in doubt, use a cake tester, pushing from the bottom up toward the top. If it comes out clean and it's not sticky, the bread is ready.

If each of us were asked to describe what a "home-baked" bread looks like, we'd probably come close to painting a word picture of a quick bread. I find that quick breads get the most comments from guests, even though my sourdough starter has been active for three years and I slave over three rises. Somehow the sourdoughs are beginning to look too professional. Slashed across the top, the crusts firm and brown, the quick breads look like they've just come from a farm kitchen. Everyone loves them.

The Bakers and 7
Their Recipes

Enough. You have read quite enough about bread. It is time to try your hand at the craft. The recipes, as I've told you, have been collected from my own files and from the friends whom you will meet on the following pages—bread winners from all over the United States. My discussions with them, my correspondence, the excitement of sharing knowledge and humorous stories, made writing this book one of the great joys of my life.

They—as you—and I—spend their working days at jobs and professions that have nothing to do with baking. But they all have one thing in common—Bread. And now, so will you.

GEORGE MELUSO

George Meluso is a New York fashion photographer who has a house on our island, but he is, first of all, my teacher. All of us here know of him and most of us have tasted his remarkably good breads, for he is the most generous of people. Some years ago, George baked the *Challah* recipe which follows for the village Sabbath services, though he himself is not Jewish. Each Sunday, hordes of his son's friends can be seen making their way from his house, each of them munching on a piece of his homemade pizza.

My own introduction to bread baking was quite unusual. George had offered to let me watch him bake, probably one of the best lessons any novice can take. Since there are no cars in our village, I rode over on my bicycle, observed the first step and then rode home. About an hour later, George telephoned to tell me that the next stage was about to begin. Back on the bicycle, over to George's house to see the rising bread pounded down, then back home again. For several hours we performed that rite of a phone call followed by my riding over for each step of the process.

Finally, when the bread was ready to come out of the oven, he telephoned for the last time and together we shared the slices of the warm loaf topped with creamy butter. I then went home and baked my own first bread. It tasted just as good.

His mother had always baked bread—huge loaves for the whole family. About 10 years ago, when George decided to try his hand at it, his loaves just didn't look right.

I had been buying bread for 10 years at a small Italian bakery in East Harlem. Two elderly brothers ran the shop, an old, dingy bakery with one of New York's last brick ovens fired by coal. I asked them if I could watch them bake bread.

The brothers agreed and George was told to appear at 5:00 A.M. the next morning. When he arrived at the appointed time, they gave him a white hat and white apron and put him to work

The Breads:

Whole Wheat Bread
Pizza Dough
(Pizza Topping)
Challah
French Raisin Bread
Pumpernickel
Italian Sesame Twist

shaping their breads. As long as he was there to observe, there was no sense keeping his hands idle.

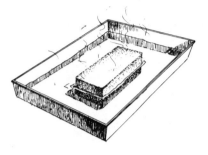

At 8:00 A.M. we all stopped for "refreshment"—a glass of red wine—and to this day I keep a small glass of red wine on my counter while I bake. Later in the day, when people bought the breads, I was delighted—they were the breads that I had shaped!

Helping out at the bakery for a few weekends, George also learned about steam in the oven and he, too, puts a hot brick into a pan of water at the bottom of the oven for each baking.

Except for the flour, he seldom measures, relying on the "feel" of the dough rather than the recipe amounts. His easy and uncomplicated attitude toward bread baking dispelled any fears I might have had about the craft. You'll notice over and over again how each baker in the book speaks of the "feel" or the texture of the dough. You, too, will learn to recognize just when it's right.

In George's recipes, you'll notice that he bases all of them on six cups of flour: "I find that six cups of flour make two perfect anythings. . . ."

After several weekends of visits, I came away with *six* Meluso recipes—plus a delicious and simple pizza topping.

This is a simple recipe that uses George's basic six cups of flour as measurement. The two loaves can be free form or you can bake them in medium-size loaf pans (8½ × 4½ × 2½ inches). I found it to be a marvelous breakfast bread when toasted, with the millet giving it a crunchy quality. If you like, you may add one-half cup of raisins to the recipe.

Dissolve the yeast in ½ cup warm water, add ½ teaspoon honey and stir. Let the mixture stand for about 10 minutes to become active.

Pour 1 cup warm water into a large mixing bowl, stir in honey, salt, and yeast mixture. Add millet and sunflower seeds. Stir. Add flour 1 cup at a time.

With each addition, stir thoroughly. Flour your hands and flour a working surface, then turn out the dough. If it seems too damp, add a bit more flour.

Knead for 8 to 10 minutes and place in an oiled bowl. Lightly brush top of the dough with oil and then cover the bowl and place it in a warm spot. When the dough is double in size (about 1 hour), turn it out onto the floured surface and pound it down. Let it rest for about 2 to 3 minutes. Then knead for about 2 to 3 minutes more. Place the dough back in the bowl, cover and let it rise again to double—about 45 minutes.

Preheat the oven to 375°F. When the dough has doubled in bulk or the indentations remain when you push 2 fingers into it, turn it out onto a floured surface again, pound it down and let it rest for 2 to 3 minutes.

Form the dough into 1 large ball and then divide it in two. Shape the dough and place on a buttered cookie sheet, allowing enough room between the loaves for expansion in the oven. Put boiling water in a pan and place a hot brick in it. Put at bottom of oven to create steam. Place the breads in the oven and bake for 45 minutes or until the loaves test done. Turn loaves or cookie sheet in the oven at least twice to allow for even baking.

When done, the bottom of each bread should be firm and sound hollow when tapped. Remove the loaves from the oven and place them on a wire rack to cool.

Whole Wheat Bread

(2 loaves)

For the Leavening:

2 packages dry yeast
½ cup warm water
½ teaspoon honey

For the Bread:

1 cup warm water
1 tablespoon honey
1 tablespoon salt (optional)
¼ cup millet
¼ cup sunflower seeds (chopped)
4 to 6 cups whole wheat or
    graham flour

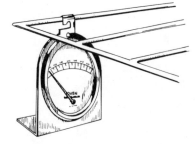

Pizza Dough

(2 large- or 4 medium-size pizzas)

For the Leavening:

1 package dry yeast
½ cup warm water
½ teaspoon honey

For the Pizza Dough:

4 to 5 cups whole wheat flour
1 tablespoon oil
1 cup water

My wife and I have been arguing the point these past few weeks—she claims that pizza isn't truly a bread. I, of course, disagree. Pizza is one of George Meluso's greatest triumphs and, if the purists will forgive me, I would like to include the recipe in this book. It is, after all, a dough. It is made with flour, liquid, and leavening—it is similar to *Pita* (see Index) and *Khubis Araby* (see Index).

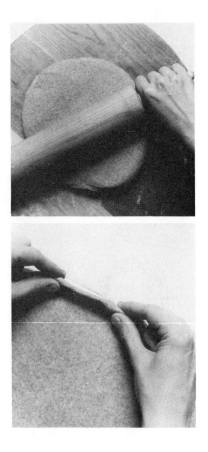

Dissolve yeast in ½ cup warm water, add ½ teaspoon honey and stir. Let stand for about 10 minutes to become active.

Put 4 cups of flour in a large mixing bowl (George does not sift), stir in oil, 1 cup water, and yeast mixture. Mix thoroughly. Coat your hands with flour and turn out the dough onto a floured surface or board. Knead thoroughly for 8 to 10 minutes. Divide the dough in half—you should have 2 pieces that weigh about 1½ pounds each (or 4 pieces of ¾ pound each). Form the dough into balls and place on a floured surface, cover with a towel and let them rise to double (about 1 hour).

Punch them down and form 2 circles. On the floured surface, roll out each circle with a rolling pin to fit a 16-inch (or 8-inch) circular tray. (George does not suggest that beginners make the circles by throwing the pizza dough into the air as he does. The technique is certainly theatrical, but it takes practice to keep from putting your fist through the dough.) When the circle is approximately the right size, place it on the circular tray and shape it exactly to the size of the tray. Using your fingers and pressing into the edges of the dough, make a small raised ridge all around the circle. This will hold the sauce. Preheat oven to 500°F.

In a large pan, sauté the minced garlic in the olive oil. Pour in tomatoes, season with salt and pepper, and cook over low heat for 30 minutes, stirring from time to time. Let cool to room temperature because a hot sauce will make the pizza dough soggy. When cooled, spoon sauce evenly over the pizza dough, lay sliced mozzarella over top, and sprinkle with basil and oregano. Place the pizza on the floor of a gas oven or the lowest shelf of an electric oven and bake for 8 to 10 minutes—until any cheese on the topping is melted and the outer crust is crisp. When it's finished, sprinkle grated Parmesan or Romano cheese on the top.

Remove the pizza from oven and let it sit for about 5 minutes before cutting it in sections.

Incidentally, both the dough and the pizza itself will hold up well if you freeze them. You might want to make only 1 large pizza, and save the rest of the dough for another time.

Suggested Pizza Topping

(for 2 large- or 4 medium-size pizzas)

For the Sauce:

1 clove garlic, minced
2 tablespoons olive oil
1 1-pound can crushed plum
    tomatoes
1 teaspoon salt (optional)
dash pepper

½ pound mozzarella cheese sliced
    finely or shredded (fontina or
    provolone may also be used)
basil
oregano
1 tablespoon grated Parmesan or
    Romano cheese

Challah

(2 loaves—braided)

For the Leavening:

2 packages dry yeast
½ cup lukewarm water
½ teaspoon honey

For the Bread:

6 cups unbleached white flour
1 tablespoon honey
2 tablespoons coarse salt*
3 tablespoons oil
3 eggs, beaten (reserve 1
teaspoon egg yolk for glaze)
1 cup water

For the Glaze:

1 teaspoon egg yolk
1 tablespoon water
poppy seeds

This is the traditional Jewish Sabbath bread—a light exquisitely designed loaf, glazed with egg yolk and topped with poppy seeds. George Meluso described his first attempt at the bread:

It was October and the weather on the island was chilly. Since my house is not winterized, there was no warm place in the kitchen to let the bread rise. I took a large board sprinkled with cornmeal and I placed the braided dough on it and put it in front of the fireplace. In about an hour, it had risen—and it was a thrill to see that beautiful loaf in all its glory, with the fire making a halo around it. It was almost too beautiful to put it in the oven to bake!

Try the three-braided *challah* first, and then you might try a six-braided loaf for a spectacular effect.

Dissolve the yeast in lukewarm water, add honey and stir. Let stand for about 10 minutes.

Put the 6 cups of flour in a large mixing bowl, make a well in the center and pour in the yeast mixture.

In a large measuring cup, combine the honey, salt, oil, and the beaten eggs, making sure that you have reserved 1 teaspoon of yolk for the glaze. Add the 1 cup of water and mix.

Add the mixture to the flour and yeast. Mix well. Turn out onto a slightly floured surface, flour your hands and knead for 10 minutes.

Put the dough in an oiled bowl, lightly brush the top with oil and cover. Set in a warm place until dough is double in size (about 1 hour).

When dough has doubled, turn out onto floured surface, punch down, and let dough rest for about 2 minutes. Gently knead the dough again for about 2 more minutes, place in oiled bowl again and let rise to double (about 1 hour).

When the dough has doubled in size or the indentations of your fingers remain when the dough is pressed down, turn out onto

---

*The salt, though traditional, may be eliminated if you choose to do so.

lightly floured counter and punch down. Knead for a few moments and then divide the dough into 6 equal parts.

Roll each part of the dough into the shape of a sausage—about 10 inches long, tapered at the ends. Braid 3 rolls together to form a loaf. (Some bakers prefer to start the braid in the middle and work toward the ends. George Meluso and I find starting at the end a great deal easier.) Make certain that the ends of the braid are firmly pressed together so that they don't unravel during baking.

Oil a large baking sheet and lightly dust the surface with the flour. Place the braided bread on the sheet and make a second loaf with the remaining 3 braids.

NOTE: For 6-braided breads, 3 larger braids are placed on the bottom and 3 smaller braids are put atop as a crown. It makes a very large loaf.

Cover the braided breads and place them in a warm place to double the size. Preheat the oven to 375°F.

When the loaves have doubled in size, combine the reserved teaspoon of egg yolk with 1 tablespoon of water, mix, and brush the tops of the loaves with the glaze. Sprinkle poppy seeds on top of the loaves and place them in the oven to bake for about 40 minutes or until browned and the bottom sounds hollow when tapped.

Remove from oven and set the loaves on a wire rack to cool.

NOTE: Tradition calls for unbleached white flour in *challah*. However, you may make this bread using whole wheat flour, if you like. It won't be traditional, but it will taste just fine.

French Raisin Bread

(2 loaves)

For the Leavening:

1 package dry yeast
½ cup lukewarm water
½ teaspoon honey

For the Bread:

1½ cups tepid water
3 tablespoons honey
1½ tablespoons salt (optional)
6 cups whole wheat flour
1 cup raisins (softened in water
and drained)

Dissolve the yeast in ½ cup of lukewarm water. Add ½ teaspoon honey and stir. Cover and set aside the yeast mixture until it foams and doubles in volume.

In a large mixing bowl, pour in 1½ cups of tepid water; then add the honey and salt. Add the foaming yeast, and beat in 2 cups of the flour, mixing well after each addition. Cover mixture and let stand for a few minutes.

Add more flour until a stiff dough is formed. Turn out onto a lightly floured board, using only enough additional flour to knead into the dough if it becomes too sticky. Knead well, about 8 to 10 minutes, until the dough is smooth and elastic. Shape the dough into a ball and place in a warm, greased bowl. Cover with a piece of buttered wax paper. Set aside in a warm place until dough doubles in bulk (about 1¼ to 1½ hours).

Turn dough out onto a lightly floured board and divide it in half; then knead each piece well until all the air bubbles have been worked out. Before shaping the loaves, add ½ cup of the drained raisins to each of the balls, kneading them right into the dough.

Now shape into 2 long loaves, tapering at the ends. Place each loaf on a greased baking pan sprinkled lightly with cornmeal. Cover lightly with a towel and set aside in a warm place, free from drafts, until doubled in bulk (about 1 hour).

Preheat the oven to 350°F.

Before putting loaves in the oven, slash each one diagonally ¼ inch deep about 2 inches apart. Brush the tops of the breads with a little saltwater before baking and then once or twice more during baking to give them a crisp, golden-brown crust. Bake about 40 to 45 minutes for crusty loaves.

When done, cool on wire racks.

You'll find this to be a dense, dark, delicious bread. You may prefer to use loaf pans instead of making the breads as free-form shapes.

Soften yeast in ½ cup lukewarm water. Add ½ teaspoon honey. Mix. Cover and set aside until foaming and double in volume.

In a large mixing bowl, stir together 1½ cups hot water, salt, honey, treacle or molasses. Cool to lukewarm. Add the foaming yeast. Add rye flour and whole wheat flour—just enough to make a stiff dough. Mix well with hands or large wooden spoon and let stand for 10 to 15 minutes. Turn out onto a breadboard that has been sprinkled lightly with whole wheat flour. Knead well for 10 minutes. Rye flour has a tendency to be slightly sticky and damper than unbleached white. Place the dough in a warm, well-greased bowl, turning the dough to grease the top. Cover with a light towel and let rise in a warm place, free from drafts, for 1½ hours or until doubled in bulk.

Turn out onto a floured board and knead again for 10 minutes. Return to the greased bowl, cover, and let rise again for about 45 minutes or until dough is not quite double in bulk. (The second rise will not be as large as the first.)

Turn out onto a lightly floured board and knead again for 2 to 3 minutes. Divide the dough in half and shape into 2 round loaves. Place in greased and floured round casseroles or on a greased and floured baking sheet. Cover with a towel or wax paper and let rise in a warm place for about 30 minutes.

Preheat oven to 375°F.

Bake loaves in oven for 1¼ hours or until bread is firm and golden brown. If a thick, crisp crust is desired, brush top of loaves with water before baking and several times during baking.

Cool on wire racks.

Pumpernickel

(2 loaves)

For the Leavening:

2 packages dry yeast
½ cup lukewarm water
½ teaspoon honey

For the Bread:

1½ cups hot water
1½ tablespoons salt (optional)
1 tablespoon honey
3 tablespoons treacle or molasses
4 cups rye flour
2 cups whole wheat flour

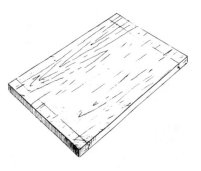

Italian Sesame Twist

(2 loaves)

For the Leavening:

1 package dry yeast
½ cup lukewarm water
½ teaspoon honey

For the Bread:

1½ cups tepid water
1 tablespoon honey
1½ tablespoons salt (optional)
5 to 6 cups whole wheat flour
sesame seeds

Aside from being downright delicious, it seems that any bread that is shaped in the form of a twist is also very impressive. This bread is one of George's (and my) favorites.

Dissolve yeast in ½ cup lukewarm water. Add ½ teaspoon honey and stir. Cover and set mixture aside until it is foaming and double in volume.

Pour the tepid water, honey, and salt into a large mixing bowl and stir. Add the foaming yeast. Begin to add the flour, 2 cups at a time, mixing well after each addition and thoroughly blending with a wooden spoon. Continue to add more flour until a stiff dough is formed. Cover with a towel and let stand for a few minutes.

Turn the dough out onto a lightly floured board and knead until it is smooth and elastic, about 8 to 10 minutes. Shape the dough into a ball and place in a warm, greased bowl, turning the dough to grease the top. Cover with buttered wax paper and a light kitchen towel and set aside in a warm place until double in size, about 1¼ to 1½ hours.

After the dough has risen, turn out onto a lightly floured board and knead again for about 10 minutes, or until any air bubbles have disappeared.

Divide the dough into 2 equal sections. Then take each section and divide it into 3 equal parts. Roll each of the 3 parts into 14-inch strands or ropes. Braid the 3 strands and seal the ends. Bring both ends around to form a circle and connect the ends by wetting your fingertips and lightly pasting the dough together. Repeat with the second set of 3 strands to form another circular braided loaf.

Place the 2 loaves, well spaced apart, on a greased and lightly floured baking sheet. Cover with wax paper or a light towel and place in a warm spot until they double in size—about 1 hour.

Preheat oven to 350°F.

When loaves have doubled in size, brush tops with water and sprinkle with sesame seeds. Bake for 40 to 45 minutes for crusty brown loaves.

Cool on wire racks.

ESTHER YANNEY

Each year in the month of June, the city of Omaha, Nebraska, celebrates with an Ethnic Festival—music and dancing and all kinds of good things to eat, a festival for the people of all the nationalities who have chosen that city as their home.

The last time I spoke with her, Esther Yanney, mother of two, grandmother of seven, was in the midst of making the last of 25 dozen *Khubis Araby,* the Lebanese flat bread that she bakes for the festival each year. By the time the week was over, her total would probably double. "They go so fast at the festival—20 dozen in less than an hour. . . ."

The recipe itself is quite simple. And it's fun to make. You have to be just a bit uninhibited, because the trick lies in making the dough as thin as possible by throwing it in the air. Esther can make an 8-inch circle into the size of a platter in just a few seconds. The finished dough is so thin that you can see light passing through it.

My mother taught me how to make the bread. I would pat out the dough and then watch her toss it in the air to make it thin. She told me not to worry about the middle, just make sure the edges were thin. The middle would thin out during the tossing. Now my husband helps me. I throw the dough while he moves the breads on the shelves of the oven and takes them out when they're ready. . . .

For the beginner, Esther suggests that a good part of the stretching of the dough be done with a floured rolling pin.

When she's not baking for the Ethnic Festival or the Lebanese Bake-O-Rama at St. Mary's Church in Omaha, Esther makes the bread for her family, all of whom love it. The best invitation I've had is an offer to visit her next time I'm in Omaha, to learn how to throw the dough.

Incidentally, *Khubis Araby* may be served soft or it may be made crisp in the oven—either way, serve it with butter.

The Bread:

Khubis Araby
(Lebanese flat bread)

Khubis Araby

(Lebanese flat bread)

(25 to 30 breads—recipe may be cut in half
for fewer breads)

2 packages dry yeast
½ cup warm water
5 pounds unbleached white flour
4 teaspoons salt*
water

In a large bowl, dissolve the yeast in warm water. Let it stand for a few minutes. Add flour and salt. Stir in enough water to make a soft dough, as for bread. Turn out onto a lightly floured surface and knead for 8 to 10 minutes, until dough is smooth and elastic. Cover and let rise until double in bulk.

Punch down dough and shape into about 25 to 30 balls, each about the size of an orange. Cover again and let rise until double in bulk.

Preheat the oven to 550° to 600°F. The bread should be made in a gas oven. See note below for electric ovens.

Place 1 ball of dough on a lightly floured surface and firmly tap it down with the fingertips to flatten it out. Do not push at an angle to flatten it—push straight down with your fingers. Occasionally, turn the dough to maintain a circular shape.

When the circle is about 8 to 10 inches in diameter, carefully lift it up on 1 hand. The dough is then tossed from hand to hand so that the dough will stretch into a circle of much larger dimension.

To maintain the circular shape, try rotating the dough about a quarter turn each time, catching the *outer* edge of the dough. As it is caught by 1 hand, it is turned, and tossed again after resting just briefly.

When the dough is as thin as possible—place it on a wide paddle

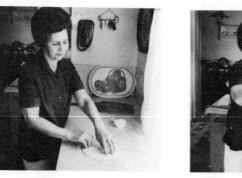

*The salt, though traditional, may be eliminated if you choose to do so.

(or baker's peel, as it's professionally called) and slide it onto the floor of the preheated oven. (If you don't have a baker's peel, any wide, flat, thin board will serve as a substitute.) Bake only a few seconds until it gets firm on the bottom. Remove the bread from the oven and place it under the broiler for a couple of seconds until it bubbles on top. Keep in mind that this bread takes very little baking because it is thin and the heat is so high.

Remove the bread from the oven and cover it with a towel. Repeat the process with the remaining balls of dough. You can have one baking in the oven while another is finishing under the broiler at the same time. Esther (along with the author) suggests that you try doing just 1 bread at a time at the beginning. It will keep you busy enough.

As the breads are finished, place them under the towel so they stay soft. They may also be frozen in a tightly sealed plastic freezer bag. When you take them out to thaw, keep them in the bag at room temperature.

NOTE: *Khubis Araby* may be baked in an electric oven, but you will need a double oven to do it. You will have to place a steel plate above the heating coil at the base on 1 oven and bake the bread on that. The other oven would be preheated for broiling and used to brown and bubble the tops of the breads.

CORINNE WASTUN

Corinne lives in Yerington, Nevada, and writes a weekly column for the *Mason Valley News*—"The Only Newspaper in the World That Gives a Damn about Yerington." Though she's now officially retired, she still travels a great deal and mails the column back when she's on the road. Of course, she is a bread baker, and through the years many of her readers have also sent in recipes for her files.

I first began baking bread when my husband and I lived in a mining camp in the early 1940s. A grocery truck came once a week to deliver bread and since week-old bread was not very good, I decided to start baking my own.

She's baked in just about every kind of oven. Her first was a kerosene stove with an oven that sat over the burner. She's also baked in the old iron variety wood stove (and thinks the results are the best of all). Her daughter also bakes bread and Corinne tells me that she uses bread pans that are now in their fourth generation and have *never been washed:*

They are tin and they've been seasoned like frying pans—never washed, just wiped out. They're now covered with brown spots but bread never sticks in them. . . .

Corinne's daughter also has one of the best bread-baking tips that I've come across. Some people complain that they are either not strong enough or tall enough to knead on the standard kitchen counter. The solution:

My daughter found that by putting the breadboard on the floor and kneading Indian fashion, she had more power with which to do a good job.

With tips like these—and after you try the superb recipes that follow—it will be more than the *Mason Valley News* that gives a damn about Yerington, Nevada!

While Corinne was visiting some friends in Green Springs, Ohio, she met Lelah Brown of Tiffin. Ms. Brown is a dedicated cook and baker and these biscuits were served for dinner while Corinne was there.

Sift together flour, salt, baking powder and gradually stir in the light cream with a fork. Then add the sour cream. Drop 6 portions about 3 inches apart on an ungreased baking sheet.

Bake at 450°F. for 12 to 15 minutes.

Melt-in-Your-Mouth Biscuits

(6 biscuits)

1 cup whole wheat flour
¼ teaspoon salt (optional)
2 teaspoons baking powder
⅔ cup light cream
2½ teaspoons sour cream

Honey Oatmeal Bread

(2 loaves)

2 cups boiling water
½ cup mild-flavored honey
2 tablespoons butter
2 teaspoons salt (optional)
1 cup uncooked rolled oats
1 package dry yeast
¼ cup lukewarm water
4½ to 5 cups whole wheat flour, unsifted

Glaze:

honey
uncooked rolled oats

This recipe was sent to Corinne by Martha McCarty of Agoura, California. She's a gourmet cook who enjoys trying new recipes and formulating many of her own. The bread is slightly different from the Honey-Oatmeal Wheat Bread baked by Valerie Rogers (see Index.)

In a large bowl, stir together boiling water, honey, butter, salt, and rolled oats. Let stand 1 hour.

In a small bowl, dissolve the yeast in the lukewarm water. Add to the oat mixture. Stir in the flour 1 cup at a time and beat well.

Turn out onto a lightly floured surface and knead until dough is smooth and elastic (about 10 minutes). If necessary, add enough flour to keep the dough from being too sticky. Place in a greased bowl, turn to coat the top, and cover with a towel or damp cloth. Place in a warm spot and allow to double in bulk—about 1¼ hours.

Turn out onto floured board, knead for 1 or 2 minutes, shape into 2 loaves, and place in well-greased loaf pans. Cover and place in a warm spot until almost doubled in bulk (about 45 minutes).

Bake at 350°F. for 40 to 50 minutes. Tops should be well browned and the bottoms should sound hollow when rapped with the knuckles.

For a tasty glaze, brush tops lightly with honey and sprinkle with uncooked rolled oats.

Cool completely on a wire rack before slicing.

My next door neighbor, Mary Sue Whatley, was widowed while young and left with four small children to raise by herself. She said she first started baking bread because she couldn't afford to buy enough for her family at store prices. She continued because she loved working with the dough and trying new recipes. This one became a holiday favorite.

Scald milk. Stir in honey, salt, and butter. Cool to lukewarm. Measure the warm water into a large warm bowl, sprinkle the yeast over the top and stir until dissolved. Stir in the lukewarm milk mixture, add the eggs and 3 cups of the flour. Beat until smooth. Stir in enough additional flour to make a soft dough. Turn out onto a lightly floured board, knead until smooth and elastic, about 10 minutes. Place in a greased bowl, turn to coat the top, cover and let rise in a warm place free of drafts until doubled in bulk (about 50 minutes to 1 hour).

Punch down. Turn out onto floured board and knead in the citron, raisins, and chopped almonds until they are well distributed. Divide the dough into 4 equal pieces and set 2 pieces aside. Divide 1 piece into 3 equal strips about 14 inches long. Place the 3 strips on a large greased baking sheet and form them into a braid. Brush the top of the braid with melted butter.

Take the second piece and divide it two-thirds and one-third. Take the larger section and divide it into 3 equal strips about 12 inches long. Form the second braid and place it atop the first one. Brush the top with melted butter.

With the remaining dough from the second piece, make a third braid about 10 inches long and place it atop the two others.

Form a second loaf in the same manner. Cover both lightly and let rise in a warm place free from drafts, until doubled in bulk, about 1 hour.

Beat 1 egg and 1 tablespoon of water together until well blended. Brush the braided loaves with the egg mixture. Decorate the top with the whole blanched almonds.

Bake in a moderate oven at 375°F. for about 40 minutes or until loaves are well browned on top.

Hoska

(a braided Czechoslovakian bread)

(2 loaves)

¾ cup milk
½ cup honey
½ teaspoon salt*
½ cup (1 stick) butter
½ cup warm water
2 packages dry yeast
2 eggs
5½ to 6 cups unbleached white flour, unsifted
¼ cup citron
¼ cup raisins
¼ cup chopped almonds
melted butter

Glaze:

1 egg
1 tablespoon water
¼ cup whole blanched almonds

---

*The salt, though traditional, may be eliminated if you choose to do so.

Sopapillas

(Mexican fried bread)

(2 to 3 dozen squares depending on size)

4 cups unbleached white flour
4 teaspoons baking powder
2 teaspoons salt*
2 tablespoons shortening
water

Mary Sue Whatley, who gave Corinne the *Hoska* recipe, also contributed this one. Served hot, with butter and jelly, *Sopapillas* are delicious with any meal.

Sift the dry ingredients into a mixing bowl. Cut in the shortening. Add a little water—just enough to hold together, as you might for a pie crust. Roll thin with a floured rolling pin and cut into small squares (about 2 to 3 inches) or in the shape of triangles.

Fry them in deep and very hot shortening and they will puff up.

Serve hot.

Cinnamon Twists

(16 twists)

1 cup sour cream
¼ cup honey
3 tablespoons butter
⅛ teaspoon soda
1 teaspoon salt (optional)
1 package dry yeast
1 teaspoon honey
½ cup lukewarm water
2 beaten eggs
3 to 4 cups whole wheat flour

Filling:

¼ pound softened butter
¼ cup honey
1 tablespoon cinnamon

My friend, Kathy Harrison, enjoys baking and she especially likes to try some of her grandmother's recipes. At the top of the card for this one, her grandmother had written: "If at first you don't succeed, try again." Good advice for any bread baker.

In a saucepan, heat the sour cream, honey, butter, soda, and salt—but do not boil. Let cool to lukewarm.

Dissolve the yeast and the honey in the lukewarm water. Add with the beaten eggs and the flour to the cooled mixture. Turn out onto a lightly floured board and knead for 5 minutes.

Roll out the dough into a square, 16 × 16 inches. Combine the butter, honey, and cinnamon and spread on the rolled-out dough. Fold into thirds and cut into 16 1-inch strips. Twist each strip and lay on an oiled cookie sheet. Cover lightly and let rise in a warm spot until light—about 1 hour.

Bake at 350°F for about 25 minutes.

When they're done, they may be frosted with your favorite icing, if you like.

*The salt, though traditional, may be eliminated if you choose to do so.

Corinne's friend, Anna Poli, was born and raised right in Yerington. A farmer's wife, she's active in many community projects including her church, and she also cooks and bakes superbly. To quote Mrs. Poli:

> . . . this bread is so simple to make that it hardly seems possible for it to be so good, but it's delicious, especially hot. . . .

In a bowl, put the dry ingredients, add the honey and then pour in the beer, stirring only until the flour is moistened.

Pour into a greased loaf pan and bake at 300°F. for 55 minutes. As soon as it's removed from the oven, rub the top and sides with butter.

Beer Bread

(1 large loaf)

3 cups whole wheat flour
1 teaspoon baking powder
½ teaspoon baking soda
2 tablespoons honey
12 ounces beer
butter

> When I was a child, my mother often made a bread cake on baking day. After I started baking myself, I often used some of the dough for the same purpose.

Beat egg, add honey and then knead into the bread dough. Add the rest of the ingredients, kneading them in thoroughly.

Line a loaf pan with wax paper and grease. Pour dough into the prepared pan.

Bake at once in a slow oven (300° to 325°F.) for about 1¼ hours.

Bread Cake

(1 loaf)

1 egg
½ cup honey
¾ pound any bread dough
½ cup melted butter
1 cup raisins
⅓ teaspoon nutmeg
⅓ teaspoon cinnamon
½ teaspoon soda

Ever-Ready Bran Muffins

(about 7 dozen muffins)

5 to 6 cups whole wheat flour
5 teaspoons baking soda
1 teaspoon salt (optional)
2 cups boiling water
2 cups cereal flakes
1 cup butter
1 cup honey
4 beaten eggs
1 quart buttermilk
4 cups unprocessed bran
½ cup nuts
½ cup raisins

Corinne's granddaughter, Laurie Sutton of Big Bear Lake, California, has become very conscious of eating for her health:

. . . all of her cooking is considered for its health attributes. She especially likes this recipe because all the ingredients are natural and there are no preservatives. She keeps some of the dough in her refrigerator all the time—it will keep up to a month.

The recipe is practical and you can make the dough, put the unused portion away in your refrigerator, and take some out to bake up right before breakfast.

Combine the flour, soda, and salt. Pour boiling water over the cereal flakes and let soak for a few minutes.

In a large bowl, cream the butter and honey together. Combine the eggs and buttermilk and blend into the honey mixture. Add flour and blend gently until well mixed.

Fold in the bran, soaked cereal flakes, nuts, and raisins. Bake in paper-lined muffin tins at 425°F. for 15 to 20 minutes. (Do not stir batter—just spoon out the amount you need, allowing room for the muffins to rise.)

If Laurie is not using all the muffin spaces in the pan, she fills the empty ones with water to keep the oven moist while baking—another variation on the "hot-brick-in-water" technique that I use for all my bread baking.

Indian Fry Bread

(2 to 3 dozen breads depending on size—recipe may be cut in half for fewer breads)

4 cups unbleached white flour
3 tablespoons baking powder
1 teaspoon salt*
2 tablespoons nonfat dry milk
1 tablespoon shortening
2 cups water

The Paiute Indians have a village on the outskirts of Yerington, and at public functions, such as fairs, the Paiute women put up a booth and sell their Indian Fry Bread. It's considered a delicacy by all of us who live here. . . .

Sift all the dry ingredients. Mix in the shortening with your hands and add enough water to make a soft dough, mixing well.

On a floured surface, knead the dough until it is smooth enough and flexible enough to be molded into little round balls. Flatten them out. Cook in deep fat and put on a paper towel to drain.

---

*The salt, though traditional, may be eliminated if you choose to do so.

BERNICE BEENHOWER

The Breads:

Basic Dough (Sponge)
Herb Bread
Fragrant Rye Bread
Wheat Bread
Light Oatmeal Bread
Sweet Dough

One of the joys of sharing bread-baking experiences with new friends is that each and every one has some tips that I never heard before. I laughed when I first heard Bernice Beenhower's suggestion about keeping a plastic bag handy: ". . . to stick your hand in when the telephone rings which, of course, it will, as soon as you are deep in dough. . . ." Now I keep a plastic bag handy—and the telephone always rings!

Bernice lives in Santa Fe, New Mexico, with her stockbroker husband, Herbert, and their four children. She's a fine pianist, an exceptional dress designer, and a dedicated community action organizer and leader. And, of course, she bakes marvelous breads.

I bake bread because I enjoy the physical process—it feels good, it smells good. It's fun to watch the changes. We usually plan dinner around the fresh bread on baking day: bread,

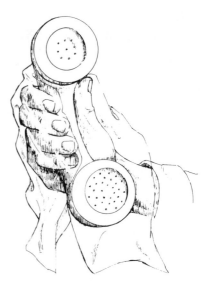

butter, cheese, salad, fruit . . . a feast and a vivid reminder of the ceremony and closeness of "breaking bread" together!

Bernice feels as I do about a baking day. You might just as well make four to six loaves, since you'll be home most of the time anyway. Where I use a large, large mixing bowl and double the recipe, Bernice uses *two* medium-size bowls and makes two different breads at the same time.

One of the best things for the beginner who might be reading this is her basic recipe for dough, with additions for each kind of bread. Once you get the knack, you can try your own variations.

Basic Dough (Sponge)

(2 loaves)

3 cups lukewarm skim milk
1 package dry yeast
¼ cup honey
4 cups whole wheat flour

Into a mixing bowl, pour the lukewarm skim milk. Add the dry yeast and mix thoroughly with a wire whisk. Add the honey and then the flour, 1 cup at a time. Keep beating with the wire whisk for at least 100 strokes. The beaten mixture will then act as a sponge, to be used with the other ingredients later on.

Cover the bowl loosely with plastic wrap and a tea towel and set it in a warm (not hot) place to rise for about an hour. Do not place the sponge near a draft. If the spot is not quite warm enough, the dough will rise anyway, but it will take a little longer.

When the sponge has doubled in size, it's time to add the rest of the ingredients.

Herb Bread

Add to sponge:

¼ cup butter
1 tablespoon salt (optional)
2 tablespoons each of chopped chives and parsley. An additional 2 tablespoons of dill, thyme, lovage, or chervil.*
3½ to 4 cups whole wheat flour

Add the ingredients to the sponge and, using a wooden spoon, blend them thoroughly into the mixing bowl. (Before you turn them out, don't forget the plastic bag for answering the phone!) Turn the dough out onto a floured board or counter. Flour the heels of your hands and knead for 8 to 10 minutes. You may have to add ½ cup or more flour if the dough gets too sticky. Every time my arms tire, I invite a passing member of the family to take a few turns with the dough.

When the dough is smooth and satiny, place it in a greased bowl and turn to coat the top. Set the bowl in a warm place again, covered with a towel. Let it rise until doubled in bulk—about 1 to

(continued on page 69)

---

*If you like, use your own favorite herb combination. (Herbs may also be added later when you are shaping the dough. Just butter dough, sprinkle herbs over it, and roll up loaf, jelly-roll fashion.)

Sweet Dough (Bernice Beenhower) page 70   67

1½ hours depending upon warmth, breezes, and humidity. When doubled, turn out onto floured board or counter and punch down vigorously several times. Return to the greased bowl, cover, and let it rise to double again.

When dough has doubled in bulk, turn out onto lightly floured board, and punch down. Divide in half and knead each piece several times. Roll each piece tightly and place in a well-greased 9-inch loaf pan or shape into 2 rounds and place on a well-greased cookie sheet.

NOTE: Bernice and I agree that smaller families may want smaller loaves. Just separate the dough into 3 or 4 pieces before baking.

Set the loaf pans or the shaped loaves in a warm place, cover lightly with a towel, and let the breads rise for about 30 minutes while heating the oven to 350°F. For a soft crust, brush the tops with butter. For a crusty top, brush with water. Bake the breads 45 minutes to 1 hour or until the tops are brown and the loaves sound hollow when turned out onto an asbestos glove and tapped on the bottom.

NOTE: I try to bake my breads as short a time as possible so I set my timer for the minimum amount of time and then check to see if they are done.

Cool on wire racks.

*Fragrant Rye Bread and Light Oatmeal Bread have delicate flavors that Bernice feels are best enhanced by unbleached white flour. However, both breads were tested in the Rodale Test Kitchens, using whole wheat flour, and the results were judged very good.

Fragrant Rye Bread*

Add to sponge:

¼ cup butter
1 tablespoon salt (optional)
1 tablespoon freshly grated orange peel
1 tablespoon caraway seeds
1 tablespoon anise seeds
3 cups rye flour
1 to 1½ cups unbleached white flour

Wheat Bread

Add to sponge:

¼ cup butter
1 tablespoon salt (optional)
4 to 4½ cups whole wheat flour (more if necessary)
½ cup wheat bran, toasted 10 minutes in slow oven
¼ cup wheat germ

Light Oatmeal Bread*

Add to sponge:

¼ cup butter
1 tablespoon salt (optional)
1½ cups uncooked rolled oats
1 cup whole wheat flour
½ cup toasted sesame seeds
2 to 2½ cups unbleached white flour

Sweet Dough

Add to sponge:

2 eggs, beaten
¼ cup honey (additional)
½ cup butter
1 tablespoon salt (optional)
3½ to 4 cups unbleached
white flour
1 tablespoon cardamom or anise
seeds—1 teaspoon cinnamon
or mace—or ½ teaspoon
nutmeg, ginger, or cloves. Pick
your favorite combination.

Glaze:

2 egg whites
1 tablespoon warm water

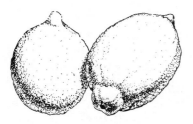

This is a variation that makes superb coffee cakes and buns. The recipe makes a fairly soft dough, quite delicate, but not quite as flaky as a true Danish pastry dough. It's fun to try the variations—use your imagination and invent your own.

You can use any of the following combinations as a delicious filling for Sweet Dough:

• mincemeat plus Mandarin oranges, pineapple, and apples soaked in rum* (If mixture seems too watery, add a tablespoon of flour.)

• poppy seeds, freshly grated lemon peel, honey

• prunes, nutmeg, and freshly grated orange or lemon peel

• cinnamon, nutmeg, butter, honey

• slivered almonds, crushed cardamom seed, freshly grated orange peel, honey

• pureed apricots, freshly grated orange peel, ginger, honey

• any good natural marmalade plus a few chopped nuts

• chopped dates, ginger or mace, plus a bit of freshly grated lemon peel

• chopped figs that have been soaked in sherry plus honey and freshly grated lemon peel*

In the mixing bowl with the sponge, add the beaten eggs, additional honey, butter, salt, and the additional flour, 1 cup at a time. Add the seasoning you have chosen and blend well with a wooden spoon. Turn out onto floured board or counter, flour your hands and knead for 8 to 10 minutes. Keep the dough quite soft—do not add too much flour while kneading.

As in previous recipes, when dough is smooth and satiny, place in a greased bowl and turn to coat the top. Set the bowl in a warm place, cover with a towel and let rise to double in bulk (about 1 hour).

---

*This recipe may be made without rum or sherry.

When dough is double in size, turn out onto a floured board or counter, punch down, knead for 2 to 3 minutes and return to the greased bowl. Again place in warm spot, cover and allow to double in size (about 1 hour).

When dough has doubled again, you are ready to shape and fill. Each bowl of dough will make 3 good-size coffee cakes or several pans of rolls. Shape them to fit the pans you have available, and be sure to allow room for expansion while it's rising. There are many ways to use the dough—and many variations of shapes—just choose the one you'd like to try:

• Divide the dough into 3 long sections; roll out each section with a floured rolling pin. Fill each section, then roll tightly into long strands and braid. Sprinkle nuts on top.

• With a floured rolling pin, roll the dough into a rectangular shape about 6 × 10 inches. Spread filling on top and roll. Turn entire roll into a ring, sealing at the joining point by just wetting your fingers a bit and squeezing the ends where they meet. With a sharp knife, razor, or sharp scissors, cut the top of the dough at regular intervals—about 2 inches apart—and just lift the cut piece slightly. When the baking is complete, the filling will show through.

• Roll into a rectangle (about 6 × 10 inches) with floured rolling pin. Cover with filling; roll up into jelly-roll shape and slice into 1-inch pieces.

When you've selected the shape you want, place the dough on a greased cookie sheet or in the pans you have available. Place in a warm spot, lightly covered, and allow to rise for about 30 minutes while you heat the oven to 350°F.

Before baking, glaze the tops with the egg white, which has been diluted with warm water. Bake the rings and braids 35 to 40 minutes, slightly less for the little pieces. Check after 20 minutes to be sure that the tops are not burning. If they are browning too fast, lower the oven temperature a bit, or lightly cover the tops with a sheet of aluminum foil.

NOTE: Bernice uses unbleached white flour here to get an especially light, flaky dough. We tried the recipe with whole wheat flour and the result, though perhaps a little less flaky, was called excellent by our tasters.

NOELLE BRAYNARD

I first met Noelle last summer when she came hobbling down our walk at the island with her foot in a cast. Since she is a ballerina and it's most awkward to dance with one's foot in a cast, I gave my sympathy and expressed my hope for a quick recovery. We discussed her father Frank, who was responsible for Op-Sail during the bicentennial year. Then I learned that Noelle spent a great amount of time (while her leg was healing) *baking bread:*

> . . . *because I'm a dancer, people are frequently surprised to learn that I love to bake and eat bread, but it's not incongruous to me. Whole grain breads contain essential B-vitamins. When I need to lose a few pounds, I cut down on the* quantity *of all foods, but I keep my diet well balanced.*

Noelle dances with the Battery Dance Corporation far down on the lower end of Manhattan Island and since the company rehearses right where she lives:

> *Many a dancer rehearsing in my loft has been distracted by the smells of baking bread coming from the kitchen. Sometimes I have to run right out of rehearsal to punch down the dough and I return with puffs of flour on my black leotards. Once, however, I was involved in a dress rehearsal and couldn't stop—I could only dance past fleeting views of the dough rising and tumbling out of the bowl onto the dining room table!*

Most of her recipes are her own, all of them based on experimentation with buckwheat, rye, uncooked rolled oats, unsweetened coconut, wheat germ, and cornmeal.

The Breads:

Sesame-Bran Bread
Oatmeal Buckwheat Bread
Buckwheat/Chopped
**   Walnut Bread**

Sesame-Bran Bread

(3 loaves)

2 packages dry yeast
1 cup lukewarm water
½ cup oil or melted butter
2 large eggs
1½ cups milk or mixed, nonfat dry milk
5½ to 6½ cups whole wheat flour
½ cup bran
1½ cups sesame seeds
butter

Empty the packets of dry yeast into a bowl. Add the lukewarm water and place in a warm spot until the surface is bubbly. This should take about 15 minutes.

While yeast is proofing, prepare the liquid for the dough by mixing the oil or melted butter, the eggs, and the milk until you have a total of 2½ cups. The liquid should be lukewarm or at room temperature.

In a large bowl, combine the yeast mixture, the liquid, and 2½ cups of flour. Let stand in a warm place until the surface is bubbly, about 30 minutes.

Then, add 3 cups of the flour, stir well, knead in the bran and then the sesame seeds. Turn out onto a lightly floured board—if the dough is still wet, add ¼ cup more flour with your hands. Knead for 10 minutes, sprinkling more flour on the board to keep the dough from getting too sticky.

Butter or grease a large bowl, put the dough into it, turning to coat the top. Cover and let rise in a warm spot for 1 to 1½ hours.

Punch the dough down with your fist and while the dough is still in the bowl, divide it into 3 parts of about equal size. Bring 1 to the floured board and roll it into a sausage shape about 2 feet long. Fold both outer ends into the center to meet and repeat the process 4 times. Now shape it into a loaf and place in a buttered 8 × 4-inch loaf pan. Do the same for the other 2 pieces. (Sometimes I like to bake the breads in soufflé dishes for festive occasions.)

Cover all 3 pans and let rise in a warm place for 1 hour or until dough has almost doubled in size. Place in an oven preheated to 375°F. about midway between top and bottom.

Bake for 40 to 45 minutes or until tops are golden brown. If you like, you may baste melted butter on top to give a richer, more golden crust.

Let breads cool in pans for 5 minutes; then turn out and cool on racks for 20 minutes before wrapping and storing.

Empty the dry yeast into a bowl, add the lukewarm water and place in a warm spot until the surface is bubbly—about 15 minutes.

While the yeast is proofing, prepare the liquid for the dough. As in all of Noelle's recipes, this liquid should total 2½ cups when mixed. Add the oil or melted butter, eggs, molasses, and potato water to measure the 2½ cups. The liquid should be lukewarm or at room temperature.

In a large bowl, combine the yeast mixture, the liquid, and 3 cups of flour. Let stand in a warm place until the surface is bubbly, about 30 minutes.

Then add 3 more cups of the flour, stir well, add the rolled oats and the buckwheat. Stir well and turn out onto a lightly floured board. If it seems too damp, add a bit more flour with your hands. Knead for 10 minutes, sprinkling more flour on the board to keep the dough from getting too sticky.

Butter or grease a large bowl, put the dough into it, turning to coat the top. Cover and let rise in a warm spot for 1 to 1½ hours.

Punch the dough down with your fist and while the dough is still in the bowl, divide it into 3 parts of about equal size. Bring 1 to the floured board and roll it into a sausage shape about 2 feet long. Fold both outer ends into the center to meet and repeat the process 4 times. Now shape it into a loaf and place in a buttered 9 × 5-inch loaf pan. Do the same for the other 2 pieces.

Cover all 3 pans and let rise in a warm place for 1 hour or until dough has almost doubled in size. Place in an oven preheated to 375°F. about midway between top and bottom. Bake for 45 minutes or until tops are golden brown. If you like, you may baste with melted butter on top to give a richer, more golden crust.

Let breads cool in pans for 5 minutes, then turn out and cool on racks for 20 minutes before wrapping and storing.

Oatmeal Buckwheat Bread

(3 loaves)

2 packages dry yeast
1 cup lukewarm water
½ cup oil or melted butter
3 large eggs
½ cup molasses
1 cup potato water
   (water in which potatoes have
   been boiled)
6 to 7 cups whole wheat flour
1 cup uncooked rolled oats
1½ cups buckwheat
butter

Buckwheat/Chopped Walnut Bread

(3 loaves)

2 packages dry yeast
1 cup lukewarm water
½ cup oil or melted butter
3 large eggs
¼ cup honey
1¼ cups warm water
6½ to 7 cups whole wheat flour
1½ cups buckwheat
1 cup chopped walnuts
butter

Empty the dry yeast into a bowl, add the lukewarm water and place in a warm spot until the surface is bubbly—about 15 minutes.

While the yeast is proofing, prepare the liquid for the dough and, here again, the total amount should be 2½ cups. The 2½ cups should be a mixture of the oil or melted butter, eggs, honey, and the additional warm water. It should be lukewarm or at room temperature.

In a large bowl, combine the yeast mixture, the liquid, and 3 cups of the flour. Let stand in a warm place until the surface is bubbly, about 30 minutes.

Then add 3 more cups of the flour, stir well, add the buckwheat and the chopped walnuts, stir well, and turn out onto a lightly floured surface. If the dough seems too damp, add a bit more flour with your hands. Knead for 10 minutes. If the dough seems too sticky as you knead, add more flour.

Butter or grease a large bowl, put the dough into it, turning to coat the top. Cover and let rise in a warm spot for 1 to 1½ hours.

Punch the dough down with your fist and while the dough is still in the bowl, divide it into 3 parts of about equal size. Bring 1 to the floured surface and roll it into a sausage shape about 2 feet long. Fold both outer ends into the center to meet and repeat the process 4 times. Shape into a loaf and place it in a buttered 9 × 5-inch loaf pan. Do the same with the other 2 pieces.

Cover all 3 pans and let rise in a warm place for 1 hour or until dough has almost doubled in size. Place in an oven preheated to 375°F. about midway between top and bottom. Bake for 45 minutes or until tops are golden brown. If you like, you may baste the tops with butter to give a richer, more golden crust.

Let breads cool in pans for 5 minutes, then turn out and cool on racks for 20 minutes before wrapping and storing.

GIRARD FRANKLIN

The Breads:

Beer Wheat Bread
Onion Poppy Seed Twists

Gerry is another one of my Fire Island neighbors who loves to bake bread. A New York psychologist and psychoanalyst in "real" life, he's been swapping recipes with me for several years. He's one of the most uninhibited bread bakers I know and many of his 25 recipes are his own inventions:

A few years ago I was alone in a restaurant waiting to be served and I began to read a book about bread. It reminded me of my pre-med days and the chemistry courses I loved so much—the challenge, the mystery of mixing things together and getting surprising results. . . .

The next weekend he baked his first bread—the basic white—and it was a disaster.

I forgot about the damp weather on Fire Island and I didn't add enough flour. Since then, I've learned how to work with the dough. . . .

And indeed he has. I have tasted both of these breads. Each one is unique and delicious.

Beer Wheat Bread

(2 medium-size loaves)

⅓ cup melted butter
¾ cup milk
1 cup wheat germ
12 ounces beer, preferably dark
2 packages dry yeast
2 tablespoons honey
1½ teaspoons salt (optional)
⅓ cup molasses
6 cups whole wheat flour

Glaze:

1 tablespoon melted butter

This is a very heavy bread, but Gerry says he loves the combination of beer, molasses, whole wheat flour, and wheat germ. It's very easy to make.

Warm the butter and milk and add the wheat germ. Warm the beer and add to the yeast in a large bowl. After it bubbles, combine with first mixture and stir in honey, salt, molasses, and whole wheat flour. If dough is too sticky, add more flour. Mix well and then turn out onto a lightly floured surface. Knead until smooth and elastic (about 8 to 10 minutes).

Place dough in a greased bowl, turn once to coat the top and cover. Place in a warm spot and let rise until double (about 1½ hours).

Turn out onto lightly floured surface, punch down and knead for 2 to 3 minutes. Form into 2 loaves, and place in 2 well-greased, medium-size loaf pans (4½ × 8½ inches). Cover, place in a warm spot and let rise until almost double (about 1½ hours).

Bake at 375°F. for 50 minutes to 1 hour. Turn the loaves out onto racks to cool and brush the tops with the melted butter.

Right after they came out of the oven, Gerry brought them over to our house on his bicycle. There was just one problem with them—he didn't bring enough. These goodies go fast! They're small dinner rolls and they can be whipped up about a half hour before lunch or dinner.

Preheat oven to 450°F.

Combine the whole wheat flour, salt, baking soda, and baking powder. In a second bowl, mix the onion, butter, yogurt, and sour cream.

Pour the wet ingredients into the bowl containing flour mixture and mix until the dough is smooth. Turn out onto a lightly floured surface and knead for about 30 seconds to combine all the ingredients thoroughly. Divide dough into 4 balls of equal size. Roll each ball into a rope about 1 inch thick and cut each rope into 8-inch lengths.

Taking 2 ropes at a time, lay 1 across the other to form an "X" and then make 2 twists on each side, pinching the ends together by wetting your fingers. Repeat the process until you have used all the dough.

Put the twists on a sheet of wax paper, brush with the beaten egg and sprinkle them with poppy seeds. Transfer twists to a baking sheet that has been greased, and bake at 450°F. for 15 minutes, or until golden brown.

Onion Poppy Seed Twists

(16 twists)

2½ cups whole wheat flour
1¼ teaspoons salt (optional)
½ teaspoon baking soda
2 teaspoons baking powder
1 tablespoon minced onion
¾ stick butter (6 tablespoons), melted and cooled
½ cup yogurt
½ cup sour cream

Glaze:

1 egg, beaten
poppy seeds

SUZANNE CORBETT

Suzanne is such a treasure of bread recipes that I asked her why she wasn't writing a book of her own. "I am," she replied, "but it's a secret."

She lives in St. Louis, Missouri, is married and has a five-year-old son. Her husband, Jim, claims that he's gained a lot of pounds in their seven years of marriage largely as a result of her gourmet cooking. She teaches cooking in the adult education programs offered through the St. Louis high schools, belongs to the Arts and Education Council of Greater St. Louis and also gives demonstrations in bread baking at the historic sites that surround the city. "What I try to communicate is that bread baking is a craft and an art and it should get as much respect as any other craft. . . ."

Her breads have won blue ribbons at the Missouri State Fair and she constantly experiments. She's baked breads in flowerpots, buckets, pie pans, oatmeal boxes and in cast-iron pots over an open fire. And she, one of the most versatile of the bread bakers I know, has also had her failures along with her huge successes (even as you and I).

How bread rises has always been a marvel to me. Once, a bowl of honey-wheat bread I had rising on my bathroom counter expanded faster than I thought it would and it climbed out of the bowl, onto the counter top, down the wall and onto the floor. . . .

One of the most common errors in bread-baking, she points out, is letting the dough rise too much before putting it in the oven:

Once, thinking that if I let the dough rise to the size I wanted the finished loaf to be, the results would be great, I let the yeast overwork. When I put it in the hot oven, the bread fell. I got the biggest, fattest pancakes you ever saw!

But most of her stories are stories of success and I think you'll find her recipes easy to follow, with a broad range of breads that you can try.

Anadama Bread

(2 loaves)

7 cups unbleached white flour
(whole wheat flour may be
substituted)
1½ cups cornmeal
2½ teaspoons salt (optional)
⅓ cup softened butter
2 packages dry yeast
2¼ cups very warm water (120° to
130°F.)
⅔ cup molasses (room
temperature)

This is one of the most famous of bread-baking tales. In fact, the story about Anadama might well be the reason that the bread has survived; it appears in every bread book. I'll not be the author who leaves it out!

The tale has it that a woman named Anna kept baking the same bread recipe over and over again through all the years of her marriage. Every day, every night, she served her husband this bread. Finally, at the end of his gustatory rope, the husband picked up a sack of cornmeal and hurled it at his wife, shouting: "Anna damn ya!" He missed Anna, but hit the bread dough sprinkling it with the cornmeal. She baked it anyway and the bread turned out quite all right. No one has ever bothered to find out what Anna baked the next night.

Mix 2½ cups flour, cornmeal, salt, butter, and yeast in a large mixing bowl. Slowly add the water and the molasses to the dry ingredients and beat for 2 minutes at medium speed of mixer or by hand with a wooden spoon. Stir in enough flour to make a stiff dough. Turn out onto a lightly floured surface and knead until smooth and elastic (about 10 minutes).

Place in a greased bowl, turning once to coat the top. Cover loosely with a towel or with plastic wrap and place in a warm spot. Let rise to double in bulk (about 45 minutes to 1 hour). Turn out, punch down, and divide in half.

Shape and place in 2 greased 9-inch baking pans. Cover and allow to rise until almost double (about 1 hour).

Bake at 375°F. for 45 minutes or until breads test done.

Cool on wire racks.

The adobe oven has a free-standing, conical shape and the resulting breads have a fine crust due to the way the heat circulates within the oven. The bread, of course, may also be baked right in your own home oven. One form of the bread symbolizes the sun and its life-giving rays.

Sprinkle yeast over warm water in a mixing bowl. Stir until dissolved. Blend in butter and salt. Beat in 3 cups of the flour until a smooth batter is made. Then add enough flour to make a stiff dough. Knead lightly in the bowl and then transfer the dough to a greased bowl. Turn once to coat the top. Cover lightly with a towel and place in a warm spot until doubled in size (about 1 to 1½ hours).

When doubled, turn out onto a lightly floured surface and knead for 5 minutes, adding more flour if necessary if the dough is too sticky. Cover and let rest for 10 minutes.

Divide the dough in half. Roll into 2 balls and place on a greased baking sheet. Allow enough room for the breads to expand. Let rise for 15 minutes. Bake in a hot 400°F. oven for 45 minutes.

Cool on a wire rack.

Molding the Sun Shape: If you'd like to make the sun shape and, thus, a more festive-looking bread, take one of the balls and roll it out into a circle. Fold the dough in half to make a semicircle. Make 6 slashes with a sharp knife or kitchen shears two-thirds of the way into the dough, cutting from the circular side. Place on a greased baking sheet and spread the fingers of dough apart. Repeat with the other dough. Cover, let rise until doubled (about 1 hour). Bake in a preheated oven at 350°F. for 50 minutes.

Cool on a wire rack.

Adobe Bread

(2 loaves)

2 packages dry yeast
2 cups warm water
3 teaspoons melted butter
2 teaspoons salt (optional)
5 to 6 cups whole wheat flour

Banana Nut Bread

(1 large loaf)

2 cups whole wheat pastry flour
1 teaspoon baking powder
½ teaspoon salt (optional)
½ teaspoon baking soda
½ cup melted butter
½ cup honey
2 eggs
1 cup mashed bananas
1 cup chopped nuts (Suzanne likes to use Missouri black walnuts)

This recipe won Third Place Ribbon at the Missouri State Fair and it's another one of the "quick breads" that evolved at about the turn-of-the-century, when yeast was so difficult to make. Women used seasonal fruits and nuts with which to make their favorite breads. In the winter months, the baker might make 20 or 30 loaves at a time and then keep them outdoors when the temperature dropped below 32°F.—Mother Nature's primitive home freezer.

In a bowl, mix flour, baking powder, salt, and baking soda together. Combine the melted butter with the honey and then add the eggs and bananas. Blend wet mixture into flour mixture. Fold in nuts. Pour into large 9-inch greased loaf pan and bake for 1 hour at 350°F.

When done, cool on a wire rack.

Buttermilk Biscuits

(12 biscuits)

2 cups whole wheat flour
2 teaspoons baking powder
½ teaspoon baking soda
½ teaspoon salt (optional)
5 teaspoons butter
¾ cup buttermilk
melted butter

This is one of the recipes that Suzanne teaches in her basic cooking classes.

Sift all the dry ingredients together in a mixing bowl. Cut in the butter until the mixture resembles coarse cornmeal. Make a well with a rubber spatula, adding buttermilk all at once and stir until a soft dough is formed and leaves the sides of the bowl.

Turn out onto a lightly floured surface and knead about 1 minute to thoroughly blend the ingredients. Pat the dough down to a thickness of about ½ inch or roll it out to that thickness with a floured rolling pin. With a floured 2-inch cookie cutter, cut the dough into rounds and place on a greased baking sheet. Take the remaining dough, make a ball and again roll it down to ½-inch thickness. Cut remainder of biscuit shapes and place on greased sheet. Brush with melted butter and bake at 450°F. for 12 to 15 minutes, or until golden brown.

These biscuits are best when eaten warm.

This is another recipe that Suzanne teaches to her basic students. It won a Third Place Ribbon in the 1978 Missouri State Fair.

Preheat oven to 425°F.

Sift dry ingredients into a mixing bowl. In a separate bowl, combine the milk, eggs, butter, and honey, stirring until well blended. With a rubber spatula, make a well in the dry ingredients and pour milk mixture in all at once. Stir in quickly and mix.

Pour batter into greased muffin tins or square pan and bake for 20 to 25 minutes.

Serve warm.

Corn Bread

(about 1 dozen muffins or squares)

1 cup whole wheat flour
1 cup yellow cornmeal
2 teaspoons baking powder
¾ teaspoon salt (optional)
1⅛ cups milk
2 eggs
4 teaspoons melted butter
3 teaspoons honey

Corn pone sometimes goes by the name of "hoe cakes" which got their name because they were originally cooked on the blade of a hoe over an open fire.

Mix cornmeal, salt, and baking soda. Cut in the butter. Add boiling water and mix. Add the buttermilk and mix to form a soft dough. Pat it into a square, greased pan or form it into about 1 dozen smaller square shapes and place on a greased cookie sheet. Bake at 350°F. for 35 to 40 minutes.

Corn Pone

(about 1 dozen squares)

2 cups white cornmeal
1 teaspoon salt (optional)
¼ teaspoon baking soda
4 tablespoons butter
¾ cup boiling water
½ cup buttermilk

Blend cheese, butter, milk, salt, cayenne pepper, and paprika together. Combine bread crumbs and flour and then add the 2 mixtures in a large bowl. Mix thoroughly.

Divide in half, wrap in wax paper and refrigerate overnight. Next day, roll out dough between 2 pieces of wax paper until thin. Take a knife or pastry wheel (called a "jagger" in the days of great-grandmother) and cut into strips 5 inches long and 1 inch wide. Put the strips on a greased cookie sheet and top with sesame seeds. Repeat with other half of dough.

Bake at 350°F. or until brown.

Country Cheddar Sticks

(about 3½ dozen sticks)

1 cup grated cheddar cheese
¼ cup softened butter
¼ cup milk
¼ teaspoon salt (optional)
dash or two of cayenne pepper
    and paprika
1½ cups fine bread crumbs
¾ cup whole wheat flour
sesame seeds

Fasnachts

(about 1½ dozen)

1 package dry yeast
4 teaspoons warm water
2 cups milk, scalded
6 to 7 cups whole wheat flour
2 eggs, beaten
4 teaspoons melted butter
¾ cup honey
1¼ teaspoons salt (optional)
oil for deep frying
honey
cinnamon

This is one of two recipes in this section from the Pennsylvania Dutch and they've become popular with the Dutch and German communities in St. Louis. Both are unusual in that they are deep fried instead of baked.

Soften yeast in the 4 teaspoons warm water. Scald milk and let cool to room temperature. Then stir in 3 cups of sifted flour. Stir in yeast. Cover, place in warm spot and let rise to double (about 1 hour).

When doubled, stir in mixture of beaten eggs, melted butter, honey, salt, and 3 to 4 more cups of flour. The dough should be stiff. Cover, place in warm spot and let rise to double.

Punch down. Roll out dough with floured rolling pin to a thickness of about ½ inch. Cut into squares about 2 × 3 inches. Make a small slit in center of each square. Cover and let rise again for about 30 minutes. Fry in deep hot oil until brown: drain on paper towels. Dip in honey and lightly sprinkle with cinnamon.

Cranberry-Orange Muffins

(about 2½ dozen muffins)

3 cups whole wheat flour
½ cup honey
½ cup chopped nuts
2 teaspoons baking powder
1 teaspoon salt (optional)
1 teaspoon baking soda
¼ cup freshly squeezed orange juice
3 teaspoons oil
1 egg
2 cups whole cranberry sauce

On Fire Island and in many northeast coastal areas, we go out into the bogs to collect cranberries. The yield is generally so large that any recipe using cranberries is always welcome. Suzanne teaches this one to her students.

Combine all of the ingredients together in a large bowl. Mix well. Fill greased muffin tins two-thirds of the way full. Bake at 400°F. for 15 to 20 minutes.

This is another recipe that requires hot, deep oil rather than an oven. It also requires a metal funnel with some kind of handle. The Pennsylvania Dutch have a special one just for funnel cakes, but any metal funnel will do.

Sift together all the dry ingredients and then add the honey, egg, and the milk. Beat until smooth. Heat about 2 inches of the oil in a large cast-iron skillet. To test the correct temperature, drop a small piece of dough into the oil. If it floats to the top and bubbles appear around the edges, you are ready to make the funnel cakes.

Hold your finger at the bottom of the funnel and pour in some batter. Then, using a spiral motion, let the batter pour into the oil. The cakes should look like free-form spiral sculpture. Fry until golden brown, turning once. Drain on paper towels. Drizzle with honey or maple syrup and serve hot.

The amount you can make will depend upon the amount of batter you use for each cake.

Funnel Cakes

1 cup whole wheat flour
1¼ teaspoons salt (optional)
½ teaspoon baking soda
¾ teaspoon baking powder
2 teaspoons honey
1 egg
⅞ cup warm milk
oil for deep frying
honey or pure maple syrup

Potato Loaves

(2 loaves)

1 medium-size potato
reserved potato water
hot tap water
2 packages dry yeast
2 tablespoons butter
2 tablespoons honey
1 tablespoon salt (optional)
1 cup warm milk
6 to 7 cups whole wheat flour

Pare and dice potato. Boil in water to cover until tender (about 20 minutes). Save the liquid and add to it enough hot tap water to make 1 cup. Mash the potato and set it aside.

When lukewarm, pour potato water in a large bowl. Sprinkle in yeast, and stir. Add butter, honey, and salt. Stir in the mashed potato (about 1 cup), warm milk, and 3 cups of the flour. Beat until smooth. Stir in enough flour to make a stiff dough. Turn out onto a lightly floured surface and knead until smooth and elastic—about 8 to 10 minutes. Place in a buttered bowl, turning once to coat the top. Cover and let rise in a warm place until doubled in bulk (about 45 minutes to 1 hour).

When doubled, punch down, return to bowl, cover and let rise again in a warm spot for about 20 minutes.

Turn out onto a lightly floured surface, punch down and knead for 1 or 2 minutes. Divide dough in half. Shape into loaves and place in large greased baking pans. Cover and allow to rise to double. Dust tops with flour.

Bake at 375°F. for about 35 to 40 minutes or until they test done.

Cool on wire racks.

Soft Gingerbread

(2 breads)

½ cup butter
½ cup honey
1 cup molasses
1 teaspoon ginger
1 teaspoon cinnamon
2½ cups unbleached white flour
1 teaspoon baking soda
1 cup boiling water
2 eggs, well beaten

At one of the historic houses in St. Louis, the General Daniel Bissell Home, a very old gingerbread recipe has been used for over 150 years. The Park Service still has custody of this recipe and has granted Suzanne the use of it to share with our bread bakers.

Stir together the butter and the honey. Add the molasses, ginger, and cinnamon. Beat in the flour and then mix the baking soda with the boiling water to dissolve it and add to the batter. Add the eggs. Mix well.

Take 2 square cake pans—the old recipe gives them as "common square bread pans"—and line them with ordinary brown, bag paper, cut to fit the pans. The ordinary 7 × 7-inch cake pan will do nicely. Butter the paper with softened butter. Pour batter into lined pans and bake at 350°F. for 40 to 60 minutes.

This bread has been a favorite of the St. Louis German community since 1880. It is another example of how a bread can be made in many different ways. Compare it with George Meluso's Pumpernickel (see Index). Each is different from the other. Each is delicious and fun to make.

Combine the whole wheat and rye flours. In a very large bowl, mix 2 cups of the flour mixture with the salt, cornmeal, and yeast. In a saucepan, heat the water, molasses, carob mixture, and butter until very warm (about 120° to 130°F.). Add this to the dry ingredients in the large bowl. Add the mashed potatoes and 1 more cup of the flour. Stir in caraway seeds and enough of the flour mixture to make a stiff dough.

Turn out onto a lightly floured surface and knead for 15 minutes. Add more flour if the mixture seems too sticky.

Place in a buttered bowl, turn once to coat top, cover and place in a warm spot to rise until doubled in bulk (about 1 hour).

Turn out onto lightly floured surface, punch down and knead for 1 or 2 minutes. Return to the bowl and cover; let rise for 30 minutes more.

On a lightly floured surface, turn out dough, punch down and knead for 1 or 2 minutes. Divide into 3 equal parts. Shape into round, long, or oval loaves (or all 3 if you like) and place on greased baking sheets. Cover, let rise in a warm spot until doubled.

Bake in a 350°F. oven for 50 minutes or until the loaves test done.

Cool on wire racks.

Pumpernickel Bread

(with potato)

(3 loaves)

9 to 10 cups whole wheat flour
4 cups dark rye flour
2 tablespoons salt (optional)
¾ cup cornmeal
2 packages dry yeast
3½ cups water
¼ cup dark molasses
3 tablespoons carob powder
    mixed with 6 tablespoons hot
    water (optional)
1 tablespoon melted butter
2 cups mashed potatoes
2 teaspoons caraway seeds

Sweet Tater Buns

(about 20 buns)

1 large sweet potato
⅓ cup sweet potato water, reserved
1 package dry yeast
1 teaspoon salt (optional)
3 tablespoons honey
1 teaspoon butter
1 cup milk
3½ to 5 cups unbleached white flour

This is a real old-fashioned Ozark treat. It is one traditional recipe that does not convert well to whole wheat flour, probably due to the sweet potato's heaviness.

Peel and cut up the sweet potato in small pieces. Cover with water and cook until tender (about 20 minutes). Drain, reserving ⅓ cup of the sweet potato water to be used in the batter. Let the water cool to lukewarm. Then stir in the yeast.

Mash the potato and mix in the salt, honey, and butter. Scald milk and let cool to lukewarm. Stir into the sweet potato mixture. Stir in softened yeast. Adding 1 cup at a time, stir in enough flour to make a stiff dough. Turn out onto a lightly floured surface and knead until smooth and elastic (about 8 to 10 minutes). Place in a buttered bowl, turn once to coat the top, cover, and let stand in a warm place until doubled in bulk (about 1 hour).

When doubled, turn out onto a lightly floured surface and punch down. Knead for 1 to 2 minutes. Then, pinch off pieces of the dough about the size of golf balls and place each one in a section of a greased muffin tin. Cover lightly and let rise until doubled (about 1 hour).

Bake at 425°F. for 15 minutes.

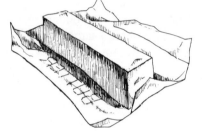

Sour Milk Corn Bread

(1 dozen squares)

1½ cups stone-ground cornmeal
½ teaspoon baking soda
1 teaspoon baking powder
½ teaspoon salt (optional)
1 egg
1 cup sour milk or buttermilk
1 teaspoon honey
1 tablespoon melted butter

Mix dry ingredients, add egg, sour milk or buttermilk, and honey. Brush a square baking tin with the melted butter. Pour in batter and bake 20 minutes in a 425°F. oven. Cut into squares with a sharp knife.

Mix the first 2½ cups of flour, salt, and yeast. In a saucepan, heat to 120° to 130°F. the milk, maple syrup or honey, and the oil. Add 2 eggs to the liquid. Then add the liquid mixture to the flour-yeast mixture and mix well. Stir in the rest of the flour.

The batter does not have to be kneaded. Cover the bowl and place in warm spot to let rise to double in bulk (about 1 to 2 hours). Turn out onto a lightly floured surface, punch down and knead for a few minutes, adding flour if dough is too sticky. Shape into loaves—any shape—or use loaf pans that have been greased. Cover and let rise until doubled. Brush tops with melted butter and bake at 375°F. for 25 to 35 minutes or until they test done.

Cool on wire racks.

Whole Wheat Bread

(2 loaves)

2½ cups whole wheat flour
1 teaspoon salt (optional)
2 packages dry yeast
1¼ cups milk
¾ cup pure maple syrup or honey
   (or use a half and half mixture
   of both)
⅓ cup oil
2 eggs
3 cups whole wheat flour
melted butter

Combine all the dry ingredients in a mixing bowl. Mix the honey and melted butter together. Add the eggs, then the vanilla and the milk. Pour liquid mixture into the dry ingredients and then add the nuts, stirring them in thoroughly. Mix well.

Place dough in a large loaf pan that has been well greased and bake in the oven at 350°F. for 1 hour.

Cool on wire rack.

Whole Wheat Nut Bread

(1 large loaf)

1¾ cups whole wheat flour
2 teaspoons baking powder
½ teaspoon salt (optional)
½ teaspoon cinnamon
¼ teaspoon nutmeg
¼ teaspoon allspice
½ cup honey
¼ cup melted butter
2 eggs
½ teaspoon pure vanilla extract
⅔ cup milk
½ cup chopped nuts

Seven
Holiday Breads

When Suzanne and I first discussed the kinds of recipes she might contribute to the book, I was delighted when she suggested the next seven breads. They're traditional, festive, and fun to make.

Though I've lived in St. Louis all my life, my mother is from the panhandle of Texas, my father comes from the Alsace region of Germany. My great-grandfather was Irish and took part in the Oklahoma land rush. My great-grandmother was a Cherokee Indian and the other two great-grandparents were from Swedish and Scottish-English backgrounds. I suppose it's only natural that I enjoy baking international breads.

Panettone

(Italian)

(makes 2 or 3 breads depending upon size of cake pans)

½ cup raisins
¼ cups slivered, fresh orange peel
1 package dry yeast
½ cup warm water
½ cup melted butter
¼ cup honey
3 eggs
2 egg yolks
1 teaspoon salt*
freshly grated peel of 1 lemon
1 teaspoon pure vanilla extract
5 cups unbleached white flour
melted butter
chopped almonds (optional topping)

This is a festive Italian holiday bread that tastes marvelous with wine as well as with coffee or tea.

Combine raisins and slivered orange peel and set aside. Sprinkle yeast over the warm water; stir well. In a large bowl, combine butter, honey, eggs, egg yolks, and salt. Mix. Add the yeast and water mixture, lemon peel, and vanilla. Stir in 2 cups of flour, then enough flour to make a stiff dough.

Turn out onto a lightly floured surface and knead until the dough is smooth and silky (about 8 to 10 minutes). Cover with a towel and let rest for 10 minutes. Then knead the fruits into the dough.

Return to bowl, cover and allow to rise in a warm spot until doubled in bulk (about 45 minutes to 1 hour). When doubled, turn out onto lightly floured surface and punch down. Divide the dough in half and place each part in a buttered, 9-inch round cake pan. (If you have smaller cake pans, the recipe will make 3 breads.)

Brush tops with melted butter and sprinkle with chopped almonds (optional). Lightly cover and let rise for about 1 hour. Brush tops with melted butter again and bake for 40 to 50 minutes in a 350°F. oven.

---

*The salt, though traditional, may be eliminated if you choose to do so.

This bread is baked both at Christmas and Easter. When done, your family and friends will admire it as an Italian work of art.

Combine yeast and water, stir with fork until dissolved and set aside. In the large bowl of an electric mixer, cream butter, honey, orange peel, almond extract, brandy, and salt until mixture is fluffy. Beat in the eggs and the egg yolks one at a time. With a spatula, blend in the milk and the yeast mixture. Beat in 2 cups of flour to make a smooth batter. Add enough flour to make a stiff dough.

Turn out onto a lightly floured surface and knead the dough for 10 minutes or until the texture is smooth. Place in a buttered bowl, cover lightly with a cloth and allow to rise in a warm place for about 1 hour, or until doubled in bulk.

In a small bowl, beat the almond paste and the egg whites into a smooth mixture and set aside.

Turn out dough onto a lightly floured surface; punch down and let it rest for 10 minutes. Divide the dough into 2 parts. With a floured rolling pin, roll 1 part into an oval shape, about 6 × 12 inches in size. Roll the rest of the dough into a triangle about the same general size as the oval.

Place the oval piece on a greased baking sheet. Lay the triangle across the oval. (The oval will form the wings and the triangle will form the head and the tail.)

Twist the top part of the triangle to form the dove's head. Pinch the tip to form a beak. Twist the bottom of the triangle to form the tail. Small cuts may be added to give a feathered look. Brush the almond paste mixture on the tail and wings. Beat the rest of the egg whites with the water and brush over the dough. Decorate with almonds. Let rise in a warm place for 25 minutes.

Bake at 325°F. for 45 minutes.

Cool on wire rack.

Dove of Peace

(an Italian Christmas bread dove)

(1 large loaf)

1 package dry yeast
¼ cup warm water
½ cup softened butter
¼ cup honey
3 teaspoons freshly grated orange peel
1 to 1½ teaspoons pure
    almond extract
3 teaspoons brandy*
½ teaspoon salt**
3 eggs
3 egg yolks
½ cup warm milk
5 to 6 cups unbleached white flour
2 ounces almond paste
1½ egg whites

Glaze:

1½ egg whites beaten with 1
    teaspoon water
sliced and whole almonds

---

*This recipe may be made without brandy.
**The salt, though traditional, may be eliminated if you choose to do so.

St. Lucia Buns

(Swedish)

(2 dozen rolls)

2 packages dry yeast
½ cup warm water
1 cup warm milk
¼ cup honey
1 teaspoon ground cardamom
pinch of saffron
1½ teaspoons salt*
½ cup butter
2 eggs
6 to 7 cups unbleached white flour
raisins (optional)
1 egg white

December 13 is St. Lucia Day, which hails the beginning of Christmas in Sweden. By tradition, the eldest girl in each household dresses up as St. Lucia and she wears a crown of holly decorated with candles. As a part of the celebration, she serves her parents these sweet St. Lucia Buns.

Combine yeast and warm water in bowl. In a large bowl, combine milk, honey, spices, and salt. Add butter, eggs, and the yeast mixture. Beat in enough flour to make a stiff dough. Turn out onto a lightly floured surface and knead until smooth—about 10 minutes.

Place in a greased bowl, cover lightly with a towel and allow to rise in a warm place for about 1 hour, or until doubled in bulk.

When doubled, turn out again onto a lightly floured surface and knead for about 3 minutes. Return to bowl, cover and let rise again for about 45 minutes.

Turn out onto floured surface, punch down and knead for about 3 to 5 minutes. Lightly cover with a towel and let it rest for 15 minutes.

Divide the dough into 2 dozen pieces and roll each piece into a rope about 12 inches long. Place each strand on a greased baking sheet and coil it into an S-shape. Then continue to coil each end until it looks like the shape of a snail shell. A raisin may be placed in the center of each roll.

Brush the tops lightly with egg white and sprinkle with sugar. Bake at 350°F. for 15 to 20 minutes or until brown.

*The salt, though traditional, may be eliminated if you choose to do so.

This Greek Christmas bread is sometimes baked with a single almond inside the loaf. Whoever gets the slice with the almond will have good luck in the coming year.

In a large mixing bowl, combine 1 cup flour and the yeast. In a saucepan, heat milk, honey, butter, and salt and cook until lukewarm. Add to flour and yeast mixture. Mix thoroughly. Add egg and lemon peel. Stir in well. Add enough flour to make a stiff dough.

Turn out onto a lightly floured surface and knead for about 8 to 10 minutes, or until smooth. Place in greased bowl, cover with a towel, and place in a warm spot to rise until doubled in bulk— about 45 minutes to 1 hour.

Knead in raisins, walnuts, and almond. Let rest for 10 minutes. Then shape into 1 large, round loaf. Place on a greased cookie sheet, cover lightly and let rise until almost double (about 45 minutes).

Bake at 375°F. for 30 minutes.

Christopsomo

(Greek)

(1 loaf)

2½ to 3 cups unbleached
  white flour
1 package dry yeast
¾ cup milk
2 tablespoons honey
¼ cup butter
½ teaspoon salt*
1 egg
½ teaspoon freshly grated
  lemon peel
½ cup light raisins
½ cup finely chopped walnuts
1 whole almond (for luck)

*The salt, though traditional, may be eliminated if you choose to do so.

Poppy Bread

(Polish)

(2 loaves)

2 packages dry yeast
5 cups unbleached white flour,
more if needed
1½ cups milk
⅔ cup honey
⅓ cup butter
1 teaspoon salt*
3 eggs
1 cup boiling water
¾ cup poppy seeds
½ cup chopped nuts
1 teaspoon freshly grated
lemon peel
1 stiffly beaten egg white

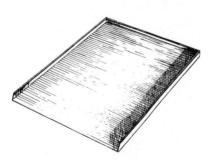

In a mixing bowl, combine yeast with 2 cups of the flour. In a saucepan, heat the milk, half of the honey, butter, and salt until lukewarm. Add the mixture to the dry ingredients. Add eggs. Stir in enough flour to make a stiff dough. Turn out onto a lightly floured surface and knead for about 10 minutes. Shape into a ball and place in a greased bowl, turning once to coat the top. Cover lightly and let rise in a warm place until doubled.

Pour boiling water over poppy seeds and let stand for 30 minutes; then drain thoroughly.

Place poppy seeds in a blender and blend until ground. Stir in nuts, remainder of honey and lemon peel. Fold in the egg white.

After dough has risen, turn out onto a lightly floured surface and punch down. Divide into 2 parts. Let rest for 10 minutes.

Roll 1 part of dough into an 8 × 24-inch rectangle; spread with half the poppy seed mixture. Roll up jelly-roll style, starting with the 8-inch side. Place it seam down in a greased loaf pan. Repeat with the rest of the dough and place in a second greased loaf pan.

Cover with a towel, let rise in a warm spot until double in bulk.

Bake at 350°F. for 35 to 40 minutes.

NOTE: This bread has been tested using whole wheat in place of unbleached white flour, and the result is very satisfying, if not traditional.

---

*The salt, though traditional, may be eliminated if you choose to do so.

Place raisins, citron, and orange peel in a bowl. Add rum and let soak for 1 hour. Drain and reserve rum.

Sprinkle yeast into warm water and let stand until dissolved. In a saucepan, heat the milk and the butter until the butter melts. Pour into a large mixing bowl, add honey, salt, lemon peel, drained rum (reserve fruits), and almond extract. Cool to lukewarm. Beat in eggs and dissolved yeast mixture. Add enough flour to make a soft dough. Dredge fruits in flour and add to dough. Add almonds. Mix well.

Turn out onto a lightly floured surface and knead until smooth (about 8 to 10 minutes). Place in a greased bowl, turn once to coat the top, cover, and place in a warm spot to rise until doubled in bulk (about 45 minutes to 1 hour).

Turn out onto a lightly floured surface, divide dough into 2 parts. Roll each piece into an oval about ¾ inch thick. Brush with melted butter. Roll up and place on a greased cookie sheet. Brush tops with melted butter, cover lightly with wax paper, and place in a warm spot until doubled in bulk.

Bake at 350°F. for 40 minutes.

Dresden *Stollen*

(German)

(2 loaves)

¾ cup raisins
⅓ cup chopped citron
2 tablespoons slivered, fresh
    orange peel
¼ cup rum*
1 package dry yeast
¼ cup warm water
1 cup milk
⅔ cup butter
¼ cup honey
1 teaspoon salt**
2 tablespoons slivered, fresh
    lemon peel
½ teaspoon pure almond extract
2 eggs
4 to 4½ cups unbleached
    white flour
¾ cup chopped almonds
melted butter

*This recipe may be made without rum.
**The salt, though traditional, may be eliminated if you choose to do so.

Kolachy

(Czechoslovakian)

(2½ to 3 dozen rolls)

1 cup warm water
1 cup warm milk
2 packages dry yeast
½ cup melted butter
⅓ cup honey
1½ teaspoons salt*
2 eggs, beaten
¼ teaspoon nutmeg
freshly grated peel of 1 lemon
1 teaspoon freshly squeezed
lemon juice
8 to 9 cups unbleached white flour
melted butter

Kolachy and Other Sweet Roll Fillings

These are Czechoslovakian sweet rolls, and not only are they eaten at Christmastime, but they're baked for all holidays, celebrations, and weddings.

Combine water and milk in a large mixing bowl. Sprinkle in the yeast and stir with a fork until dissolved. Blend in the butter, honey, salt, eggs, nutmeg, lemon peel, and juice. Beat in 3 cups of flour until mixture is smooth. Gradually add enough flour to make a stiff dough. Turn out onto a lightly floured surface and knead until the dough is smooth (about 8 to 10 minutes). Place in a greased bowl, turn once to coat the top, cover, and place in a warm spot to rise until doubled in bulk.

When dough has doubled in size, turn out onto lightly floured surface, punch down and let rest for 15 minutes.

Pinch off bits of dough the size of golf balls. Roll each piece into a ball and place on a greased baking sheet, allowing each enough room to expand during baking. Using your thumb, make a depression in the center of each ball. Fill with any one of the fillings recommended below—or use your own favorite combination of jellies, jams, or other fillings.

Brush dough around the edges with melted butter. Cover with plastic wrap and let rise for 20 minutes.

Bake at 375°F. for 15 to 20 minutes. Remove to wire racks.

NOTE: *Kolachy* may be made substituting whole wheat for unbleached white flour. They may be served hot or cold and, if you like, you may also frost them with your favorite icing.

Poppy Seed Filling: Combine 1 cup poppy seed, ¼ cup butter, ¼ cup honey, 1½ teaspoons freshly squeezed lemon juice, ¼ cup milk, and ½ teaspoon cinnamon in a saucepan. Stir and bring to a simmer. Cook for 5 minutes. Set aside and cool. Store in refrigerator.

*The salt, though traditional, may be eliminated if you choose to do so.

Date Filling: Combine 2 cups pitted, chopped dates, ⅓ cup water, ⅓ cup honey, and 3 tablespoons butter in a small saucepan. Cook, stirring constantly until thick. Add ½ teaspoon pure vanilla extract. Allow to cool.

Cheese Filling: Combine 1 cup dry cottage cheese with 2 egg yolks, 3 tablespoons honey, 1 tablespoon softened butter, and 1 teaspoon freshly grated lemon peel. Mix and keep chilled. Raisins (¼ cup) and/or almonds (¼ cup) may be added to filling.

Prune Filling: Combine 2 cups dried, pitted prunes with 1½ cups boiling water in a saucepan. Bring to a simmer and let cook until the water has been absorbed. Add ½ cup honey, ¼ teaspoon ground cloves, freshly grated peel of 1 lemon, and 1 teaspoon freshly squeezed lemon juice. Stir in till well mixed. Set aside to cool.

Berry Fillings: Combine 2 cups fresh or frozen berries with ¼ cup honey, 3 teaspoons cornstarch, and 2 teaspoons freshly squeezed lemon juice. Bring to a boil; lower heat to simmer and cook until thick. Cool. For a smoother filling, the berries may be crushed or pureed before cooking.

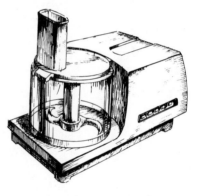

TONY DORSCH

The Breads:

Garden Cracked-Grain Bread
French *Baguettes*
Raisin Coffee Breakfast Bread
Brioche à Tête

Tony is a biology teacher in Redmond, Oregon, and he started baking bread because his wife, a French teacher, missed the *baguettes* and *croissants* that she'd eaten while spending a year in France. He's now reached the point where he grinds all of his own grains with a hand stone grinder.

My Grandmother Dorsch's bread was always fresh in the morning and I remember that she always baked in round bowls or tins, which is why I use hand-thrown pottery bowls and coffee cans to make mushroom-shaped loaves.

Tony buys his yeast in one-pound cakes and cuts them to size, just as I do, but he never preheats the oven because he feels it kills the yeast too soon. I've always loved discussing "mistakes" with fellow bread bakers while the long-distance telephone bills mount up:

I've had burned bread, raw bread, salty bread, flat bread, dead bread, sour bread. We ate the mistakes and I was very frustrated. The hardest part was to find the right temperature with the oven I was using . . . .

Tony recommends buying a good oven thermometer rather than depending upon the dial calibrations. He also has a marvelous way to correct the errors you might make in your first attempts:

If you want to feel better about mistakes, invite a bunch of hungry kids in from the neighborhood. They can make you feel really successful!

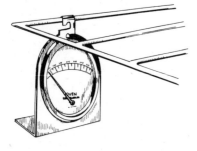

The four recipes that follow are Tony's favorites.

Country Cheddar Sticks (Suzanne Corbett) page 85 *101*

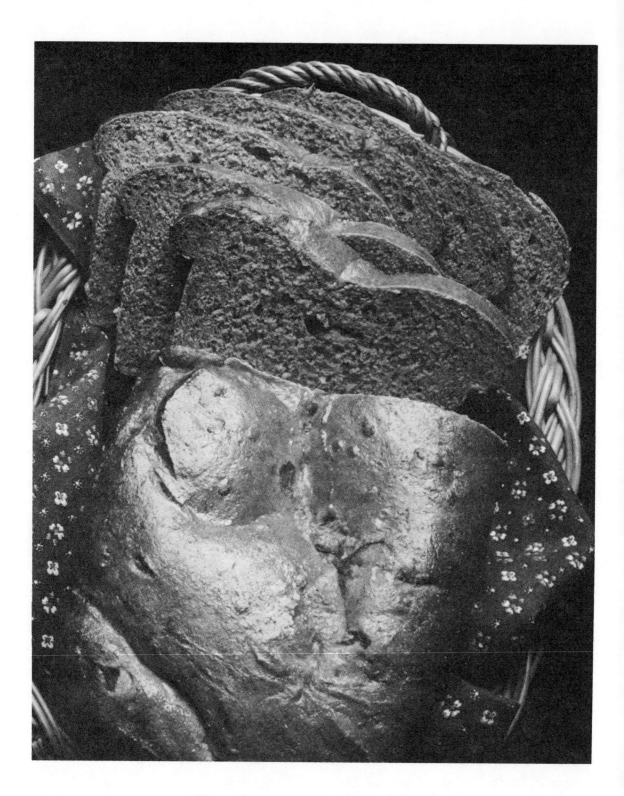

This bread was worked out by Tony on his own and has been his most consistent bread. "When I finally perfected my garden grain bread, and the first loaves came out correctly—ah, ambrosia!" I provide Tony's recipe for this ambrosia just as he gave it, a formula carefully arrived at. However, you may want to try the recipe using whole wheat flour in place of the unbleached white.

Combine boiling water with cold milk. Sprinkle the yeast over the lukewarm liquid and add white flour. Allow this mixture to sit for 6 to 12 hours in a warm spot.

The next morning, combine the above batter with eggs, honey, butter, and salt. Beat with a wooden spoon; then add cornmeal, cracked wheat, wheat germ, wheat flour, and white flour.

Mix thoroughly and then turn out onto a lightly floured surface. Knead well, about 8 to 10 minutes, and then roll in a greased bowl to coat all parts of the dough. Cover and let rise to double (about 1 hour) in a warm spot. Turn out onto lightly floured surface, knead for a few seconds, then form into 2 loaves. Put in greased loaf pans or bowls and cover. Let rise for 1 hour in a warm spot.

Bake at 350° to 375°F. to 35 minutes or until done. Test by tapping on bottom; if loaves sound hollow, they are finished.

Cool on wire rack.

Garden Cracked-Grain Bread

(2 loaves)

1 cup boiling water
1½ cups cold milk
1 package dry yeast
3 cups unbleached white flour
3 eggs
¼ cup honey
¼ cup butter
1 tablespoon salt (optional)
¼ cup cornmeal
¼ cup cracked wheat
¼ cup wheat germ (optional)
2 cups stone-ground wheat flour
2½ to 3 cups unbleached
   white flour

French Baguettes

(3 long loaves)

1 tablespoon melted butter
1 tablespoon salt*
1 tablespoon honey
2⅔ cups lukewarm water
1 package dry yeast
6 to 6½ cups unbleached white flour

Combine butter, salt, honey, and lukewarm water. Sprinkle yeast over this mixture and add flour.

If using a dough hook attachment, place liquids into a bowl and add dry products slowly to form dough. Otherwise, add dry and wet ingredients as above, mixing thoroughly until they are blended. Turn out onto a lightly floured surface and knead thoroughly (about 8 to 10 minutes) or until dough is smooth and elastic. Roll in greased bowl to coat all of dough and cover; place in a warm spot to rise until doubled in size (about 1½ hours). Turn out onto floured surface and punch down. Return to bowl and let rise again for about 1 hour (covered).

Butter a cookie sheet and sprinkle cornmeal on it. Roll out dough into a flat sheet about 30 × 15 inches and then divide into thirds so that each section measures about 10 × 15 inches in size.

Each loaf is formed by rolling the rectangle into a narrow, even loaf. Seal the ends by pinching. Place the loaves on the cookie sheet and cover lightly with a piece of plastic film and let rise for 1 hour. (These free-form French loaves may be made to look even more professional if they're baked in the long, black, French-loaf pans, especially designed for the purpose.)

Spray or brush the loaves with ice-cold water and cut 3 or 4 diagonal slashes on the tops with a sharp knife or razor blade.

Bake at 400°F. for 55 minutes or until crust is browned top and bottom. More water may be brushed on the loaves if desired, but keep in mind that the more water you use, the harder the crust you get. (I spoke with Tony while writing his chapter and questioned him about what seemed to be a long baking time at such a high temperature. He explained that the French *baguettes*, to be authentic, must have a crusty texture on the outside, unlike many of the American, long loaves. His neighbors, who have also lived in France, pronounce Tony's *baguettes* "*très bon et magnifique!*")

NOTE: These are traditional *baguettes*. If you should decide to replace the unbleached white flour with whole wheat flour—and you certainly can!—the bread would be called *pain complet*.

---

*The salt may be eliminated if you choose to do so.

Combine boiling water and cold milk; sprinkle yeast over this lukewarm liquid and add flour. Allow this mixture to sit for 6 to 12 hours in a warm spot.

The next morning, combine the above batter with eggs, honey, melted butter, and salt. Beat in with a wooden spoon and mix thoroughly.

Add remaining flour and raisins, mixing well.

Turn out onto a lightly floured surface and knead well (about 8 to 10 minutes). Roll in a greased bowl to coat the dough and then cover and let rise in a warm spot until doubled (about 1 hour).

Turn out onto floured surface and punch down, kneading for about 2 to 3 minutes. Form 2 loaves and put in greased pans or bowls. Cover and let rise in a warm spot for 1 hour. Bake at 375°F. for 35 minutes.

Cool on wire racks.

NOTE: This is one of those breads that tends to come out on the heavy side when whole wheat flour is used, so Tony believes unbleached white flour makes the best version. Try it both ways and have it the way you like it best.

Raisin Coffee Breakfast Bread

(2 loaves)

1 cup boiling water
1½ cups cold milk
1 package dry yeast
3 cups unbleached white flour
3 eggs
¼ cup honey
¼ cup melted butter
1 tablespoon salt (optional)
5 to 6 cups unbleached white flour
1 cup raisins

Brioche à Tête

(1 large *brioche*)

1 package dry yeast
½ cup lukewarm water
2 teaspoons honey
1¼ teaspoons salt (optional)
3 eggs (reserve 1 egg yolk
for glaze)
½ cup melted butter, unsalted
3½ to 4 cups whole wheat
pastry flour

Glaze:

1 egg yolk
2 tablespoons milk

Tony's recipe brings back memories of my own trips to France and the first time I discovered *brioche*. It's a superb breakfast bread and it's also very impressive.

Combine yeast, lukewarm water, honey, and salt. Blend well and then add eggs, melted butter, and whole wheat pastry flour, mixing in 1 cup at a time.

Turn out onto a lightly floured surface and knead until smooth and elastic (about 8 to 10 minutes). Place in a greased bowl and turn to coat the dough. Cover and let rise in a warm spot for 1½ hours or until doubled in size.

Turn out onto floured surface, punch down and knead for 2 to 3 minutes. Return to greased bowl, turn to coat the dough, cover with plastic or a plate and place in the refrigerator for 12 hours or overnight.

The next morning, turn dough out onto floured surface and knead for 2 to 3 minutes. Pull off a small piece of dough about the size of a lemon or a golf ball. Set aside. With the remainder of the dough, shape into a smooth, round ball and place in a greased, fluted 2-quart *brioche* pan, or 2-quart round pan if a *brioche* pan is not available.

Take the small piece of reserved dough and shape it into a large teardrop or ellipse. With a floured knife, cut about a 1-inch deep slash into the top of the larger piece and insert the pointed end of the small piece into it. Push the edges together to hold the "cap" firmly.

Cover and let rise in a warm spot for 1 hour. Glaze with mixture of egg yolk and milk. This may be done with a soft pastry brush.

Bake at 350°F. for 1 hour. Allow it to brown well on top.

Let cool 15 minutes and then turn out to wire racks.

AMY SELTZER

The Breads:

Italian Bread Sticks
Applesauce Raisin Bread

At the age of 13, Amy was the youngest of my bread-baking students in the Fire Island classes. As a matter of fact, she could roll out a long sourdough much better than her instructor, something I've never quite been able to forgive. She's now 16 and she still bakes bread: "My family complains that my breads keep the freezer so full that there's no room for anything else."

She's currently a student at the Brearly School in New York City. Her bread baking continues on weekends, however, and she has learned her bread philosophy well: "I believe in trial and error bread baking. If it looks done, it's done!"

Italian Bread Sticks

(about 3 to 4 dozen bread sticks)

1 package dry yeast
⅔ cup warm water
½ teaspoon honey
½ teaspoon flour
2 tablespoons oil
2 tablespoons olive oil
1 teaspoon salt (optional)
1 teaspoon honey
2 to 2½ cups whole wheat flour
1 egg, beaten
poppy or sesame seeds (optional)

There's one problem with these delicious bread snacks. You spend so much time rolling them out, Amy says, that by the time you have rolled the 48th, the first one has been rising for 30 minutes! "It sure helps to have a friend with you to help roll out when you're baking them."

Dissolve yeast in warm water, add honey and flour. Wait until the yeast solution bubbles (about 5 to 10 minutes). Then add oil, olive oil, salt, honey, and 1 cup of the flour. Beat until smooth. Add enough of the remaining flour to make a stiff dough.

Turn the dough out onto a lightly floured surface and knead until smooth and elastic (about 8 minutes). Use extra flour if you need it to keep the dough from becoming too sticky. Place the dough in a greased bowl and brush a small amount of oil on top to keep it from drying out. Cover with a towel and let rise in a warm place until doubled in bulk (about 1 hour).

When doubled, turn out onto a lightly floured surface, punch down dough, and knead for about 2 to 3 minutes. Divide the dough in half, then divide each half into 18 to 24 equal pieces. Roll each piece into 6 or 8-inch lengths, about ½ inch thick. Place them in rows on a greased baking sheet about ½ inch apart. Brush the tops of the sticks with the egg and sprinkle with poppy or sesame seeds, if desired. Let them rise in a warm place until almost doubled (20 to 30 minutes).

Bake in a 325°F. oven for 30 minutes (less if the sticks are thinner and longer) or until golden brown.

This is a quick bread that is fairly moist. Amy says that she generally increases the amount of raisins because she likes a "cakier" bread. It's marvelous hot with melted butter on it.

Preheat oven to 350°F.

In a bowl, combine the eggs, applesauce, melted butter, and honey, mixing thoroughly. Stir in the flour, baking powder, salt, soda, cinnamon, and nutmeg. Stir until smooth. Stir in the raisins and nuts. The batter will *not* be doughlike, but slightly wet and gooey. Turn the batter into 2 well-greased 5 × 9-inch loaf pans and bake in a moderate oven (350°F.) for 1 hour. Cool.

This bread slices the best on the second day.

Applesauce Raisin Bread

(2 loaves)

2 eggs, slightly beaten
2 cups natural applesauce
½ cup melted butter
½ cup honey
5 cups whole wheat flour
4 teaspoons baking powder
1 teaspoon salt (optional)
1 teaspoon baking soda
1½ teaspoons cinnamon
¾ teaspoon ground nutmeg
2 cups seedless raisins
1½ cups coarsely chopped pecans
   or walnuts

The Saga of Sourdough

At some point in our bread-baking "careers," all of us try sourdoughs. The starter is made or borrowed, stored and treasured, sniffed and hoarded, given as a gift, talked about, written about, possibly even lied about when we tell one another how old our starter is.

Each of my bread-baking friends has at least one recipe that includes a sourdough starter. In each of the files collected for this book, I found recipes for sourdough breads, rolls, and muffins and thus decided that I would include the best in one chapter dedicated to sourdough baking, and to that alone.

I covered the brief history of sourdough in earlier pages (see Index), and more is added to the lore on the pages that follow. The important thing, perhaps, is that each of us would like to pass on to you the excitement of a type of bread that seems difficult at first, but is, in reality, quite simple and certainly rewarding. The taste is like no other taste in the bread world!

Once the starter has been made (or a cup borrowed), it is only a matter of keeping it properly—many have kept for 25 or 30 years. When a cup is used, flour and water replace the amount you've taken from your cache, and the concoction continues to bubble on for as many years as you care to tend to it.

Since the starter acts as the leavening, some bakers use no yeast, like the pioneers of so many years ago. However, there is no law that says you can't use "a belt *and* suspenders" by adding yeast in addition to the starter. This will guarantee the rise, and still keep the distinctive sour taste of the bread. Purists will "pooh-pooh" this grossness, but I am a great believer in encouraging the beginner.

I've listed the breads under the names of the people who have given me the recipes, and I have again taken the author's privilege of adding some notes and recipes of my own.

BEATRICE SEAL

Get to know the incredible Bea Seal better by turning to page 188.

I've read and been told many times that sourdough breads are probably hundreds of years old, possibly the first leavened breads known to man. Webster's Dictionary says: "fermented dough for use as leaven in bread . . . a Canadian or Alaskan prospector—so called from the habit of carrying sourdough, the fermented dough used as a leavening in bread baking." Whatever its origin, sourdough is something special to bread cookery. . . .

Sourdough Starter

Bea goes on to explain how to make your first starter, an easy recipe—in fact, the way I began my first starter almost seven years ago:

Most sourdough bakers will tell you the best way to start your sourdough stock is to get a starter from someone who has a good bubbly batch going, but there are other good alternatives, such as this yeast starter. . . .

1 package or cake of yeast
2 cups warm water
2 cups whole wheat flour

Combine the ingredients in a glass or pottery container. NEVER USE METAL! Cover with cheesecloth and let stand at room temperature for 48 hours, stirring it down several times. Potato water is an even better liquid than tap water. Each time you stir, you may notice a clear, yellowish liquid on top of the starter. This is natural—just stir it down. Do the same before using.

Using the Starter: Each time you use your starter, replenish it with equal amounts of flour and water. The starter should be kept in the refrigerator when not in use, then taken out and brought to room temperature before using it.

If you do not use the starter weekly, take it from the refrigerator about every 10 days to be freshened. Discard half the starter, feed it with equal parts of flour and water, keep it at room temperature until it bubbles, and then refrigerate, lightly covered.

Old-Fashioned Traditional Starters: The starter that Bea describes for us is quite simple, of course. The smell will tell you when you have a pungent, active starter, and the taste of the breads will tell you even more strongly that you are a sourdough baker, equal to anyone in San Francisco! However, many years ago, the starters were made differently, by capturing the "wild yeast" in the air. Bea Seal tried it:

My favorite starter was developed as a result of following a suggestion from my husband's medical/pharmaceutical background. He suggested that I simply capture "wild yeast" in the air outside.

Traditional Starter

2 cups sweet acidophilus low-fat milk (regular low-fat milk may be used)
2 cups hard wheat flour (whole wheat flour may be used)
1 teaspoon honey
glass or ceramic container

Put the low-fat milk into the container, cover with cheesecloth and leave at room temperature for 24 hours. Add 2 cups of flour and honey and stir well to blend the mixture. Cover the container with cheesecloth and put it outside in warm weather. After 24 more hours, take the starter inside and put it in a warm place where the "captured" yeast will be activated. This may take from 2 to 3 days. When the starter becomes bubbly and begins to expand in size, it is ready for use. Handle the same way as the yeast starter recipe, refrigerating when not in use, and adding flour and water to refresh or replenish the starter.

Bea, wanting to begin a second starter, tried the same recipe, but:

. . . after 24 hours, I went outside and found no activity, so I just let it stay in the shade on the patio and forgot about it. Mid-afternoon, during a light sprinkle of rain, I remembered my starter. I ran to take it in, found a light settling of raindrops on top of the mixture, but no bubbles. My curiosity encouraged me to stir the mixture lightly and set it in a warm, sunny corner. In less than an hour, it was boiling out of the jar.

Of course, if the weather is inclement or too cold, the kitchen of your house will do nicely to begin this starter. But, however you begin, whether you beg or borrow your sourdough starter· or make your own, you are ready to try the recipes that call for it.

You're going to love the breads that result!

This is a crunchy, delightful treat that makes outstanding breakfast toast. Steel-cut oats may be found in any natural foods store.

Pour the boiling water over the steel-cut oats and let stand until lukewarm. Then stir in the honey, 2 cups of whole wheat flour, and the starter. Blend thoroughly and let stand for several hours—or if the weather is quite cold, let the mixture stand overnight. This is called the "sponge."

When the sponge is ready, dissolve the yeast in warm water and add to the sponge with the rest of the ingredients. Blend well and turn out onto a lightly floured surface. Knead for about 8 to 10 minutes, adding more flour as necessary to make a firm, unsticky dough. It should be smooth and elastic.

Place in a buttered bowl, turn to coat all sides, cover and let rise to double in a warm place (about 1 hour). Turn out onto floured surface and knead again for about 2 to 3 minutes.

Divide into 3 portions, shape into loaves and place in 3 buttered 9 × 5-inch loaf pans. Cover and let rise in a warm place until almost doubled in size.

Bake at 350°F. for 45 to 55 minutes.

Cool on wire racks.

Sourdough Steel-Cut Oats Bread

(3 loaves)

2 cups boiling water
2 cups steel-cut oats
¼ cup honey
2 cups whole wheat flour
1½ cups sourdough starter
1 package dry yeast
½ cup warm water
⅓ cup melted butter
⅓ cup pure maple syrup
2 teaspoons salt (optional)
4½ to 5 cups graham flour or
    whole wheat flour

Combine the water, starter, and 2 cups of whole wheat flour. Stir well and let rest for about 2 hours, or overnight in cooler weather.

Pour the scalded milk over the butter, salt, and honey. Stir to melt the butter and cool to lukewarm. When cool, stir in yeast, add to sourdough batter and blend well. Then stir in remaining whole wheat flour and all other ingredients, using enough graham flour to make a firm dough that is easily workable. Turn out onto lightly floured surface and knead thoroughly for about 8 to 10 minutes.

Return to a greased bowl, turning to coat all sides; cover and let rise to double (about 1 hour) in a warm spot.

Turn out onto floured surface, knead for 1 or 2 minutes; then divide into 3 parts, shape into loaves and place them in buttered 9 × 5-inch loaf pans. Cover, place in a warm spot and let rise to double (about 45 minutes to 1 hour). *(continued on page 114)*

Sourdough Graham Bread

(3 loaves)

2 cups water
1 cup sourdough starter
6 cups whole wheat flour
1 cup milk, scalded
¼ cup butter
2 teaspoons salt (optional)
⅓ cup honey
1 package dry yeast
2 teaspoons baking soda
½ cup wheat germ
3¾ to 4 cups graham flour

Bake at 400°F. for 15 minutes. Reduce heat to 325°F. and bake until breads are done—about 30 minutes more.

Remove from pans and cool on wire racks.

Sourdough English-Style Muffins

(about 1 dozen muffins)

1 cup sourdough starter
2 cups milk
1 cup yellow cornmeal
3⅔ cups whole wheat flour
3 tablespoons light honey
1 teaspoon salt (optional)
1 teaspoon baking soda
1 large egg

These are great when served piping hot. The ones that are left over may be split and popped into a toaster. Either way, they're a taste treat!

Combine starter, milk, cornmeal, and 1½ cups of the flour. Stir to blend well, cover bowl and let rest overnight.

Stir mixture down, then add the remainder of the flour and all other ingredients. Mix well and turn out onto a lightly floured surface. Knead thoroughly for about 8 to 10 minutes.

Roll or pat dough into a thickness of about ½ inch. Cut with a large (about 3½ inches) biscuit cutter. Cover muffins and let rise for about 45 minutes.

Bake on top of stove on a lightly buttered griddle (Bea uses an electric fry pan) at about 300°F. for 10 to 12 minutes on each side. Turn only once.

Sourdough Whole Wheat Biscuits

(about 1½ dozen 2½-inch biscuits)

2 cups whole wheat flour
2 teaspoons baking powder
½ teaspoon salt (optional)
½ cup butter
2 cups sourdough starter

Bea warns that you watch these carefully since they burn quickly if you're not careful.

Sift the dry ingredients into a bowl. Cut in the butter well. Work in starter until well blended.

Turn out onto a lightly floured surface and knead VERY GENTLY for 2 or 3 minutes. Then roll or pat the dough to a thickness of about ½ inch. Cut into small rounds and place on lightly greased cookie sheet.

Bake at 425°F. for about 10 minutes.

Serve warm.

When I first saw this recipe, I called Bea at her home in North Carolina and commented about the fact that there was no flour in the list of ingredients. Bea reassured me that there is, indeed, no flour!

Combine the cornmeal, molasses, salt, scalded milk, and butter. Stir to melt butter and let mixture cool to lukewarm.

When cool, stir in remainder of ingredients and beat well. Pour into a 9 × 13-inch or 8 × 12-inch well-buttered cake pan. Bake at 425°F. for 35 to 45 minutes or until golden brown.

Serve warm.

Sourdough Corn Bread

(2 to 3 dozen squares)

2 cups stone-ground
    white cornmeal
3 tablespoons light molasses
1 teaspoon salt (optional)
2 cups milk, scalded
½ cup butter
2 cups sourdough starter
2 large eggs
2 teaspoons baking powder

Soften yeast in warm water. Add to starter with oil. Sift the dry ingredients and then blend well with yeast mixture. Cover and let rise to double (about 1 hour).

Punch down and shape into small balls, putting 2 into each greased or buttered muffin cup. Cover and let rise for about 45 minutes.

Bake at 350°F. for 12 to 15 minutes.

Sourdough Rolls

(about 1 dozen rolls)

1 package dry yeast
½ cup warm water
1 cup sourdough starter
4 teaspoons oil
2 cups whole wheat flour
2 teaspoons baking powder
½ teaspoon salt (optional)

DEBORAH FOUGHTY

Sourdough Tomato-Cheese Bread

(2 loaves)

1 cup sourdough starter
1 28-ounce can tomatoes, undrained
2 packages dry yeast
¼ cup warm water
1 pound grated sharp or longhorn cheese
½ teaspoon baking powder
2 to 3 teaspoons safflower oil
1 tablespoon honey
2 tablespoons salt (optional)
6½ to 7½ cups whole wheat flour

Debbie is an elementary school teacher in Devils Lake, North Dakota, and she makes this bread with a starter that is seven years old—not at all unusual for confirmed sourdough bakers. She uses the starter for most of her baking as well as for desserts and pancakes.

Put the starter in a large bowl. Add the tomatoes—cut and mashed—and include the liquid.

Dissolve the yeast in the warm water. Put aside to proof. Add the cheese, baking powder, safflower oil, honey, and salt to the starter-tomato mixture. Add the dissolved yeast and gradually beat in the flour 1 cup at a time. The dough will be fairly thick.

Turn out onto a lightly floured surface and knead for 8 to 10 minutes. Add more flour if necessary. Place in a greased bowl, turn to coat the dough, and cover. Let rise in a warm spot until double in size—about 1 hour.

Punch down knead for 1 or 2 minutes; then divide into 2 loaves, and place in well-greased loaf pans (9 × 5 inches). Cover with a towel or plastic wrap and let rise in a warm spot until almost doubled in size (about 1½ hours).

Bake at 375°F. for 40 minutes or until loaves test done.

Cool on wire racks.

GERRY FRANKLIN

Meet my delightful neighbor, Gerry, more formally on page 77.

One summer Sunday morning, Gerry rode his bicycle over to our house and presented us with some slices of this marvelous bread. The sample was devoured in about two minutes!

Dissolve the yeast in water, add the flour and the onion and stir well in a container that is at least 2 quarts in size. Cover loosely and leave at room temperature for 2 days. Stir before using. As with any other starter, you can keep it going by adding equal parts of rye flour and warm water to replace the amount that you've used. Or—when not in use—keep it in the refrigerator, tightly covered and add some additional flour and water about once a week.

The night before baking, make a sponge.

Stir together in a large bowl, cover loosely and keep at room temperature overnight.

Next morning, make the dough.

Dissolve yeast in warm water, then add to the sponge prepared the previous day. Stir in the remaining ingredients, turn out the dough onto a lightly floured surface and knead until smooth and not sticky (about 8 to 10 minutes). If necessary, add additional flour. Place the dough in a lightly greased bowl, turn to coat all sides, and let rise in a warm spot until doubled (about 1 hour).

Punch down, divide into 2 large or 4 small loaves, and place them on a greased baking sheet that has been sprinkled with cornmeal. Cover loosely and let rise until almost doubled—about 1 hour. Before baking, brush the loaves with the glaze and then liberally sprinkle the tops with the seeds.

Bake at 425°F. for 40 to 50 minutes. Cool on wire racks.

Sourdough Onion Rye Bread

(2 large or 4 small free-form loaves)

The Starter:

1 package dry yeast
2 cups warm water
2 cups medium rye flour
1 finely chopped onion,
   medium size

The Sponge:

1 cup starter
1½ cups warm water
3 cups medium rye flour
1 finely chopped onion,
   medium size

The Dough:

1 package dry yeast
¼ cup warm water
1 tablespoon salt (optional)
1 tablespoon caraway seeds
1 tablespoon poppy seeds
1 cup gluten flour (or whole wheat)
2½ cups whole wheat flour

The Glaze:

1 egg beaten with 1 teaspoon water
caraway seeds or onion flakes
   (or black caraway seeds)

SUZANNE CORBETT

Suzanne is a gold mine of fantastic bread recipes. For the full story, see page 80.

Sourdough Rye or Whole Wheat Bread

(3 loaves)

1½ cups sourdough starter
1½ cups warm water
3 cups rye flour
2 packages dry yeast
¼ cup water (120°F.)
2½ teaspoons salt (optional)
1½ tablespoons caraway seeds
¼ cup molasses, dark
½ cup melted butter
4 to 4¼ cups whole wheat flour

Light Brown Glaze:

1 egg white
1 tablespoon water
caraway or sesame seeds

Deep Golden Glaze:

1 egg yolk
1 tablespoon water
caraway or sesame seeds

Combine the starter, warm water, and rye flour. Cover with plastic wrap and let stand overnight or for 12 hours.

Next day, stir the mixture, add the yeast dissolved in the ¼ cup water, salt, seeds, molasses, and butter. Stir in enough whole wheat flour to make a workable dough. Turn out onto a lightly floured surface and knead for 10 minutes.

Place the dough in a greased or buttered bowl, turning once to coat the top. Cover and let rise in a warm place until doubled in bulk, about 1 hour.

Punch down, knead for 1 or 2 minutes, and shape into 3 round or long loaves. Place on greased baking sheets sprinkled with white or yellow cornmeal. Slash tops and let rise to double (lightly covered with plastic wrap).

Brush with egg wash, and sprinkle tops with seeds. Bake at 375°F. for 30 minutes.

Cool on wire racks.

MAGGIE MARTHEY

Treat yourself to Maggie's Southwestern specialties by turning to page 137.

This is a simple biscuit recipe that is baked in an iron skillet.

Mix all the ingredients, except butter, to make a firm dough. Grease a black, iron skillet with the butter.

Pinch off balls of dough the size of walnuts and place in the skillet. Set the biscuits in a warm place to rise for about 15 minutes.

Bake at 400°F. for 25 to 30 minutes.

Sourdough Biscuits

(about 1½ dozen biscuits)

2 cups whole wheat flour
1 tablespoon honey
1 tablespoon baking powder
¾ teaspoon salt (optional)
2 cups sourdough starter
2 to 3 tablespoons butter

MEL LONDON

Sourdough Notes

As the author, I could not resist interjecting some thoughts at this point, plus two of my favorite recipes and a new type of starter. There is no doubt that the word "sourdough" conjures up exciting images—either in terms of its history or in memories of visits to San Francisco. Watch the reaction of your dinner guests when they look at you and ask, "What kind of bread is this?" When you tell them it's a sourdough, you will have secured a permanent place in their Gourmet Hall of Fame.

If you really find sourdough baking as intriguing as most of us do, I would strongly suggest that you acquire the long, black, French-bread pans. If your local market doesn't carry them, I've given addresses for mail order at the back of the book. The beauty of baking sourdough in loaf form is that you can make as many as 10 at one time in your standard oven. I now have two 5-loaf pans that do the job.

It is amazing just how long you can keep a starter bubbling and active—as long as you take good care of it. If it should die, a couple of days and you have another one started and on its way. One summer, I left on a long trip and entrusted my starter to a friend. When I returned, I found that it had not been used, had been sitting in the sun for six weeks and had made their kitchen unlivable because of its funky smell. I felt as though I had lost a friend!

The night before you bake, mix the ingredients with a wooden spoon in a medium-size bowl. Cover lightly and place in a warm spot. This will be your sponge. The next morning, it should be bubbly and will have risen in the bowl. I generally tiptoe out of bed in the early morning, trying not to awaken my wife, and I lift the towel to look at the miracle that has occurred while I slept!

Next morning, make the dough.

Mix the yeast, warm water, and honey. Set aside to proof. In a large bowl, blend the sponge, the yeast mixture, salt, and the flour, 1 cup at a time. Turn out onto a lightly floured surface and knead for 8 to 10 minutes or until dough is smooth and elastic. If you find the dough sticky, add more flour.

Place dough in a greased bowl, turn once to coat the top, cover lightly and place in a warm spot to double in size (about 50 minutes to 1 hour).

Turn out onto lightly floured surface, knead for 1 or 2 minutes and return to the greased bowl; cover and let rise again for about 45 minutes. This recipe calls for 3 rises, as you will notice. Actually, you can use only 2 rises, but I find that the bread has a finer texture when given the additional rise.

After the second rise, turn out again onto lightly floured surface, knead for 1 or 2 minutes and shape into 4 long loaves. Place in greased French-loaf pans sprinkled with white cornmeal (or use a cookie sheet treated in the same way), cover lightly and let rise to almost double (about 45 minutes).

Using a razor blade, slash the tops of the loaves diagonally about 2 inches apart. Don't be afraid—the loaves won't fall. Spray with water and sprinkle with sesame seeds. Bake at 425°F. for 25 to 30 minutes. About 15 minutes into the baking, spray the loaves with water again—this will give you a superb crust. Incidentally, I always use a hot brick in a pan of boiling water on the bottom of my oven.

When breads test done, cool on wire racks.

San Francisco Sourdough Loaves

(2 to 4 long loaves)

The Sponge:

1 cup starter
2 cups unbleached white flour, unsifted (whole wheat flour may be used)
1 cup warm water

The Dough:

2 packages dry yeast
1 cup warm water
1 teaspoon honey
1 tablespoon salt (optional)
4 cups unbleached white flour (whole wheat flour may be used)
sesame seeds for top

Sourdough Yogurt Starter

1 cup skim milk
4 tablespoons yogurt (unflavored low-fat)
1 cup unbleached white flour
(whole wheat flour may be used)

Since San Francisco is famous for its sourdough breads, it seems only right that I should have discovered this new starter idea while discussing recipes with a friend in a coffee shop on Polk Street in that city. That was about three years ago, and I've been experimenting ever since. In fact, this year's Christmas gifts (next recipe) used this very same starter. Once it's made, you keep it in exactly the same way as you do any other starter by replenishing it with equal parts of warm milk and flour. And—as with other starters—the older it gets, the better it seems to be.

Take a 1- to 2-quart container—it may be a glass jar, a ceramic bowl, or strong plastic. Warm the container by pouring hot water into it and letting it stand for several minutes.

Heat the milk to a temperature of about 95°F. (use a thermometer for this), then remove from heat and stir in the 4 tablespoons of yogurt. Pour the mixture into the warmed container, cover tightly and place in a warm spot. I use the oven with only the pilot light providing the heat. Just remember to take it out if you're going to bake. I forgot one time and the plastic wrap melted into the starter!

After about 24 hours, the starter will have formed a curd, possibly covered with clear liquid. Merely stir the liquid back into the starter. NOTE: If the liquid is pink, discard the entire starter and begin again.

When the curd has formed, stir in the flour, blending the mixture with a wooden spoon until it is smooth. Cover tightly and let it stand again in the warm place for 3 to 5 days. It should be bubbly, just as any other starter and you will notice a superb, sour smell when you lift the wrap. Use it when it's ready or store it in the refrigerator, tightly covered.

We find that this is an ideal starter for our Fire Island sourdough baking. We put it in the oven on Sunday and when we return on Friday evening, the starter has been working for just the right amount of time.

I chose this bread for the Fire Island Christmas gifts this year, since I felt that they were festive, delicious and very unusual. As always, they were loaded into the wagon—16 this year—and delivered to everyone before the sun went down. My wife and I had been making the starter for some weeks, but I had no idea how long it would take me to bake 16 breads, since only 4 would fit in the oven at one time. By planning the day, working on a schedule that had 4 loaves being mixed and kneaded while 4 were rising for the first time, and still another 4 were formed and on their second rise—with the first 4 breads in the oven—it took only 4 hours from start to finish! With the winter sun fast disappearing, we made the rounds on our bicycles, the wagon trailing me, each package decorated with fresh holly and sunlight reflecting off the aluminum wrap.

Fifteen were delivered. The 16th rested lonely and unloved in the wagon, for the final intended recipients were not at home. The house was locked and dark. They would not be there for Christmas at all. My wife and I sat atop the steps overlooking the beach, the sun now near its final plunge into the water and the smell of the bread came through the wrapping and wafted up to our noses. Like two naughty children, we tore it open and tasted it—still warm. One piece led to another. And—in five minutes—the bread was gone. Eaten. Devoured. Giggling, we went home, just in time to hear the phone ring.

It was our friend, Florence McManus, to whom we had delivered a bread not 15 minutes before. "Would it be greedy," she asked, "to eat the whole bread at one sitting? It's delicious. I want the recipe!"

Indeed, my Christmas was complete!

Spoonhandle Sourdough Rye

(2 loaves)

1 package dry yeast
2 teaspoons honey
1 cup warm water
1 tablespoon salt (optional)
2 teaspoons oil
3 tablespoons caraway seeds
¾ cup yogurt starter
1½ cups rye flour
2 to 2½ cups whole wheat flour
melted butter
caraway seeds

Mix the yeast, honey, and warm water and set aside to proof.

In a bowl, put the salt, oil, caraway seeds, and the yogurt starter (make sure starter is at room temperature if you have refrigerated it). Add the yeast mixture, then stir in the rye flour and mix well. Gradually mix in the whole wheat flour, 1 cup at a time until the dough pulls away from the sides of the bowl and cannot be mixed with the wooden spoon. Turn out onto a lightly floured surface and knead for 8 to 10 minutes, adding flour if the dough becomes too sticky as you knead.

Place in a well-greased bowl, turn once to coat the top; cover and place in a warm spot until doubled in bulk—about 50 minutes to 1 hour. (continued on page 124)

Punch down, knead for 1 or 2 minutes, and divide into 2 equal parts. Place each part on a lightly greased baking sheet and press down with the heel of your hand until you make a round flat shape about 8 inches in diameter. Each baking sheet should hold 2 breads. Cover lightly with plastic wrap and place in a warm spot to rise for about 45 minutes. The loaves will puff up to almost double.

Take a long wooden spoon, flour the handle (and keep putting flour on the handle through this next process) and, using a rolling motion, press into the dough about 1½ inches apart. I find that the breads will take about 4 of these creases. Don't be afraid to roll the handle all the way down to the bottom. Brush with melted butter and sprinkle with caraway (I used black caraway this year).

Bake at 375°F. for 35 minutes or until brown. Brush with melted butter while still hot from the oven and cool on wire racks.

Two Sourdough Free Spirits

As a final tribute to the marvelous sourdough breads, I have separated two of my friends and placed them here, at the end of this chapter.

Both Sylvia Moore and Max Schubel are, first of all, unusual and interesting people. But, more important, perhaps, is the fact that they both have a free, spirited, inventive, joyful approach to bread baking.

The stories are theirs—told, for the most part, in their own words.

SYLVIA MOORE

I met her while waiting to check in at an airline counter in Billings, Montana. Looking over her shoulder, I could see that the book she was reading was all about sourdough breads. Naturally, I asked about it. She was, she said, a flight attendant for an international airline. She was based in San Diego, California— and, yes, she loved to bake bread. In fact, she told me, she had always wanted to bake bread on board a jumbo jet. After that first meeting, we talked by long distance phone occasionally, and we corresponded. Within a few months, a letter arrived on the stationery of the Conquistador-Sheraton Hotel in Guatemala.

You aren't going to believe it! Yesterday, I successfully baked 747 Sourdough Banana Bread on board a jumbo jet bound for Guatemala.

I left San Diego for Los Angeles at 4:30 A.M. to catch Flight 515. The night before I had packed: one glass mixing bowl, measuring cups, wooden spoon, spatula, whole wheat flour, nuts, coconut, bananas, eggs, starter, and butter, plus two bread loaf pans.

We were to fly at 33,000 feet with a cabin altitude of between 5,000 and 6,000 feet.

I was assigned the forward, economy galley and, after takeoff, we all attended to bar service, hot lunch, and then started our in-flight movies. That's when I got to work. I assembled all my tools and ingredients and started mixing the bread. The starter, which had been out of the refrigerator since 4:30 A.M. was warm and bubbly.

I mixed the batter and greased the bread pans. Meanwhile, I had preheated one of the five large ovens in my galley. Normally they hold 42 casserole-type entrées and they have three

settings—high, medium and low. I put one pan on the bottom rack and one on the center rack and set the temperature at medium—between 300° and 400°F., I guess. (Contrary to popular opinion, aircraft ovens are not microwave!)

The entire aircraft was permeated by the aroma of the banana bread, and the crew members and passengers wandered up front to see what was happening! After about 50 minutes, the breads were ready—the one on the center rack was better than the one on the bottom—but both were superb. We were all going crazy sampling the products. Of course, I went up to the cockpit to offer the bread to the captain and his crew. One of the comments was, "Sure beats a box lunch!" After my friend Crystal Thurston took pictures, we passed around platefuls of bread to the passengers and landed in Guatemala!

747 Sourdough Banana Bread

(2 loaves)

½ cup honey
¼ cup sorghum molasses
⅓ cup butter
1½ cups sourdough starter
1 teaspoon baking soda
1 teaspoon salt (optional)
1 egg
1½ cups mashed bananas
1 to 1½ cups whole wheat pastry flour
½ cup unsweetened coconut
1 cup chopped walnuts

Of course, these loaves can be baked right in your home oven. You don't need a 747 jumbo jet for your kitchen. But the story is so delightful and so charming, that I could not resist relating it exactly as it happened. Sylvia got her original starter from her neighbor, Suzi Splinter. It was a 25-year-old wild yeast culture from a Durango woman in the San Juan Mountains of Colorado. Yours does not have to be quite that exotic. Any sourdough starter will do.

In a mixing bowl, combine the honey, sorghum, and butter. Mix well. Add the starter, soda, and salt. Lightly beat the egg and add to the batter. Stir in the bananas and the flour. Add the coconut and nuts, stir well and pour into 2 small, greased loaf pans. Bake about 40 to 50 minutes at 375°F.

Cool on wire racks.

The story has not ended. . . . There is a postscript.

After arriving at the hotel in Guatemala, I was cleaning my pans and noticed that I still had one cup of the starter left, plus lots of flour. I thought I would attempt another recipe—a long sponge sourdough whole wheat bread—on the flight the next day.

So there at the sink, I added a cup of water and two cups of whole wheat flour to my starter, covered the bowl, set it on a towel rack high on the wall, filled the bathtub with hot water to keep the bathroom warm—and left it overnight.

The next morning, the dough was bubbling nicely and I flew out on a 707 to Mexico City with the added challenge of a short flight time—only 1½ hours! Before the passengers boarded, I took the dough out, added the honey, butter and about one-and-a-half cups more of the whole wheat. I kneaded the dough and while the passengers boarded and we took off, it doubled in bulk. I formed two loaves, took care of my passengers, and preheated the oven to medium (350°F.) and popped the loaves in. By the time the passengers had been served, the aroma of fresh-baked bread again permeated the cabin. It was a success!

What amazed me most was how easy it all was—even on the short flight. And, what a conversation starter! Several of the passengers told me of their experiences with sourdough baking and were flabbergasted that I actually baked bread at 33,000 feet in the air. I told them I might try baking bread next at 120 feet below sea level while scuba diving. Now wouldn't that make an interesting chapter in your book!

Knowing Sylvia, I'll be looking for a letter from underneath the Atlantic Ocean anytime now.

For long sponge recipes, you add all the liquid in the recipes to the starter and up to four-fifths of the flour called for and then leave it overnight, covered, in a warm place. Then, the next day you bake it, omitting any yeast or soda—and the bread rises quickly and is even more sour and tastier.

Mix ingredients together in a large bowl. Cover and let stand until the next day. In the morning, it will be bubbly and have a sour smell.

Next morning, make the dough.

Mix honey, butter, and flour together and add to the sponge prepared the previous day. Mix well, turn out onto a lightly floured surface and knead for about 8 minutes. Return to a greased bowl, turn once to coat all sides and cover. Place in a warm spot to rise to double (about 1 hour or less).

When doubled, turn out onto lightly floured surface, punch down, knead for 1 or 2 minutes and form into 2 loaves—either long shape or made to fit 2 small, loaf pans.

Cover and let rise for about 30 minutes. Bake at 350°F. for 55 minutes.

Long Sponge Sourdough Bread

(2 loaves)

The Sponge:

1 cup starter
1 cup water
2 cups whole wheat flour

The Dough:

½ cup honey
2 tablespoons butter
1½ to 2 cups whole wheat flour

MAX SCHUBEL

Island Sourdough

Since Max lives on an island and has no telephone, our communications have relied upon letters relayed through the surprisingly reliable mail service from New York to Greenville, Maine, and back again. Though he approaches bread baking with a joy that I find inspiring, he wrote in his August letter: ". . . no, I don't think there's anything special about a composer on an island baking his own bread. . . ."

Of course, being the author, it was my prerogative to disagree and the mail has brought both photographs and Max's comments about his bread-baking activities, specifically with regard to his Island Sourdough, a combination of techniques, ingredients and inventiveness that might well give the reader some new ideas. In fact, you will find that Island Sourdough is not so much a recipe as a way of life for the bread baker. In fact, Max's last letter (most of which is transcribed below) actually has a title: "Adventures in Sourdough."

There I was one day, standing before the rack in Greenville's A&P, unable to reach out and take a sack of the supermarket's "finest"—physically unable, psychologically unwilling. After years of fulfilling the simple, conditioned art of being a packaged bread consumer, something basic within me finally said "NO". . . .

That was about 15 years ago—Max bought flour and yeast, got out some cookbooks and set out to make his own:

. . . of course, like all good Aries, I knew it all. The first attempts were bread jawbreakers. Slowly I learned. . . . Several years ago, I read a sourdough maker's tried-and-tested guide for making a really pure, no-nonsense bread. Since the cheesemaking suggestions I'd gotten from that magazine earlier had turned me into a productive cheesemaker, using

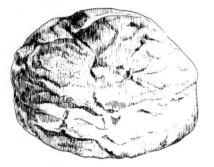

penny-a-quart "pig milk" (outdated milk, which local farmers buy from their dairy processing plant as the returns come in and then feed to their pigs), I launched into the sourdough recipe. I did exactly what the writer outlined—no prideful deviations. My restraint ate at my quelled gumption. The first starter and batch of bread were made on the kitchen table on my island. . . .

Max says that the first group didn't rise much, but it *was* sour and it tasted good. The bread improved with each baking and, gradually, as his confidence grew, he began giving his sourdough breads to others.

Soon, my zeal about the goodness of sourdough began to take on some of the qualities of religious fanaticism. In my travels as a composer and producer of recordings, I'd try to turn people on to making their own sourdough. It wasn't until years later that I realized that some people were just too polite to say "no" when I invaded their kitchens, brought in flour and honey, took them to the local health foods store, dug around for bowls and showed them how to begin starters. I received a letter from a composer friend in Maryland, saying: ". . . do come visit, if you promise not to bake bread again. . . ."

One of the fascinating things to me about Max's sourdough experiences is his observation of how the process differs in various parts of the country:

. . . in Albuquerque, New Mexico, people said, "Oh, it'll NEVER rise, we're too high up!"—yet the results there were fast. My place in Maine, I'm sorry to say, produces slow and relatively inactive yeasts. New York City has produced the most vigorous and high rising dough . . . and in all that pollution and noise. . . .*

Max is beginning to think that both yeasts and humans are sparked by the same invisible forces in certain towns, lakes, elevations or zones.

The Starter

Max claims that the record for starters is 80 years, though I have not checked it in the *Guinness Book of World Records*. However, as I've mentioned before, many of us have starters that have gone on for 5 to 10 years with no trouble at all.

---

*The author takes exception to this statement. As our former Mayor Lindsay once said, "You can't trust air you can't see."

. . . I make my starters by mixing one cup of a high gluten flour in a bowl with three-fourths cup lukewarm water and one teaspoon of honey. Place the uncovered bowl on an outdoor porch or other place, protected from direct sun, winds, insects, birds and animals. If the starter dries or cakes on the surface, add a small amount of water and mix that in. After the mix has been outdoors for about three hours collecting neighborhood, airborne yeasts (which feed on the honey), bring the bowl indoors, mix again with a wooden spoon, cover it with a tight-fitting lid or plastic wrap and put it in a warm (85°F.—no higher) place either indoors or out.

Check the contents after several hours. You should see a bubbling action on the surface plus a slight rising in the mix. Check again in a few more hours. When there is no new bubbling or rising, add another cup of fresh stone-ground whole wheat or rye flour. Make sure it's fresh, because flour that has been in your pantry for a few months loses something of its "life" and causes the rising in sourdough to stop. Also add about one-half cup more water to keep the mix spongy. Mix in another teaspoon of honey. Cover the bowl and store in a warm place overnight. When more bubbling and rising is visible, add two more cups of flour and enough water to maintain the sponge—plus another teaspoon of honey. (I usually transfer the starter to a larger bowl at this time.) Cover and keep warm for several hours.

Max warns that new starters are temperamental and if the action seems sluggish, don't be disturbed. In time, the starter will acquire its own peculiar identity. When you're ready to bake, take about a pint of the mix and put it in a covered bowl. This is the primary starter and should be stored in the refrigerator.

With the remainder of the sourdough starter, I add increasingly larger parts of flour and water. How much depends upon the quantity of bread and rolls I want to bake. Now is the time to try out soy flour (usually no more than 20 percent of the total flour used in a mix, since it is nonglutenous and has no rising power), rye, and different wheat flours. Add enough water to keep the sponge spongey—plus honey. Keep the bowl (or garbage can) covered in a warm (80°F.) place. . . .

Baking Island Sourdough

Max now approaches what he calls *The Final Installment,* and you will begin to see why Island Sourdough is not made up of one specific recipe. It is for the bread baker who has experimented for some time and is ready for a new experience:

. . . the following list contains additions I include in my bread, though not necessarily all at the same time. Some things are used because they're seasonal:

eggs: 6 to 8 per 8-loaf batch, beaten
onions: many, and chopped finely
garlic: as you please
wheat flakes
rye flakes
cayenne pepper: not too much—or black pepper
caraway seeds
peanuts: shelled and smashed with a hammer
nuts (other than peanuts)
raisins, strawberries, rhubarb, blueberries, raspberries
grated cheese
grated potatoes, drained
beer
milk
melted butter

None of the above is essential; they are purely for your own taste.

You have added the sponge, new flour, water or other liquid, more honey, some of the ingredients listed above, and you begin to mix the batter just as you would any other bread. It is all in the "feel" of the dough:

You should now be working and feeling as though you wish your arms could have the help of an electric motor. I know there are machines to help you do the mixing, but I prefer the hard way—by hand. I perceive in this the similarity between this and cement mixing. Cement is easier in a trough, and I always wish I had a bread trough in which I could use a hoe instead of my arms and a wooden spoon!

When you've got the mix really stiff, stop. Take a deep breath, cover the receptacle as tightly as you can, place it in a warm spot (I use my mini-greenhouse) and let it rise very slowly.

Max's sourdough, with many of the heavy ingredients listed above, often takes 10 to 12 hours to rise. Then, turn the dough out onto a well-floured board and knead for a minimum of five minutes, adding flour as you need it.

Take a chunk of dough out of the mix—knead it some more. Roll it into a long roundish shape. It should fit into the greased loaf pan so that the ends almost touch the walls of the pan and it should occupy about two-thirds the area of the pan. Rolls can be made by taking a blob of the dough about the size of a tennis ball, kneading, and placing it on a greased cookie sheet. After you put the rolls on the sheet, pull them skyward into a cone-shape so that their rising tendencies will be upward and not sideways. I also use sections of cardboard, taped together into long, thin shapes, to make Italian or French bread. Foil may also be used to make different-looking loaves, but there is a danger of burning the lower surface on the inside of an enclosed wrapper.

Once the bread is laid out, you can score the tops of the loaves with a knife, write inscriptions, coat the surface with egg white, sprinkle with sesame, caraway, poppy, or anise seeds, or slices of onion.

Place all your goodies in a cool oven—one that has been preheated on "low" for 5 minutes and then turned off. Rising will take about two hours at this stage. If, after 45 minutes, the breads don't seem to be rising, heat oven at "low" for 5 minutes more. Don't open the oven or disturb the bread more than necessary.

When bread has risen, fire the oven to 350°F. Rolls take about 20 minutes, loaves take about 10 minutes longer, depending upon their shapes. They are done when the bottoms sound hollow when tapped with your fingers. Remove the rolls and let them cool. For loaves, shut off the oven, remove the loaves from their pans, turn them sideways, put them back in the pans and into the oven (which is turned off now) to finish cooking their interiors. I leave the loaves in the oven overnight. I avoid the strong temptation of eating the bread fresh from the oven by baking this way. Also, by baking late at night, when the bread is finished, I'm so sleepy that I don't want to eat. Of course, baking too late at night also incurs the risk of forgetting the oven and ending up with burnt rocks—and this, too, has happened. . . .

And so, Island Sourdough is a bread that is made in any way that you would like to bake it—with freedom, with a sense of fun, with the flexibility and ingenuity that characterizes so many of my bread-baking friends.

Too, you can now see why, when Max wrote: "I don't think there's anything special about a composer on an island baking his own bread," I drew myself up haughtily to my full height and snorted, "Indeed!"

Poppy Seed Braid (Elizabeth Ebbott) page 160   *135*

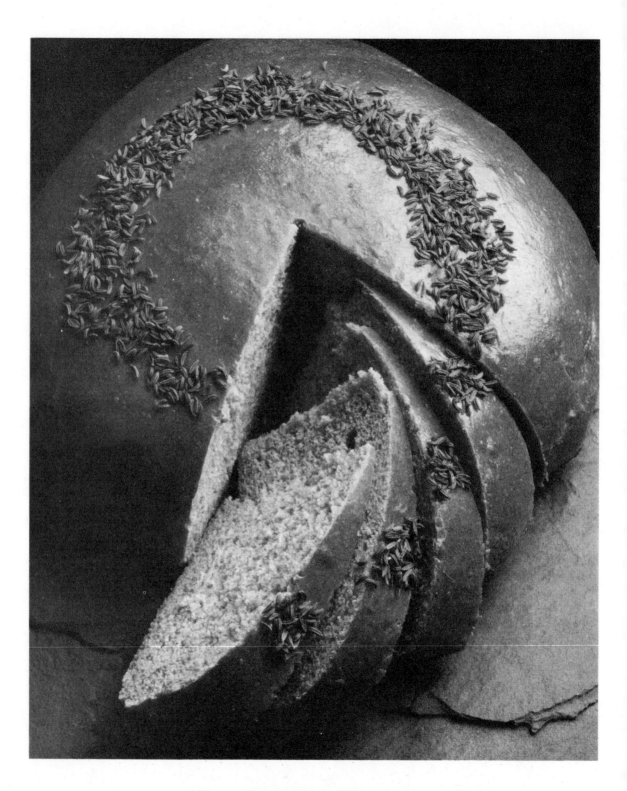

MAGGIE MARTHEY

It's amazing to me that coincidence plays so great a role in all of our lives. Because I've spent years of "running into" old acquaintances, I finally named my little Fire Island boat *Piccolo Mondo* (Small World).

As the files for this book began to grow, one of my friends in New Mexico suggested that I get in touch with Maggie Marthey, which I promptly did. It turns out that her husband, Ken, is an old film acquaintance of mine from New York! Some years back Ken and Maggie moved to the small village of Chamita, close to San Juan Pueblo in New Mexico, to escape the big city and the pollution. *Piccolo mondo* indeed!

Maggie teaches art and film and, of course, she bakes bread, with many of her recipes having originated in the Southwest. ". . . and, you might find this unusual and not normal, but when I'm sick I love to file and read my bread recipes. . . ."

Here are three of her favorites.

The Breads:

New Mexican Spoon Bread
Wheat Germ Zucchini Bread
Pueblo Indian Bread

New Mexican Spoon Bread

(1 large loaf)

1 14- to 16-ounce can cream-style
corn (1¾ cups)
¾ cup milk
⅓ cup butter
1½ cups cornmeal
2 eggs, slightly beaten
½ teaspoon baking soda
1 teaspoon baking powder
1 teaspoon salt (optional)
1 teaspoon honey
1½ cups grated cheddar cheese
1 4-ounce can chopped
green chilies

In a large bowl, combine all the ingredients except the cheese and the chilies. Mix well.

Pour half the batter into a greased 9-inch square pan. Sprinkle with half the cheddar cheese and half the chilies. Add the remaining batter and top with the rest of the cheese and chilies.

Bake at 400°F. for 45 to 50 minutes. Cool slightly and serve warm with butter.

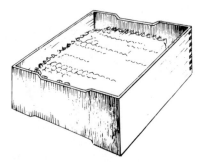

Wheat Germ Zucchini Bread

(2 large loaves)

3 eggs
1 cup oil
¾ cup honey
3 teaspoons pure maple syrup
2 cups zucchini, shredded and
drained
½ teaspoon baking powder
2½ to 3 cups whole wheat flour
½ cup wheat germ
2 teaspoons baking soda
1 teaspoon salt (optional)
1 cup chopped walnuts
½ cup sesame seeds

In a large bowl, beat the eggs, oil, and honey. Stir in the maple syrup and the zucchini.

Mix baking powder, flour, wheat germ, baking soda, salt, chopped walnuts, and sesame seeds and add to the mixture above. Blend well.

Divide dough in half and place in 2 well-greased loaf pans.

Bake at 350°F. for 1 hour or until breads test done.

The ingredients for this recipe remind me of the amounts used for our Signal Corps platoon during "our war." But, as Maggie writes:

> . . . *Pueblo Indian Bread is usually baked in large amounts in preparation for fiestas. The bread is baked in an outdoor beehive-shaped mud oven called an* horno.

The recipe is printed as Maggie sent it on. You may, of course, divide the amounts in half or by one-fourth and try a smaller batch for your own baking needs.

Maggie also says that the amount of salt can be changed to suit your own taste—and that this bread keeps quite well in a bread drawer (wrapped) or in the freezer for future use. I questioned her about the small amount of yeast she specifies for so large an amount of flour. She answered simply that the 8-hour rising time compensated for the balance of yeast-to-flour. It's a fairly dense bread, in any case.

Empty flour into a large tub. Then dissolve yeast in 1 quart of the lukewarm water and set aside.

With your hands, thoroughly mix the salt into the flour. Add the yeast mixture and then enough extra water to make a moist dough. Add the lard and knead until the dough is soft, but not wet or sticky. All of this is done with the dough right in the tub.

Grease the dough on all sides to keep it from sticking to the tub and then cover and let rise in a warm place for 8 hours or overnight.

The next day, punch down the dough. Form into loaves in any shape that you please. Place on greased baking sheets and let rise again.

Bake in a 350°F. oven for about 1 hour.

Pueblo Indian Bread

(22 to 25 round loaves—enough for a *fiesta!*)

25 pounds unbleached white flour
2 packages dry yeast
1½ gallons lukewarm water
1 cup salt (optional)
2 pounds lard

VALERIE ROGERS

When I commented that contributor Suzanne Corbett might well write her own bread book, I thought it might be wise to also mention that Valerie Rogers has already written hers (*Up to My Elbows* Louisville, Kentucky: Royal Corporation, 1973). Though she still works as a systems designer for computer operations, Valerie has also had time to raise two children, write her book, and teach bread baking to her classes in Louisville, Kentucky.

Though my schedule has been quite full, I have always had time to prepare bread. Raising two children didn't hamper me, though kneading the dough became a bit of a challenge during the last month of pregnancy. Standing sideways at the counter and kneading with one hand just took a little bit longer. . . .

Valerie began to bake bread full-time when she became aware of the additives and preservatives in "store-bought" bread.

The texture of homemade bread holds up well in sandwich preparation. It's filling, tasty, and my family is not eating empty calories.

Many of her students have gone on to win ribbons in the Kentucky State Fair. Valerie's husband won one for his whole wheat bread and her daughter won her first ribbon for her southern biscuits when she was only nine years old. She later went on to win Blue Ribbons for her white bread and dinner rolls.

Since she is a teacher and bread-baking author in her own right, I asked Valerie to pass on some of her own tips for this book. Here they are:

• Use your bread pans only for bread. Never make meat loaf or batter breads in them.

• I never use a counter surface for kneading. A kneading cloth is the best method followed by a breadboard. A cloth keeps the dough from sticking and picking up extra flour, so it always stays light and airy. The dough should be soft and light, quite like the feel of your earlobe. (Now go look in the mirror; I'm sure you have some flour behind your ear.) One of my students says it feels more like her baby's bottom!

• Don't give up. The bread will rise. A story comes to mind of a farmer who one summer found an enormous mushroom growing at the edge of his field. The farm extension agent was called in only to discover that the "mushroom" was really the farmer's wife's bread dough, a failure she had buried in the ground the previous fall. Almost a year later, the warm sun had made the dough rise.

• If the bread does not seem to be done when you cut it, don't hesitate to return it to the oven and continue the baking.

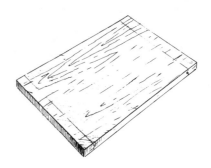

• Always add the honey to any bread recipe before adding the salt. This eliminates the danger of killing the yeast.

• I start my breads in a cold oven. Since I use my oven as a special "rising place," there's no need to take the loaves out into the cold kitchen and then shock them by putting them back in a preheated oven. Why not just turn the heat on after rising and just bake them?

Valerie has given me permission to print the following recipes from her book and I think you'll find them easy, rewarding, and delicious. One basic preliminary procedure fits every bread, with the exception of the last recipe.

Basic Procedure

Place the yeast in a large bowl, add water to dissolve the yeast, put in additional milk or water, if listed, and stir. Then add the oil or melted butter, honey or molasses, salt, and any other ingredients that appear before the flours in the ingredients list. Stir well again.

Add the flours 1 cup at a time mixing well between each cup and adding enough flour to make the dough manageable for kneading. The flour may vary from recipe to recipe.

Knead the dough 8 to 10 minutes on a kneading cloth or wooden board. Return to bowl for rising. Let rise to double, knead again, and shape into loaves. Place in lightly oiled pans, and let rise.

Bake at 375°F. (for all recipes) for 40 to 50 minutes. Remove bread from pan immediately following the baking. For crisp crust, air cool. For soft crust, cool 5 minutes, then place in plastic bag, and let steam for 5 to 10 minutes. Wipe excess moisture from bag, and continue to cool bread in bag.

Don't slice bread until it has cooled at least 5 minutes. It cuts better.

Since the first recipe calls for sprouted wheat, I thought it might be wise to give Valerie's instructions for sprouting your own wheat kernels. Wheat for sprouting can be found in all natural foods stores, but if you want a substitute, use wheat pilaf soaked overnight in half cup of water.

Begin with one-third cup of wheat for sprouting. This will be enough for the following recipe. Put the wheat in a quart canning jar, place a thin layer of cheesecloth over the mouth of the jar and secure tightly with a rubber band. Run enough warm water into the jar to just cover the wheat. Shake gently and pour off the water. Add one cup warm water and let it stand for one hour. Drain well. Lay the jar on its side; rotate so that the kernels stick to the inside of the jar. (Not all of them will stick.) Turn the jar upright and put in a warm, dark place such as a kitchen cabinet.

The next day you'll notice that the kernels and the water seem a little milky. You'll also see a few roots popping out of the kernels and the ones that had been stuck to the outside of the jar are now bunched up in the bottom. Rinse the sprouts with fresh, warm water poured through the cheesecloth. Drain and try rotating the jar again to get the kernels to adhere to the sides. Don't be too concerned if they don't stick. Return to the warm, dark place for another day.

On the third day, the sprouts have grown to half an inch long and have little roots that resemble fuzzy hair. Rinse and drain the sprouts again, but this time you don't have to rotate the jar. They will not stick and you'll notice that some of the kernels have begun sending out little sprouts while others have just become swollen. Not all the kernels will sprout, but they will be soft enough to chew.

The fourth day is bread-making day—and the roots will be an inch long and the sprouts will show signs of turning green. While you're preparing the dough, set the jar on the windowsill to absorb energy from the sun.

The sprouts are added to the dough on the last kneading. I like to chop them up a little with a heavy knife before adding them to the dough. Do not put the sprouts in the blender.

How to Sprout Wheat Kernels

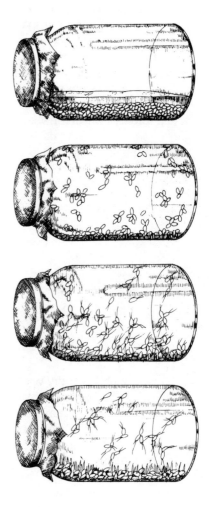

Sprouted Wheat Bread

(2 large loaves)

2 packages dry yeast
2 cups warm water
3 tablespoons oil
3 tablespoons honey
2 teaspoons molasses
1½ teaspoons salt (optional)
½ teaspoon vinegar
¼ cup mashed potatoes
3 tablespoons sesame seeds
¼ cup chopped sunflower seeds
2 tablespoons soy flour
5 cups whole wheat flour
¾ cup sprouted wheat (or wheat pilaf)
½ teaspoon freshly squeezed lemon juice

This bread uses the sprouted wheat described on the preceding pages (or wheat pilaf soaked overnight in one-half cup of water). It's a moist, heavy, and very nutritious bread.

Use Basic Procedure (page 142). The dough will be very sticky when you knead. This is a slow-rising dough. Sprinkle the sprouts with lemon juice before adding them to the last kneading.

Bake at 375°F. for 45 to 50 minutes. The sprouts will show slightly when this loaf is sliced, and this bread slices better when thoroughly cooled.

Wheat Germ Bread

(1 large loaf or 2 small loaves)

2 packages dry yeast
¼ cup warm water
¼ cup warm milk
1 cup warm water
2 tablespoons oil
4 tablespoons honey
1 teaspoon salt (optional)
½ cup wheat germ
2½ to 3 cups whole wheat flour
1 cup brown rice flour

This is a delightful, light bread, full of goodness.

Use Basic Procedure (page 142).

Bake at 375°F. for 40 to 50 minutes. This bread looks lovely when done in round loaves.

This is another bread that looks good in round loaves. The dough is soft and it rises well, has a good texture, and stays fresh for a long time. Valerie uses this bread for gift giving.

Use Basic Procedure (page 142).

Bake at 375°F. for 40 to 50 minutes.

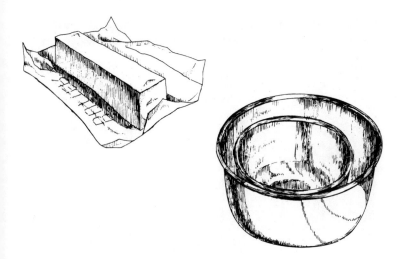

Hearty Graham Bread

(2 loaves)

2 packages dry yeast
¼ cup warm water
1   13-ounce can evaporated milk
1 cup warm water
¼ cup melted butter
3 tablespoons honey
1½ teaspoons salt (optional)
7½ to 8 cups graham flour

This bread is packed full of goodness, but it's a slow riser due to the weight of the wheat and the sunflower seeds.

Use Basic Procedure (page 142).

Add the sunflower seeds on the last kneading.

Bake at 375°F. for 50 minutes.

Health Loaf

(3 large loaves)

2 packages dry yeast
3 cups warm water
¼ cup oil
¼ cup honey
½ cup nonfat dry milk
1 teaspoon salt (optional)
1 egg
3 tablespoons wheat germ
½ cup soy flour
8 cups whole wheat flour
1 cup ground sunflower seeds

Honey-Oatmeal Wheat Bread

(3 large or 4 small loaves)

2 packages dry yeast
3 cups warm water
⅓ cup melted butter
⅓ cup honey
2 teaspoons salt (optional)
1 teaspoon ground cardamom
2 cups uncooked rolled oats
3 cups whole wheat flour
3½ to 4 cups unbleached white flour

The texture is coarse, the flavor is truly natural. Make sure you thoroughly cool this bread before you slice it.

Use Basic Procedure (page 142).

Bake at 375°F. for 40 to 50 minutes.

NOTE: This bread can be made—and beautifully—with unbleached white flour or whole wheat flour. We have tested it both ways.

Sunflower Surprise Bread

(2 large loaves)

2 packages dry yeast
¼ cup warm water
1 cup warm milk
1 cup warm water
1 tablespoon melted butter
1 tablespoon honey
½ teaspoon salt (optional)
1½ cups uncooked rolled oats
¾ cup ground sunflower seeds
5½ cups unbleached white flour

Use Basic Procedure (page 142).

If you like, you may decorate the loaf with whole sunflower seeds. Bake at 375°F. for 45 to 50 minutes.

Incidentally, you'll find the dough quite sticky and the bread heavy textured.

NOTE: We tested this bread using whole wheat flour instead of unbleached white. It's heavy, but good.

The texture of this bread is fine and light, though the dough will be heavy, bold, and quite sticky. Don't add too much flour. This rye bread has been a multiple state fair prizewinner for Valerie.

Use Basic Procedure (page 142).

Before baking, add a sprinkling of caraway seeds to the top. Bake at 375°F. for 40 to 45 minutes.

NOTE: Valerie suggests unbleached white flour in this one because of the texture it gives. However, we tested the bread using whole wheat flour and liked it very much.

Valerie's Rye Bread

(2 or 3 round loaves)

1 package dry yeast
1 cup warm water
1 cup warm milk
2 tablespoons melted butter
3 tablespoons dark molasses
1 tablespoon salt (optional)
1 tablespoon caraway seeds
2 cups rye flour
4½ to 5 cups unbleached white flour

This one is a winner with children. It's a sure riser, packed with flavor, and is a fine-textured, beautiful tan color.

Use Basic Procedure (page 142).

Bake at 375°F. for 40 to 50 minutes.

NOTE: This bread may be made with whole wheat flour and the result is fine.

Molasses Bread

(2 large or 3 small loaves)

1 package dry yeast
1¼ cups warm water
1 cup warm milk
2 tablespoons oil
3 tablespoons molasses
2 teaspoons salt (optional)
5 to 6 cups unbleached white flour

Cheese and Pepper Loaf

(2 large or 3 small loaves)

2 packages dry yeast
1½ cups warm water
½ cup warm milk
2 tablespoons melted butter
¼ cup honey
1 teaspoon salt (optional)
1 egg
1 teaspoon freshly ground pepper
¼ teaspoon sweet basil
5½ to 6 cups unbleached white flour
1 cup grated sharp cheese

Valerie uses this recipe for serving snacks at her card parties.

Use Basic Procedure (page 142).

Knead the cheese in just before shaping.

Bake at 375°F. for 40 to 45 minutes.

NOTE: You won't be disappointed in the whole wheat flour version of this one—we tried it and found it delicious, though we decided to cut down on the pepper a bit next time we make it.

Fantastic Shredded Wheat Bread

(1 large or 2 small loaves)

2 large shredded wheat biscuits
2 cups boiling water
½ cup light molasses
2 tablespoons butter
2 packages dry yeast
¼ cup warm water
1 teaspoon salt (optional)
4 to 4½ cups whole wheat flour

This is the only one of Valerie's breads that uses a slightly different procedure.

Put the shredded wheat biscuits in a large bowl, pour boiling water over them and add the molasses and butter. Set aside to swell and to cool.

Dissolve the yeast in the warm water and then add the yeast mixture to the cooled ingredients. Blend well.

Continue with Basic Procedure (page 142).

Bake at 375°F. for 40 to 45 minutes.

MARGARET PEABODY

I suppose that I accept too easily the fact that my closest Fire Island neighbor, Margaret Peabody, is one of the best bread bakers I know—and one of the most relaxed. I did mention earlier that Margaret is the one who taught me the knack of pounding the dough after the first rising. However, it never occurred to me until well into the writing of this book that I had failed to include even one recipe of hers.

One autumn weekend she arrived with a gift, an absolutely marvelous Wheat Germ Bread that she had just taken from the oven. The very next weekend, the prize was a Raisin Wheat Bread and I have three slices of it in the toaster as I write this.

Both recipes were breads that her grandmother had baked and both now have their place in my own bread files. As a matter of fact, Margaret still uses her grandmother's bread mixer—a large pail of tin-covered steel with a crank handle and a large dough hook that extends down into it. On the cover, the instructions are raised right into the metal:

> Put In All Liquids First Then Flour
> Turn Three Minutes
> Raise In Pail
> After Raising
> Turn Until Dough Forms A Ball
> Take Off Cross Piece Lift Out Dough With Kneader

Her grandmother's instructions for kneading with this machine included the words, "When making four loaves, knead until the dough forms a swan, with the dough going right up the turner to look like the neck."

With tribute to my neighbor and friend, Margaret, here are her recipes.

The Breads:

Wheat Germ Bread
Raisin Wheat Bread

Wheat Germ Bread

(4 large loaves)

2 packages dry yeast
2½ cups warm water
3 tablespoons honey
1 cup lukewarm milk
¼ cup oil
2 tablespoons salt (optional)
2 eggs, lightly beaten
10 to 11 cups whole wheat flour
1 cup wheat germ
butter

Mix dry yeast with ¼ cup of the warm water, add a small amount of the honey and set aside to proof.

In a large bowl, put all of the liquids—the remainder of the warm water, the milk, honey, oil, and then add the yeast mixture. Stir and then add the two eggs, lightly beaten.

Then, work in half the flour, mixing well—add the cup of wheat germ and then the remainder of the flour until the dough is firm and ready for kneading.

Turn out onto a lightly floured surface and knead for 10 minutes, until dough is smooth and elastic. Place in a greased bowl and cover. Let rise in a warm spot for 1½ to 2 hours or until doubled in bulk.

When dough has doubled, turn out onto floured surface and punch down. This is the place where Margaret gets rid of all her aggressions. Don't be afraid to punch it down. Pick it up and slam it down on the counter. Do it again. And then again. Knead for another 2 to 3 minutes and then divide the dough into 4 equal parts.

The loaves can be shaped free form, baked in round clay forms or in large loaf pans. Just grease the surfaces well and place the dough in the pan or on the sheet, cover and let rise to double in a warm spot (about 1 hour).

Bake in a 375°F. oven for 10 minutes and then lower the temperature to 350°F. for 35 to 40 minutes longer. When loaves test done, butter the tops while they're still hot and turn them out onto wire racks to cool.

Mix the yeast with ¼ cup of the warm water, add a small amount of the honey and set aside to proof.

In a large bowl, put all of the liquids—the remainder of the warm water, the milk, honey, oil, and then add the yeast mixture. Stir and then add the salt and the 2 eggs, lightly beaten.

Work in half the flour, mixing well, and then add the remainder of the flour to make a firm dough, ready for kneading. Before kneading, work in the cup of raisins.

Turn dough out onto a lightly floured surface and knead for 10 minutes, until dough is smooth and elastic. Place in a greased bowl and cover. Let rise in a warm spot for 1 to 1½ hours or until doubled in bulk.

When dough has doubled, turn out onto floured surface and punch down. Knead for another 2 to 3 minutes and then divide the dough into 2 equal parts.

Place the dough in 2 well-greased, large loaf pans, cover and let rise to almost double in a warm spot (about 1 hour).

Bake at 375°F. for 10 minutes and then at 350°F. for another 35 minutes or until sides are browned and the bread loosens slightly in the pan. While still hot, butter the tops of the loaves.

Cool on wire racks.

Raisin Wheat Bread

(2 large loaves)

2 packages dry yeast
2 cups warm water
3 tablespoons honey
1 cup warm milk
3 tablespoons oil
1 tablespoon salt (optional)
2 eggs, lightly beaten
6 to 8 cups whole wheat flour
1 cup raisins
butter

The Minnesota State Fair Bread Bakers

The State Fair Bakers

Patricia Nodo
Elizabeth Ebbott
Yvonne Rodahl
Kathy Strunc
Marjorie Johnson
Maxine Goldberg

As a part of our film for the National Council of Farmer Cooperatives and the American Institute of Cooperation, we were sent to Minnesota to do a sequence at the State Fair. Being a little boy at heart, I spent my lunch hours quickly wandering through the exhibits while the film crew overate at the marvelous food stands on the midways. One warm, exquisite afternoon, a young woman caught my eye as she made her way through the crowds and into an exhibition hall. Her sash read: Minnesota Honey Queen and her name was Pam Anderson. Together we toured the Honey Building where the prizewinning breads were exhibited, all of them baked with honey.

I jotted down the names of the winners and contacted them by mail. The results are here in this chapter in all the glory of prizewinning breads. Since then, I've spoken to each of the bakers and, of course, the long distance phone bills keep mounting while we exchange recipes, stories about raising honeybees, and just how close I came to their homes while driving around on the job, never realizing that I was but a loaf's-throw from another bread baker as I sped down the highway past White Bear Lake or Rice or Edina.

What began as an hour of wandering during lunch hour has turned into a wealth of recipes for me and for the readers of this book. In addition to being ribbon winners at the State Fair, each of the women in this chapter has also become a warm, generous, delightful bread-baking friend, and I now have six invitations to return to Minnesota. And I shall.

NOTE: This is another instance in which I have not converted the recipes to whole grain flours unless they were originally submitted as such. Since they are all prizewinners, I have left them intact—just as they were submitted to the State Fair. However, I'm sure that most of the recipes may be made with whole wheat flour and that the result will be a super loaf of bread.

PATRICIA NODO

The Breads:

Honey Date Nut Bread
Orange Honey Bread
Banana Honey Tea Loaf
Honey Maple Nut Bread
Modern Health Muffins

Pat might well be called the ultimate bread baker, since almost all the ingredients she uses are homegrown. She and her husband, Nick, and their two children live in Rice, Minnesota, and they raise honeybees and grain. They have an unbelievably productive, organic garden, and a ready supply of goat's milk right in the backyard. In fact, Pat's best goat, Poplar Hill Shani Sheleighleigh, gave 18 pounds, 11 ounces of milk *in one day* back a few years ago.

> *Nick has been keeping honeybees for five years. This year he worked 12 hives and they averaged 250 pounds of honey per hive! This is extraordinary, even for Minnesota. All that lovely, golden sweetness is what our family uses instead of sugar or sorghum molasses. Our early (spring) honey is light, mild and almost water-white. The summer honey goes from light and mild (clover, alfalfa) to dark amber and richly flavored (sunflower). . . .*

Pat always uses dolomite or bonemeal powder (or both) in her breads, and she says that it's an economical method of adding calcium and magnesium to her children's diet without increasing the cholesterol or sodium intake. She also uses granulated kelp for her dough instead of salt.

> *The first time I entered any kind of bread-baking competition, I didn't expect great success, particularly since all my loaves contained whole grain and mineral supplements. I entered my Trio of Quick Breads in the State Fair—and they took the Sweepstakes Prize!*

The first three breads in the recipes that follow won First Prize in the Trio of Breads competition and also took the Sweepstakes Ribbon in the Bee Division. They can be baked in fancy little molds before the holidays and stored in the freezer—to be given as gifts. Or they can be sliced thin as small tea sandwiches and put together with softened cream cheese to serve when company comes.

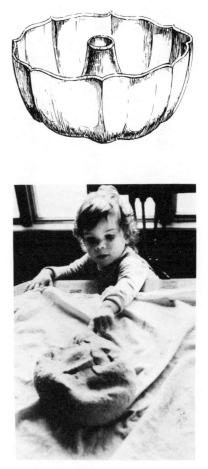

Honey Date Nut Bread

(2 small loaves)

1 cup chopped dates
1 cup boiling water (or sweet
whey or light-flavored
vegetable cooking water)
¾ cup mild-flavored honey
2 tablespoons softened butter
1 egg
1 cup coarsely chopped walnuts
1 cup whole wheat flour
½ cup unbleached white flour
¼ teaspoon salt*
2 teaspoons baking powder

Optional:

¼ teaspoon dolomite powder
1 tablespoon wheat germ
1 tablespoon bran

This bread has been the subject of several long-distance telephone conversations. For "city folk" like me, a description of "whey" is necessary when I find it in a recipe. Pat reminds me to think of Little Miss Muffet who sat on her tuffet eating her "curds and whey." Whey is simply the liquid that's left over after making cheese. As a substitute, you can use boiling water or any mild vegetable cooking water as I have in the recipe that follows.

In a saucepan, mix the chopped dates with the cup of boiling water and cook until the mixture thickens. Cool.

Cream the honey with the soft butter. Beat in the egg and the cooled date mixture. Stir in the chopped walnuts.

In a separate bowl, add the flours, salt, baking powder, and the dolomite powder, wheat germ and bran (if you care to use the last three ingredients). When the dry ingredients are blended, stir them into the date mixture.

Pour into 2 well-greased, small, loaf pans and bake for 1 hour at 325°F. or until a cake tester comes out clean and dry.

Cool on wire racks. Wrap snugly and refrigerate overnight before slicing.

NOTE: Can be baked in 2 pans, 7 × 3 inches, or in 4 round 1-pound cans.

---

*The salt may be eliminated if you choose to do so.

Cream the butter and honey. Beat in egg and orange peel. In a separate bowl, combine the dry ingredients (including the optional ingredients, if you choose to use them). Add to the butter-honey mixture, blending alternately with the orange juice. Stir to blend well and mix in the pecans. Pour into 2 well-greased, small, loaf pans and bake at 325°F. for 1 hour or until cake tester tests done. Cool on wire racks. Wrap snugly and refrigerate overnight before slicing.

NOTE: Can be baked in 2 pans, 7 × 3 inches, or in 4 round 1-pound cans.

Optional:

¼ teaspoon dolomite powder
¼ teaspoon bonemeal powder
1 tablespoon wheat germ
1 tablespoon bran

Orange Honey Bread

(2 small loaves)

2 tablespoons softened butter
1 cup mild-flavored honey
1 egg
1½ tablespoons freshly grated
   orange peel
2 cups whole wheat pastry flour
⅔ cup unbleached white flour
2½ teaspoons baking powder
½ teaspoon baking soda
¼ teaspoon salt*
¾ cup freshly squeezed
   orange juice
1 cup chopped pecans

This recipe was originally given to Pat by Tammy Jo Inman, who was the 1976 American Honey Queen. It is the third of her prizewinning Sweepstakes Trio.

Mix honey and oil. Stir in bananas, vanilla, and eggs. Combine all the remaining ingredients (including the optional ingredients, if you care to use them) in another bowl and then add all at one time to banana mixture and stir until just mixed.

Pour into 2 well-greased, small, loaf pans and bake at 325°F. for 1 hour or until cake tester tests done. Cool on wire racks, wrap snugly and refrigerate overnight before slicing.

NOTE: Can be baked in 2 pans, 7 × 3 inches, or in 4 round 1-pound cans.

Optional:

¼ teaspoon dolomite powder
¼ teaspoon bonemeal powder
If you add these ingredients, cut
   salt above to ¼ teaspoon.

Banana Honey Tea Loaf

(2 small loaves)

⅓ cup mild-flavored honey
½ cup light oil
3 medium ripe bananas, mashed
   (makes 1 cup)
1 teaspoon pure vanilla extract
2 eggs, well beaten
½ cup wheat germ
2 teaspoons baking powder
½ teaspoon salt*
½ teaspoon cinnamon
½ cup chopped walnuts
1½ cups whole wheat flour

*The salt may be eliminated if you choose to do so.

Honey Maple Nut Bread

(2 small loaves)

¼ cup wheat germ
1 tablespoon bran
2⅓ cups whole wheat pastry flour
3 teaspoons baking powder
½ teaspoon salt*
½ teaspoon baking soda
3 tablespoons light oil
¼ cup pure maple syrup
⅔ cup mild-flavored honey
1 egg
1½ cups milk
1 cup chopped walnuts or pecans

This bread was Third-Prize winner at the Minnesota State Fair.

Mix together the wheat germ, bran, whole wheat flour, baking powder, salt, and baking soda. (If you use the bonemeal and dolomite powder, mix them in at this time with the other dry ingredients.)

Cream the light oil with the maple syrup and the honey. Beat in the egg and the milk. Combine the wet and dry ingredients and the nuts. Stir only enough to dampen all the dry ingredients. Bake in 2 well-greased, small, loaf pans at 325°F. for 50 to 60 minutes or until a cake tester tests done. Cool on wire racks, wrap snugly, and refrigerate overnight before slicing.

NOTE: Can be baked in 2 pans, 7 × 3 inches, or in 4 round 1-pound cans.

Optional:

¼ teaspoon bonemeal
¼ teaspoon dolomite powder
¼ teaspoon kelp (in place of salt)

Modern Health Muffins

(1 dozen muffins)

1 cup raisins
1 cup boiling water (or sweet whey or light-flavored vegetable cooking water)
1 egg
½ cup honey
¼ teaspoon salt*
1 cup buttermilk or sour milk
1 cup whole wheat flour
1 cup uncooked rolled oats
1 cup whole bran
2 tablespoons wheat germ
1 teaspoon baking soda

These muffins were Second-Prize winners at the Minnesota State Fair. *They do not peak—they're flat—and delicious!*

Simmer the raisins and the boiling water (or whey or vegetable water) for 5 minutes. Cool and place the mixture in a blender container along with the egg, honey, salt, and buttermilk (or sour milk). Blend only until raisins are coarsely chopped.

In a bowl, mix the whole wheat flour, oats, bran, wheat germ, baking soda (and dolomite powder and bonemeal if you choose to use them). Mix wet and dry ingredients only until moistened. Place in 12 well-greased muffin cups and bake at 325°F. for 35 minutes or until a cake tester tests done. *Remember that these muffins do not peak.*

Optional:

¼ teaspoon dolomite powder
¼ teaspoon bonemeal
½ teaspoon kelp (in place of salt)

---

*The salt may be eliminated if you choose to do so.

ELIZABETH EBBOTT

Though she now lives in White Bear Lake, Minnesota, Elizabeth grew up in Iowa on a farm, went to college in Wisconsin, then lived in New York City, Connecticut, and Milan, Italy.

It was a tough challenge to make bread at home in Italy. No one in Italy bakes bread at home—they go out to the store two or three times a day and buy it fresh. The flour composition was a problem—a different ratio of hard wheat and semolina, generally used for making pasta. But the biggest problem was to find yeast—the grocery store and the various kinds of food shops had never heard of it. After great effort, we found that it was called lievito de birra *(riser of beer), and the only place to get it was at the nearby bakery. They couldn't understand why I wanted to bake bread at home when I could buy it at the store!*

Another of those amazingly busy people who still finds time to bake bread and to enter State Fair competitions, Elizabeth was trained as a therapeutic dietician and her activities have included work for the Minnesota Ethical Practices Board, the school board, Minnesota League of Women Voters, Cub Scouts and Brownie Scouts, and the United Nations Association. Of all her recipes, I loved the Poppy Seed Braid the best. It was a Second-Prize winner at the Minnesota State Fair a few years ago.

The Bread:

Poppy Seed Braid

Poppy Seed Braid

(3 or 4 braided breads, depending upon the size you prefer)

For the Dough:

2 packages dry yeast
¼ cup lukewarm water
¾ cup milk
½ cup butter
¾ cup honey
1 teaspoon salt*
5 cups unbleached white flour
3 eggs

For the Filling:

1 cup poppy seeds
1 cup hot water
1¼ cups milk
1 cup honey
2 tablespoons butter
½ teaspoon freshly grated lemon peel
butter

NOTE: You can make several braids with the remainder of the dough, refrigerate it to use at a later time, or make other breads, rolls, or coffee breads.

Dissolve the yeast in the lukewarm water, stir and set aside to proof.

In a saucepan, scald the milk and then add the butter, honey, and the salt. Cool to lukewarm and then add the yeast mixture. Pour into a large mixing bowl, add 2 cups of the unbleached white flour and beat well. Add the 3 eggs, mixing well and then add 3 more cups of the unbleached white flour. Add more flour if the mixture seems too wet.

Turn out onto a lightly floured counter top or board. (Elizabeth's pride and joy is a large marble slab that was originally designed for candy making but is just perfect for kneading or rolling out dough.) Knead for 8 to 10 minutes or until dough is elastic and smooth. Place in a well-greased bowl, turn to coat all sides and cover. Put in a warm spot to double in size (about 1 hour).

While dough is rising, prepare the filling by grinding the poppy seeds in a blender, then mixing them with the hot water and the milk. Cook the mixture in a deep frying pan for 5 minutes; then add the honey, butter and grated lemon peel. Cook down slowly on low heat, stirring frequently for about an hour or so—until all the liquid is absorbed.

When the dough has risen to double, punch down and knead for a minute or so on a lightly floured surface. Take one third or one fourth of the dough, depending upon how large a loaf you want, and roll it out into a rectangle ⅜ to ½-inch thick and about 9 × 15 inches in size. Cut the dough lengthwise into thirds, so that you now have 3 strips 9 × 5 inches in size.

Lightly spread the center of each section with butter and put the poppy seed filling down the center of each strip. Using your fingers and some warm water, dampen both ends of each strip and also dampen 1 long side. Roll each third lengthwise, so that the poppy seeds are rolled into the dough in the form of a rope. Use the wet edge as a seal and then seal both ends of the strands.

Braid the 3 strands together, seal the ends with your fingers and some additional water. Place on a well-greased cookie sheet and cover. Let rise for about 20 minutes, then bake in a 350°F. oven for 15 to 20 minutes.

---

*The salt may be eliminated if you choose to do so.

YVONNE RODAHL

Our food bill has never been a problem, what with two large gardens, fruit trees, honey, canning, and freezing. We buy wheat, rye, corn, and buckwheat in 50-pound bags and grind our own flour in a grist mill. Put together freshly ground grain and honey and you can't miss!

Dale and Yvonne Rodahl live in St. Paul, Minnesota, and they have five children, one of whom is married. They entered state and county fair competition only two years ago and they have already won ribbons for flowers, vegetables, sewing, canning, honey—and, of course, for baking.

This year we had 1,200 pounds of honey from our nine hives. We just give it away to customers and to friends, and then we sell the rest to help pay for new kitchen equipment.

Even as a superb cook and bread baker, Yvonne has had her failures:

I just call them "croutons." I cube the bread and put the cubes on a cookie tray coated with sunflower oil, sprinkle garlic or onion powder on them, brown them in the oven and I use them on green salads or in place of crackers in hot dishes.

Yvonne does as most of us do when we find sugar in some of the bread recipes that otherwise sound delicious. She merely substitutes two-thirds cup honey for each cup of sugar (small amounts such as a tablespoon can be substituted one-for-one) and then she adds one-third cup more flour to the batter.

I've chosen five of her prizewinners for the book. The rest of them were omitted because of space limitations. I plan to try them personally the next time I pass through St. Paul.

The Breads:

Holiday Dinner Rolls
Light Rye Bread
Honey Crescent Rolls
English Raisin Muffins
Corn Bread

These are perfect for Thanksgiving dinner or Christmastime meals, though I'm sure that the family would enjoy them whenever you baked them, even at nonholiday times.

Holiday Dinner Rolls

(5 dozen rolls)

1 package dry yeast
1½ cups warm water
½ cup honey
½ teaspoon salt*
⅔ cup oil
2 eggs
1 cup mashed potatoes (or 1 cup mashed sweet potatoes or 1 cup mashed carrots)
7 to 8 cups unbleached white flour
butter

In a large bowl, dissolve the yeast in warm water. Add the honey, salt, oil, eggs, potatoes, and 3 cups of the flour. Beat thoroughly. Then add enough of the remaining flour to make the dough easy to handle.

Turn out onto a lightly floured surface and knead for 10 minutes, or until dough is smooth and elastic. Place in a lightly greased bowl, turn to coat top, cover, and let rise 1 hour in a warm spot. When dough has risen, turn out onto lightly floured surface, punch down and shape into cloverleafs, Parker House or crescents. Place rolls in a greased baking pan or cookie sheet. Cover lightly with plastic or a cotton towel and place in a warm spot to rise until light (about 20 to 30 minutes).

Bake in a 375°F. oven for 15 to 20 minutes.

Remove from pans or sheet. Brush tops with butter while still hot, and cool on a wire rack.

*The salt may be eliminated if you choose to do so.

This recipe was winner of the Blue Ribbon at the Washington County Fair and it won the Yellow Ribbon at the Minnesota State Fair.

Light Rye Bread

(2 loaves or 16 large rolls)

2 packages dry yeast
1½ cups warm water
⅔ cup honey
1 teaspoon salt*
3 tablespoons butter
2 tablespoons caraway seeds
2¾ cups rye flour
2 to 3 cups unbleached white flour
butter (optional)

In a large bowl, dissolve the yeast in the warm water. Add the honey, salt, butter, caraway seeds, and the rye flour. Beat until smooth.

Add enough unbleached white flour to make the dough easy to handle. Cover and let rest for 15 minutes. Turn out onto a lightly floured surface and knead until smooth—about 8 to 10 minutes. Place in a greased bowl, turn once to coat, cover and let rise in a warm spot for about 1 hour. When dough has risen, turn out onto a lightly floured surface, punch down and form 2 loaves or 16 rolls. Place in well-greased pans or on well-greased cookie sheet, cover lightly and place in a warm spot to rise for 1 hour. Bake at 350°F. for 35 to 40 minutes. When done, butter tops to make a soft crust or leave plain. Cool on wire racks.

This recipe was White Ribbon winner at the Washington County Fair.

Honey Crescent Rolls

(2½ dozen rolls)

2 packages dry yeast
¾ cup warm water
½ cup honey
1 teaspoon salt*
2 eggs
½ cup butter
4 cups unbleached white flour (or
    2 cups whole wheat flour and 2
    cups unbleached white flour)
melted butter
celery seeds or sesame seeds

In a large bowl, dissolve the yeast in warm water. Add the honey, salt, eggs, butter, and half of the flour. Beat until smooth. Add the rest of the flour, mix well until blended. Cover bowl with a damp cloth and let rise until double, about 1½ hours.

Turn out onto a lightly floured surface, knead for 1 or 2 minutes, then roll out with a floured rolling pin and shape into crescents. Place on a greased cookie sheet and cover. Let rise to double in a warm place—about 1 hour. Brush with butter, sprinkle with celery seeds or sesame seeds, and bake in a 375°F. oven for 12 to 15 minutes. Remove from tray and cool on a wire rack.

*The salt may be eliminated if you choose to do so.

English Raisin Muffins

(10 muffins)

1 package dry yeast
1 cup warm water
1 teaspoon salt*
2 tablespoons honey
¼ cup oil
½ cup raisins
3 cups unbleached white flour
2 tablespoons cornmeal

In a large bowl, dissolve the yeast in warm water. Add the salt, honey, oil, raisins, and the flour and stir until smooth.

On a floured surface roll out dough and cut into 3½-inch circles. Use a cookie cutter, the edge of a drinking glass, or a small can.

Sprinkle cornmeal on an ungreased cookie sheet, place the muffins on the sheet and sprinkle the remaining cornmeal over the muffins. Cover and let rise in a warm spot for about 1 hour.

Heat a griddle; transfer muffins onto griddle and cook over the burner of the stove for about 7 minutes on each side. Keep the flame low so the muffins don't scorch.

Cool, split and toast or serve warm with butter and comb honey.

 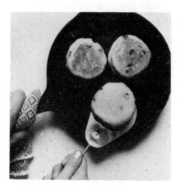 

Corn Bread

(1 to 1½ dozen squares)

1 cup unbleached white flour
½ teaspoon salt*
4 teaspoons baking powder
1 cup cornmeal
½ cup honey
2 eggs
¼ cup sunflower oil
1 cup buttermilk or sour milk

Sift together in a bowl, the flour, salt, baking powder, and the cornmeal. Then add the honey, eggs, and the oil. Add the buttermilk or sour milk and beat until just smooth.

Pour into a greased 9 × 9-inch baking pan and bake at 400°F. for 15 to 20 minutes.

Cut into squares and serve warm.

*The salt may be eliminated if you choose to do so.

KATHY STRUNC

The Breads:

Honey Bran Muffins
Honey Dinner Rolls
Honey Rye Bread

The first time Kathy and Gary Strunc entered the State Fair they both won Blue Ribbons—she for her dinner rolls and rye bread and he for his honey frame (the frame as it comes from the hive with the honey not yet extracted) in the professional beekeeping competition. Gary also took a Red Ribbon for his creamed honey. They live with their two children in Maple Grove, Minnesota, and they raise as much food as possible right on their property. "Getting back to the land is as good for our bodies as it is for our spirits. . . ."

Kathy suggests visiting an experienced bread baker to get tips and to observe special tricks (very much the way I began baking bread). She also suggests that you remain calm at all times and set aside a day when you have nothing else to do before your first try:

The first time, I started at 10:00 A.M. and the recipe said to use warm water to dissolve the yeast. I thought, "If warm water is good, boiling water should be better," and I proceeded to kill the yeast. My husband called his mother long distance to see what could be done with all the dough—a double batter, no less! She told me to add more yeast and mix it in. I did and it worked, but it was 1:00 A.M. when I finished baking the rolls. . . .

Kathy, of course, has improved, as her ribbons attest. Here are three of her favorite prizewinning recipes. All three were awarded the Blue Ribbon.

Honey Bran Muffins

(12 muffins)

1½ cups bran cereal
1¼ cups milk
½ cup honey
1 egg
⅓ cup oil
1¼ cups unbleached white flour
1 tablespoon baking powder
½ teaspoon salt*

In a mixing bowl, combine the bran cereal and the milk. Let stand for several minutes until the cereal is softened. Add the honey, egg, and oil and beat well.

In a separate bowl, combine the flour, baking powder, and salt and then add to the cereal mixture, stirring only enough to combine the ingredients.

Pour into 12 well-greased muffin cups and bake at 400°F. for 25 minutes or until browned.

Serve warm.

---

*The salt may be eliminated if you choose to do so.

Sprinkle yeast over warm water in a small bowl. Set aside and do not stir.

Put flour in a mixing bowl and stir in the honey, dry milk, and salt. Blend in the butter until mixture is fine as meal. Make a well in the center of the flour mixture and add the unbeaten egg and then the yeast mixture. Beat well until a soft dough is formed. Let rest for 10 minutes.

Turn out onto a lightly floured board, knead for 8 to 10 minutes or until dough is smooth and elastic. Place in a greased bowl, turn once to coat the top, cover and place in a warm spot for about 45 minutes to 1 hour (or until doubled in size).

Punch down, cover and let rise again for about 45 minutes. Turn out onto lightly floured surface, punch down and form into rolls. Place on a greased cookie sheet, leaving space between the rolls to allow them to expand; cover and let rise for about 20 to 30 minutes.

Bake at 375°F. for 20 minutes.

Honey Dinner Rolls

(about 2 dozen rolls)

1 package dry yeast
1 cup warm water
3½ cups unbleached white flour
¼ cup honey
¼ cup nonfat dry milk
½ tablespoon salt*
¼ cup butter
1 egg

Mix together the butter and honey; add the salt. Pour boiling water over this mixture and stir. Add the rye flour, cold water, and anise seeds and mix together. Add the yeast and the white flour. Mix well.

Turn out onto lightly floured surface and knead for 8 to 10 minutes or until dough is smooth and elastic. Place in a greased bowl, turn once to coat the top, cover and let rise to double in a warm spot—about 1 hour.

Turn out onto lightly floured surface, knead for 1 or 2 minutes, shape into 3 loaves and place in well-greased loaf pans. Cover and let rise until almost doubled (about 45 minutes); then bake at 350°F. for 1 hour.

Cool on wire racks.

Honey Rye Bread

(3 loaves)

½ cup butter
½ cup honey
1 tablespoon salt*
1¾ cups boiling water
1 cup rye flour
1½ cups cold water
½ teaspoon anise seeds
1 package dry yeast
7 to 8 cups unbleached white flour

---

*The salt may be eliminated if you choose to do so.

MARJORIE JOHNSON

The Breads:

Butter Horn Rolls
Honey Orange Rye Bread
Orange Bow Knot Rolls

Marjorie is a 4-foot-10-inch dynamo who has won a total of *102* ribbons at the Minnesota State Fair over the past five years, in addition to entering bake-off contests all over the country. A writer for a Minneapolis newspaper described talking to Marjorie as "being caught up in a benevolent tornado." As she herself puts it, "I love to bake and I love to talk, but I can't do both!"

She, her husband LeRoy ("a Blue Ribbon dentist," she calls him), and their three children live in Robbinsdale, Minnesota, where Marjorie develops many of her own recipes through testing and experimentation.

100% Whole Wheat Bread (Howard and Agnes Arns) page 245   *169*

Refrigerator Rolls (Bea Seal) page 197

Minnesota's climate seems especially conducive to baking—all those wintry days when it's cold and snowy outside. It's so cozy and warm inside with the oven full of wonderful baking odors. Is there any better smell?

Marjorie also recommends watching an experienced bread baker if you get the chance. Also, purchase a thermometer to test temperatures until you begin to learn just how warm the liquids should be.

With 102 prizewinners from which to choose, I've taken these three. Each of them has at least one Blue Ribbon and the Orange Bow Knot Rolls were also the Sweepstakes Winner at the State Fair.

Butter Horn Rolls

(32 rolls)

½ cup butter
¼ cup honey
1 teaspoon salt*
2 eggs, well beaten
2 packages dry yeast
1 cup warm water
   (105° to115°F.)
⅔ cup nonfat dry milk
4 to 4½ cups unbleached
   white flour
softened butter

Cream butter, honey, and salt together, then beat in eggs. Soften the yeast in warm water and add to the egg mixture. Blend in the dry milk and half the flour on low speed of an electric mixer or with a large wooden spoon. Add the rest of the flour with the wooden spoon and mix well.

Turn out onto a lightly floured surface and knead for 5 minutes. Put in a greased bowl, turn to coat top, cover with plastic wrap, and place in refrigerator overnight.

Next day, take half the dough and roll it out into a 12-inch circle. Spread with soft butter and cut into 16 pie-shaped pieces. Beginning with the outer rounded edge, roll each piece into a crescent-horn shape. Place on a greased baking sheet with the point underneath. Repeat with other half of dough.

Cover rolls lightly and place in a warm spot; let rise until light.

Bake at 425°F. for 12 to 15 minutes or until golden brown.

Cool on wire racks.

*The salt may be eliminated if you choose to do so.

Honey Orange Rye Bread

(2 round loaves)

2 packages dry yeast
2½ cups warm water
(105° to 115°F.)
1 tablespoon salt*
2 tablespoons butter
¼ cup honey
⅔ cup nonfat dry milk
2 tablespoons freshly grated
orange peel
2 teaspoons anise seeds
2½ cups rye flour
3½ to 4 cups unbleached
white flour

Soften dry yeast in warm water in a large bowl. Add the salt, butter, honey, dry milk, orange peel, anise seeds, and rye flour. Blend on low speed of an electric mixer until thoroughly mixed. Change to bread hooks, add white flour 1 cup at a time and beat at Speed 4 until blended; then increase to Speed 8 and beat for 5 minutes more. (Of course, you—and I—can also do it with a wooden spoon and then knead by hand for 8 to 10 minutes on a lightly floured surface.)

Shape into a ball and place in a greased bowl, turn once to coat top, and cover. Place in a warm spot to rise until doubled in bulk (about 45 minutes to 1 hour).

Punch down, turn out onto a lightly floured surface, knead for 1 to 2 minutes and then divide the dough in half. Form 2 balls and place on greased cookie sheet, leaving room between the loaves for expansion in the oven. Cover lightly with a towel or plastic wrap, place in a warm spot, and let rise again until light.

Bake at 400°F. for 10 minutes; then lower the temperature to 350°F. and bake for 20 to 25 minutes more or until breads test done and the bottoms sound hollow when tapped.

Cool on wire racks.

Orange Bow Knot Rolls

(about 2 dozen rolls)

2 packages dry yeast
1¼ cups warm water
(105° to 115°F.)
½ cup butter
¼ cup honey
1 teaspoon salt*
2 eggs, well beaten
¼ cup freshly squeezed
orange juice
2 tablespoons freshly grated
orange peel
⅓ cup nonfat dry milk
5 cups unbleached white flour
butter

Soften yeast in warm water. Add the butter, honey, salt, eggs, orange juice, orange peel, dry milk, and half the flour. Blend on low speed of an electric mixer, then beat at medium speed for 3 minutes. Add the rest of the flour by hand or use dough hooks. If you use dough hooks, blend for about 5 minutes. If you are mixing by hand with a wooden spoon, turn out onto a lightly floured surface and knead for 10 minutes or until dough is smooth and elastic.

Place in a greased bowl, turn once to coat the top, cover and let rise in a warm spot until doubled in bulk (45 minutes to 1 hour).

Punch down, turn out onto a lightly floured surface and roll dough to ½-inch thickness. Cut 10-inch strips about ½-inch wide. Knot each strip and arrange on a greased baking sheet. Cover lightly and let rise in a warm spot until rolls are almost doubled in size.

Bake in a hot (400°F.) oven for about 15 minutes. While rolls are still hot, brush the tops with butter. Serve warm.

*The salt may be eliminated if you choose to do so.

MAXINE GOLDBERG

I suppose I was most influenced by Grandmother Fenner Kasuske, who was very well-known for her baking skills. Her farm neighbors knew of her prowess and the threshing crews would beg her for her breads and doughnuts, which she'd bring right out into the fields, freshly made.

And, as Grandmother Kasuske never had any store-bought breads in her house, Maxine Goldberg bakes all her own breads too, still using the pans that her mother used over 20 years ago.

The Breads:

Swedish *Limpa* Rye Bread
Honey Wheat Nut Bread

There are four generations of bread bakers in the Goldberg household in Edina, Minnesota, and Maxine's accomplishments not only include her Blue Ribbons from the Minnesota State Fair but a continual stream of compliments from the family, the best of which is her Aunt Bea's statement that: "I'm so proud of you—you bake just like your Grandmother Fenner Kasuske!"

Maxine is currently teaching her granddaughter Elizabeth (age 10) how to bake bread.

Swedish *Limpa* Rye Bread

(2 loaves)

1½ cups hot water
2 tablespoons honey
2 tablespoons butter
2 teaspoons salt*
1 package dry yeast
½ cup warm water
3 cups rye flour
2½ to 3 cups unbleached white flour

Put the hot water into a mixing bowl, then stir in the honey, butter, and salt. Cool to lukewarm. In a cup or bowl, dissolve the yeast in the ½ cup of warm water and add to the first mixture. Stir in the rye flour gradually, mixing with each addition until all 3 cups are stirred in. Beat well. Then, gradually add the white flour to make a soft dough. Turn out onto a lightly floured board and knead for 10 minutes. (Add more white flour if the dough seems too sticky.)

Place in a greased bowl and turn once to coat the top, cover and let rise to double in a warm spot (about 1 hour). Punch down, turn dough out onto lightly floured surface, knead for 1 or 2 minutes, and then divide into 2 parts.

Shape as desired—oval or round—and place on greased baking sheets. You can also bake the loaves in standard loaf pans, if you prefer, but the breads look more festive as free-form loaves.

Cover lightly with a towel or with plastic wrap and let rise to almost double in a warm spot (about 45 minutes).

Bake at 400°F. for 25 to 35 minutes or until loaves test done and bread bottoms sound hollow when tapped.

Cool on wire racks.

*The salt may be eliminated if you choose to do so.

A simple, quick recipe for either bread or muffins.

Cream butter thoroughly, add the honey and beat well. Add the eggs and vanilla and again beat well. Alternately add the dry ingredients and the milk, stirring as you add. Stir in the nuts and pour into 2 well-greased 9 × 5-inch loaf pans. (You may also bake these in greased, muffin tins.)

Bake in a 325°F. oven for 1 hour. (If you are making muffins, bake for about 20 minutes.)

When breads test done or a cake tester comes out clean, remove from oven and cool on wire racks.

Honey Wheat Nut Bread

(2 loaves)

½ cup butter
1 cup honey
3 eggs
1 teaspoon pure vanilla extract
4½ to 5 cups flour
4 teaspoons baking powder
1 teaspoon baking soda
1 teaspoon salt*
1½ cups milk
1½ cups chopped wheat nuts or
  grape nuts

*The salt may be eliminated if you choose to do so.

MICHAEL MCKNIGHT

The Breads:

Indian *Puris*
Sweet-Sunday Bread

Michael and Karen McKnight live in Winooski, Vermont, where he is a professor at the university (he holds a doctorate in Eastern religions) and she is a student in South Asian studies. Since they both spent time in India, the *puri* recipe was one that I considered a prize for this book. But even more delightful is the fact that Michael has a great excitement about his bread-baking efforts.

As all bread makers know, the preparation of any kind of bread can become a very personal and meaningful experience. It can be either a solitary or communal experience, but the personal rewards of bread baking seem to multiply when the experience is shared with others. "A joy to be a true joy must be shared," as the poet William Blake observed.

I like to reflect on the joy of bread making as a communal event. I don't mean that many people have to participate in the actual mixing and kneading of the bread. Just to have a number of people present as guests when bread making is occurring tends to turn the event into a communal experience.

In our house, there are two bread-making times which usually have the quality of being communal events. The first comes when we have friends in our home to sample the delights of Indian cuisine, the second comes on special Sunday mornings when the event centers around a totally seductive bread ring which we call Sweet-Sunday Bread.

Here are Michael's further comments about these two unusual breads and, of course, his fabulous recipes for each of them.

When we entertain, we are accustomed to serving puris, a variety of Indian unleavened bread. We were originally introduced to the art of puri-making by friends of ours from India and then, in 1972, we vastly increased our knowledge of Indian culture and cuisine by visiting India and dining in Indian homes.

In India, bread is made almost everywhere. You can see it being prepared by the roadside, on the street corner, or within the distinctive confines of the traditional Indian kitchen.

The same bread dough can be used to make a number of different varieties of breads, including chappatis, parathas, or puris. Puris are the most exciting and dramatic variety since they explode into hollow bread globes when placed in hot oil. Although they can be eaten cold, puris are at their very best when served hot and puffy. The secret of proper puri preparation centers around a combination of the right ingredients and a firm hand in mixing and kneading them together. The firm hand comes with experience.

Indian *Puris*

(20 to 30 *puris*)

1 cup whole wheat flour
1 cup unbleached white flour
1 teaspoon salt (preferably slightly
less than 1 teaspoon)*
2 tablespoons oil
¾ cup hot water
hot oil for frying

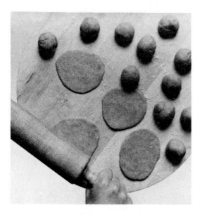

Combine all the ingredients with the exception of water in a mixing bowl and proceed to pinch them until the flour becomes crumbly to the touch. When the ingredients have reached the crumbly stage, it is time to start adding the hot water in small installments. The batter will, of course, become mushy as water is added. Keep kneading the dough vigorously as you add the water. I've found that the actual kneading time for the basic dough is 10 to 15 minutes, depending upon how much energy one puts into the process. You know that the kneading job is over when the dough ball takes on an elastic, springy quality. A good test is the "poke test." If the dough springs back to the touch, it's ready. Let the dough rest for 15 minutes. A slight rubdown with oil will prevent the dough from drying out.

The next step on the road to perfect *puris* is the process of rolling the dough into neat little pancakes, approximately 4 inches in diameter. Prior to the actual rolling with a rolling pin, it is helpful to hand pinch and roll the dough into Ping-Pong ball shapes (larger if larger *puris* are desired). Use a floured surface on which to roll out the *puris*.

The final stage is the actual cooking. The temperature of the oil is a crucial factor in making successful *puris*. The easiest method of checking this is to drop a small piece of dough into the oil as a "tester." If the little piece sinks, rises to the surface and bubbles up, the oil is ready. Be cautious not to overheat the oil, since this will make the *puris* cook too quickly. Here again, experience is the best teacher.

(We sometimes have our dinner guests participate while we make the *puris*. One person rolls, while the other handles the cooking.)

A large pan should be set aside to hold the *puris* as you take them out of the hot oil. Line the pan with paper towels to absorb the excess oil. Then, the same pan may be used to carry the *puris* to the table. Serve them in small batches as soon as they are ready, hot from the stove, since they tend to deflate and lose their character if you wait too long or pile too many atop one another.

They are traditionally consumed by filling the hollow space with all kinds of rice, lentil, and vegetable dishes. Yogurt is also quite good with *puris*.

---

*The salt, though traditional, may be eliminated if you choose to do so.

The addition of ½ teaspoon of turmeric powder will change the color of your *puris* from a rather bland, wheat color to a lovely shade of gold. The taste will be the same, but the color seems to add to their *eye* appeal.

NOTE: Two cups whole wheat pastry flour may be substituted for the flour combination listed in the ingredients.

A Delightful Variation:
Golden Puris

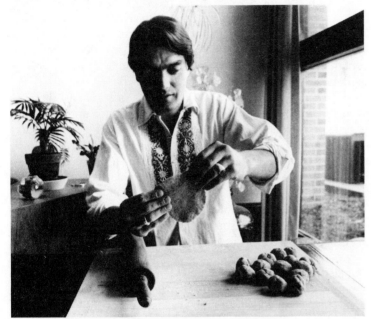

Sunday brunch is a special occasion for our family, sometimes with a gathering of friends. Our favorite for this time of the week is a bread as delicious as it is eye appealing and we found that it magically vanishes almost as soon as it touches the table.

Sweet-Sunday Bread

(1 large or 2 small rings)

1 package dry yeast
¼ cup warm water
½ cup milk, scalded
¼ cup butter
4 tablespoons honey
½ teaspoon salt (optional)
1 egg, slightly beaten
½ teaspoon pure vanilla extract
1 teaspoon freshly grated lemon peel
1 cup whole wheat flour
3 teaspoons soy flour
1½ cups whole wheat flour
2 tablespoons melted butter
1 cup diced apples (skins on)
½ cup slivered almonds, toasted
½ cup raisins
1½ teaspoons cinnamon

Add dry yeast to the ¼ cup of warm water and set aside. In a large bowl, combine the scalded milk, butter, 2 tablespoons of the honey, and the salt. Cool to lukewarm. Add the egg, vanilla, lemon peel, and first quantity of whole wheat flour. Mix well and then add the soy flour. Gradually stir in the softened yeast while continuing to mix well. Then add the remaining flour to make a moderately soft dough.

Turn the dough out onto a lightly floured surface and begin the kneading process. When dough has reached the smooth and elastic stage (about 8 to 10 minutes), place in a well-greased bowl, turn to coat all sides, cover and let rise in a warm place until double in size (about 1½ hours).

When doubled, punch down and cover dough for an additional rising period of about 10 minutes. Then, on a floured surface, roll the dough into a 21 × 7-inch rectangle about ¼ inch thick.

Lightly brush the dough with melted butter. Mix the diced apples, almonds, raisins, the remaining 2 tablespoons of honey, and the cinnamon. Then spread this mixture on the dough. Roll and seal the long edge. Shape into a ring, seam-side down and place on a greased baking sheet.

Using a pair of scissors, snip to within an inch of the center at 1-inch intervals. Pull sections apart and twist slightly. Place in a warm spot, lightly covered, and let rise until it reaches double its original size (about 50 minutes).

Bake in a 375°F. oven for 20 minutes. When done, you may top it with your favorite icing to make a sweeter and fancier bread.

STACIE HUNT

As a part of the publicity campaign for my first book, I was sent to Los Angeles to appear on a syndicated radio show called "Some Kind of People," and I was interviewed by the dynamic, charming and very clever young woman whose name heads this chapter. When we had finished the interview, I told her I'd be back to talk about my next book when it was completed—it was to be a book about bread. The next hour was spent in animated discussion outside the studio door for it turned out that Stacie Hunt is also a bread baker and her specialty is baking in *clay* containers and flowerpots! "It all began in the Girl Scouts, when I discovered that I enjoyed raw dough better than the cookies we were constantly baking at our meetings. . . ."

She continued experimenting all through school and into adulthood. Today, as president of The Production Group, a Hollywood-based company that does production in radio and television and also develops syndicated radio programs, Stacie still bakes her favorite breads in her own special way.

My love for bread baking comes from a funny (read: "peculiar") dichotomy: one part of me loves what I do for a living and the other would just as soon stay home all day preparing great and huge meals for large groups of people, teaching cooking and baking classes on weekends.

Baking bread in a clay or a brick baking dish can be done without using a commercial product. If you'd like to try some unusual shapes for your bread, Stacie recommends that you buy the clay flowerpots available at any nursery. Just be sure you purchase one that has been "heat-tested." They will generally be a bit higher priced than the others, but they won't crack in the oven.

The method dates all the way back to the Etruscans and once you've tried it, you'll understand why it has persisted through the centuries.

The Breads:

Pesto Bread
Apple, Raisin, Honey
   Munchy Bread

The Italians love to entertain with good food, bread and wine, so this recipe brings together all of the best with which to celebrate. When possible, use fresh basil. During the winter months Stacie uses the dried herb. The bread will fill the house with a sweet, delicious aroma while baking.

Pesto Bread

(1 large long or oval loaf)

1¾ packages dry yeast
1½ cups lukewarm water
5 to 5½ cups whole wheat flour
2 tablespoons butter
5 tablespoons olive oil
4 large cloves of garlic, minced
⅓ cup fresh basil, finely chopped
and packed (or 1 cup dried
basil leaves, packed firmly)
1 teaspoon salt (optional)
¼ teaspoon freshly
ground pepper
½ cup dry white wine
⅓ cup grated Romano cheese
⅓ cup grated Parmesan cheese

In a small bowl, allow the yeast to dissolve in 1 cup of the lukewarm water. Use a wooden spoon to stir out any lumps.

Put 1½ cups of the flour in a large bowl, add the yeast mixture and stir with a wooden spoon. Keep mixing until all the flour and dissolved yeast come together to form a ball of dough. Add another cup of flour by lightly sprinkling over the ball of dough, cover the bowl with a cotton cloth and place in a warm spot, free from drafts, until it doubles in size—about 1 hour.

Now, in a saucepan, melt the butter and add the olive oil. Then add the minced garlic, chopped basil, salt and pepper, and sauté lightly. (Hint: When mincing the garlic, add a small amount of olive oil and the garlic will not stick to the chopping knife.) After sautéing, allow the mixture to cool to room temperature.

The remaining flour should now be poured onto a large cutting board or pasta board to form a mound. Make a well in the center of the mound and place the risen ball of dough inside the well. Add the garlic, basil, olive oil, butter, salt and pepper mixture and then add the wine very slowly.

With a wooden spoon, very carefully mix in the remaining ½ cup of the lukewarm water. At this time, begin mixing with your hands, taking up all of the flour from the inside of the mound and working it to the outside. Continue this hand mixing until all but about 6 to 7 tablespoons of the flour are included. Now begin kneading the dough with your hands, folding it and kneading for about 5 minutes. Add the grated Romano and Parmesan cheese, then continue kneading for another 10 minutes. Add a bit more lukewarm water if you feel that the dough is not kneading smoothly enough.

After kneading, you can form the dough into whatever shape you desire—either long or oval. Sprinkle with a little more flour and wrap the dough in a cotton towel. Put it in a warm place (like your unheated oven) and it will double in size in about 1 hour.

Transfer the dough to a floured clay or brick baking dish as soon as it has doubled. DO NOT PREHEAT THE OVEN. Place the dish in your oven and set the temperature for 400°F. and bake for about 1 to 1½ hours or until you can insert a toothpick and bring it out clean. (DO NOT open the oven for the first 45 minutes, no matter how curious you are to see how the bread is baking.)

Now, remove the bread from the oven and allow it to cool for several hours. It can be reheated later. When cooling, place the bread on its side rather than letting it lie flat.

You can serve it with freshly sliced tomatoes, pasta with oil and garlic, assorted Italian cold cuts or thick and hearty soups. Or just enjoy it with a glass of wine and some cheese.

Apple, Raisin, Honey Munchy Bread

(1 loaf)

4 to 4½ cups whole wheat flour
1 package dry yeast
⅓ cup honey
1 tablespoon salt (optional)
1 cup lukewarm milk
⅓ cup lukewarm water
½ cup softened butter
½ cup raisins
2 cups peeled, chopped apples

This is a superb recipe for an autumn or winter bread, since it features fresh Pippin apples, raisins, and honey. It makes an excellent breakfast bread or dessert bread and it's especially good when used as a bottom for an ice cream dessert.

In a mixing bowl, combine 2½ cups of the flour with the yeast, and add the honey and salt. Using a beater, add the milk slowly and then the water and continue beating for about 2 to 3 minutes. Add the softened butter and mix well.

Then add the remainder of the flour or enough to make a stiff dough. You can do this either by kneading it in with your hands or with the beater. Let rest for a few minutes while you grease a larger bowl. Now come back to the dough and add the raisins and apples. Knead the dough for about 5 to 7 minutes or until all the fruits are evenly distributed throughout the dough.

Place the kneaded and fruited dough into the greased bowl, swirling it around until all sides are evenly coated. Place the bowl, covered with a damp cotton towel, in a warm place (the unheated oven would be good) and let rise until doubled in size (about 1 to 1½ hours).

Sprinkle your choice of baking dish (clay flowerpot or commercial, brick bread baker) with some flour. Uncover the risen dough and punch it down (good for any frustrations that ail you) and turn it out onto a lightly floured board. With your hands, knead the dough for another 3 to 4 minutes. Shape into a large ball, place in baking dish of your choice and let rise uncovered, in a warm place. Let it rise about 20 minutes.

Preheat the oven to 425°F. Place a pan of hot water on the floor of the oven or the lowest shelf rack. Make a knife slash across the top of the dough. Bake the bread on the middle rack for 30 minutes. At the end of that time, remove the pan of water, reduce the heat to 300°F. and bake about 35 to 40 minutes longer. Remove from oven and test for doneness. The bread should sound hollow when tapped on the bottom.

Cool on a wire rack.

THE FARM

It is not just a farm. It is a spiritual community that covers over seventeen-hundred acres in southern Tennessee about two hours from Nashville, and it was started in May 1971 when a caravan of 270 people made their way from San Francisco to settle the land. Now The Farm has a population of twelve hundred, with 17 sister farms all over the United States and an outreach relief program (PLENTY) that reaches Guatemala, Bangladesh, and the South Bronx.

> . . . I think when we first got here, there were 17 English teachers with master's degrees and only 1 carpenter. The carpenter had to teach the English teachers how to build houses. . . .

Not too long ago, I visited The Farm. I had some business in Nashville and I couldn't resist spending the afternoon with people I had spoken to on the telephone so many times. Daniel Lloyd showed me the new solar schoolhouse that was being built of recycled materials, the clinic, the canning house, the "neighborhoods" and the book publishing company. And, of course, we visited the bakery, where over two-hundred breads a day are turned out for the community families. Everything is grown right on the land. The grains are ground in their own mill and—since the community members are all vegetarians—they rely heavily on their own soybean products.

> . . . you can raise eight times as much vegetable protein as animal protein on an acre of land. When there are so many hungry people in the world, it seems wasteful to run it through a cow first. . . .

The two recipes I've used come right from *The Farm Vegetarian Cookbook* (Summertown, Tennessee: The Book Publishing

The Breads:

High-Protein Soy Bread
Onion Rye Bread

Company, 1978.) published by The Farm right in their own very busy printing plant.

NOTE: Both recipes use unbleached white flour. The bakers told me that a change to whole grain would change the lightness of the Onion Rye Bread and that the High-Protein Soy Bread would lose its special flavor. In any case, the unbleached white flour used by The Farm contains the germ of the wheat since it is milled on the property and used immediately.

High-Protein Soy Bread

(2 loaves)

3 cups soy milk, scalded
2 packages dry yeast
¼ cup oil
1 tablespoon salt
2 tablespoons honey
7 cups unbleached white flour
2 cups soy flour
oil

Scald the soy milk and then cool to warm. Sprinkle over the lukewarm soy milk the yeast, oil, salt, and honey and let sit for 10 minutes until the yeast foams.

Beat in 4 cups of the white flour and then the soy flour. Knead in the remaining 3 cups of white flour, turn out onto a lightly floured surface and knead for 10 minutes or until the dough is smooth and elastic.

Place in a greased bowl and let rise, covered, until the dough doubles in size. Punch down and shape into 2 loaves. Place in 2 well-greased, 9 × 5-inch loaf pans, brush tops with oil, cover and place in a warm spot to rise to double.

Bake at 350°F. for about 45 minutes or until golden brown.

Cool on wire racks.

Sprinkle the yeast over warm water and let sit for 10 minutes until dissolved.

Then add the molasses, salt, and the rye flour 1 cup at a time, stirring well after each addition. Add the unbleached white flour 1 cup at a time, stirring well, and then the caraway seeds and the onion.

Turn out onto a lightly floured surface and knead well for about 10 minutes, adding more flour if necessary. Place in a greased bowl, cover and let rise in a warm place until doubled in size. Then punch down, separate into 2 loaves, place in oiled bread pans and cover. Let rise again in a warm place until doubled in size.

Bake at 375°F. for 30 to 45 minutes or until breads test done. Cool on wire racks.

NOTE: This recipe may be made with whole wheat flour in place of unbleached white flour by reducing the quantity of rye flour to 2 cups and the quantity of unbleached white flour to 2½ to 3 cups of whole wheat flour.

Onion Rye Bread

(2 loaves)

2 packages dry yeast
1½ cups warm water
¼ cup molasses
3 teaspoons salt
2½ 3 cups rye flour
3 cups unbleached white flour
1 tablespoon caraway seeds
1 small chopped onion

BEATRICE SEAL

The Breads:

*I. A Basket of Luscious Southern
Bread Recipes:*

Antebellum Rice Bread
Applesauce Raisin Nut Loaf
Beekeeper Honey Bread
Buttermilk Corn Bread
Cheese Pone Crunch
Cheese Straws
Corn Pouches
Crispy Corn Flowers
Extra Corny Bread
Fig Muffins
Fig-Nut Bread
Fresh Corn Spoon Bread
Homegrown Crackers
Orange Oatmeal Muffins
Pone Bread
Refrigerator Rolls
Rice Muffins
Rye/Wheat Germ Batter Bread
Savannah Bread
Sharp Cheddar Batter Loaves
Spicy Southern Cheese Bread
Yummy Yam Buns

II. Southern Holiday Breads:

Holiday Hospitality Loaf
Old Christmas Bread
(continued on next page)

I have not dared to count them, for Bea Seal is another of those gold mines of bread recipes—unusual, simple, many of them carrying a story or an enthusiastic description of just why the bread is special to her.

Since becoming a happy North Carolinian more than eight years ago, many new-to-me recipes have found their way into my oven. I test them and adapt them to my needs, and every day becomes an adventure. . . .

Bea is a lady preacher in Washington, North Carolina, works in the hospitals and prisons as a chaplain, fills in for vacationing preachers, does child guidance and alcoholic rehabilitation work and also teaches round dancing. In addition, she and her husband travel on round dancing tours, where some of the recipes printed here were acquired. The most remarkable thing is the fact that she even has the time to collect and test the recipes that fill her files! (Some of her sourdough recipes are also included in the section of the book devoted to those most special breads—see Index.)

As a young child, I occasionally ate a meal with Aunt Trudy and Uncle Bill and I loved her hot breads. My mother also baked, but she thought that the great treat—bread right from the oven—was too "difficult to digest."

Some of Bea's recipes are from Aunt Trudy, some from her mother's original files, but most have been collected from friends, created through her own experimentation, and picked up on her round dance trips.

III. Breads from Friends and from Travel:

Bermuda Tea Biscuits
Caraway Swiss Biscuits
Cornish Splits
Egg Oatmeal Biscuits
**Fruit-Nut-Butter
   Casserole Bread**
Texas Corn Bread
Tortillas **(Mexican)**

Antebellum Rice Bread

(1 to 1½ dozen squares)

1 tablespoon melted butter
½ tablespoon melted shortening
1 cup cooked rice
½ cup cornmeal
1 teaspoon salt*
dash cayenne pepper (optional)
1 cup milk
3 eggs, beaten

This recipe was given to me by an old friend in Savannah, who told me that it was a favorite breakfast bread on the plantations.

Place the melted fats and the rice in a heavy saucepan, covered, over very low heat. Mix cornmeal and salt and pepper, then stir milk into beaten eggs and blend in the cornmeal. Blend together with the rice mixture and put into greased 8- or 9-inch square pan.

Bake at 450°F. until firm when tapped with finger and well browned on top—about 25 minutes.

Cut into squares to serve.

Applesauce Raisin Nut Loaf

(1 loaf)

½ cup softened butter
⅔ cup honey or molasses
2 eggs
1 cup light applesauce
1¼ teaspoons baking powder
2 cups whole wheat flour
½ teaspoon cinnamon
¼ teaspoon nutmeg
¾ teaspoon baking soda
½ teaspoon salt (optional)
¾ cup coarsely chopped walnuts
½ cup raisins, washed and plumped

Cream butter and honey or molasses in an electric mixer (or by using a wooden spoon, hand beater, or wire whisk). Add the eggs and beat them in one at a time. Add the applesauce and blend well.

Sift together all the dry ingredients with the spices and then add, a little at a time, to the applesauce mixture. Toss the nuts and raisins in a little of the flour mixture to completely coat them and then add slowly to the batter. Blend well and put mixture into a greased 9 × 5-inch loaf pan.

Bake at 350°F. for 45 to 60 minutes, or until done. Remove and let cool in pan for 10 minutes before removing carefully to rack to finish cooling. Store in an airtight container.

---

*The salt, though traditional, may be eliminated if you choose to do so.

Bea says that this is a light bread that keeps well and can be reheated briefly before serving for breakfast. It's also good lightly toasted.

Sift together flour, salt, cinnamon, and nutmeg. Combine the milk, honey, and butter in a saucepan and cook slowly over low heat, stirring constantly. When the butter melts, slowly add the baking powder and stir well.

Add the milk-honey mixture and the lemon peel to the dry ingredients, stir very well and pour into a greased and floured 9 × 5-inch pan and bake in a preheated 350°F. oven for approximately 50 minutes.

Warning: This is a delicate bread that burns easily, so watch it closely while baking. It will be golden brown when done. Let it stand on a rack for 15 minutes before removing it from the pan, then let cool on a wire rack.

Delicious served warm.

NOTE: This is 1 bread that does not convert well to whole wheat flour. The essential lightness is lost without the lift of unbleached white flour.

Beekeeper Honey Bread

(1 loaf)

2 cups unbleached white flour
½ teaspoon salt (optional)
1 teaspoon cinnamon
¼ teaspoon nutmeg
1 cup milk
¾ cup good quality light honey
1 tablespoon butter
1¼ teaspoons baking powder
½ teaspoon freshly grated
   lemon peel

Blend cornmeal, soda, and salt. Mix the buttermilk with the egg, add the cornmeal mixture and stir until thoroughly blended and smooth.

Put butter in a flat baking pan (about 8 inches square) and put it in a preheated oven at 450°F. Be careful that the butter doesn't burn—just keep the pan in the oven long enough to melt the butter.

Pour in the corn bread mixture and bake on top shelf for about 30 minutes or until shiny brown.

Cut into squares and serve warm.

Buttermilk Corn Bread

(1 to 1½ dozen squares)

1 cup cornmeal
1 teaspoon baking soda
1 teaspoon salt (optional)
2 cups buttermilk
1 egg, slightly beaten
2 tablespoons butter

Cheese Pone Crunch

(3 to 4 dozen squares)

1 cup yellow cornmeal
½ cup butter, divided in half
⅛ teaspoon salt (optional)
dash cayenne pepper
3 cups cold water
½ cup grated Parmesan cheese
paprika

Cook the cornmeal, half the butter, salt, and pepper in the water. The mixture should have an oatmeal consistency. Remove from the heat and gradually add enough cheese to suit your taste. (You may not want to use the entire ½ cup.)

Rinse an 8- or 9-inch square pan in cold water and pour in the cornmeal mixture. It should be about ½ inch thick. Smooth it out evenly and cover the surface with wax paper or plastic wrap and chill thoroughly in the refrigerator.

Melt the other ¼ cup butter in a somewhat larger pan and cut the chilled cornmeal mixture into 1½-inch squares. Dip all sides in the melted butter and place about ½ inch in the pan. Sprinkle tops lightly with paprika and bake at 400°F. until golden brown and crunchy, about 20 minutes.

Cheese Straws

(12 dozen or more)

1 pound sharp, natural cheddar cheese
¼ pound softened butter (½ cup)
1 egg
1 tablespoon cold water
1¾ cups whole wheat flour
½ teaspoon salt (optional)
½ teaspoon paprika
¼ teaspoon cayenne pepper

I don't think I've ever attended a wedding reception, picnic or homecoming where cheese straws were not served. They're another Southern tradition. This one is my favorite recipe.

Grate the cheese and cream with the butter until soft. Add the egg to the water and beat well. Sift all dry ingredients together and add to the cheese mixture in 3 portions, beating well after each addition. Chill for at least 10 minutes in the refrigerator.

Pack into a cookie gun, attach the small saw-toothed tip and make 3½-inch strips on an ungreased cookie sheet.

Bake at 350°F. for 10 to 12 minutes.

This is one of the recipes from my mother's old card file. It's an old family favorite with a light and delicate corny taste.

Sift flour, resift several times with the cornmeal, salt, and baking powder. Beat the whole egg with the additional egg yolk, add the milk and beat together.

Pour in the cooled melted butter and beat again. Add the flour mixture and blend well. Roll out about ¼ inch thick on floured board. Cut with a round cutter and smear with additional softened butter. Fold each one in half to form little pouches. Place on a buttered and floured baking sheet and bake at 450°F. for about 15 minutes.

NOTE: Be sure melted butter is cooled when adding to the egg mixture; otherwise, the batter will curdle.

Corn Pouches

(about 2 dozen pouches, depending on size)

1½ cups whole wheat flour, sifted
1 cup yellow cornmeal
1 teaspoon salt (optional)
2 tablespoons baking powder
1 whole egg
1 egg yolk
1 scant cup milk
2 tablespoons melted butter, cooled
additional softened butter

Blend together the cornmeal, butter, salt, celery seeds, and onion and stir in enough boiling water to make a mixture firm enough to shape into balls (about 1 tablespoon in each).

Place each one about a half inch apart on a greased baking sheet, pat into flat rounds, and imprint a design in each one with the tines of a fork.

Sprinkle very lightly with paprika and bake in a very hot oven at 450°F. until firm and lightly browned—about 20 minutes.

Serve hot.

Crispy Corn Flowers

(about 2 dozen rounds)

1 cup yellow cornmeal
1 tablespoon melted butter
½ teaspoon salt (optional)
½ teaspoon celery seeds
1 tablespoon minced onion
1 cup boiling water (approximately)
paprika

Extra Corny Bread

(1 to 1½ dozen squares)

1 cup sour cream
1½ cups yellow cornmeal
2 eggs
1 small can cream-style corn
(about 1 cup)
½ teaspoon salt (optional)

Bea says that this has a scrumptious taste, is very moist and is a favorite with the family. It freezes well, ". . . if you have a crumb left over!"

Blend all ingredients well and pour into preheated corn-bread molds or an 8- or 9-inch square buttered, preheated pan. Bake 30 to 40 minutes or until done, in a 375°F. oven.

Cut into squares and serve warm.

Fig Muffins

(about 1 dozen muffins)

2 cups whole wheat flour
2 teaspoons baking powder
½ teaspoon salt (optional)
¾ cup chopped figs
¼ cup melted butter
2 tablespoons light honey
1 cup cold milk
1 egg, beaten

We pick our own figs right in our backyard. They're delicious and a favorite food of all Carolinians. They also add a marvelous flavor to home-baked breads, as in the next two recipes.

Sift the dry ingredients and toss the figs lightly to coat. Add the liquid ingredients all at once. Stir just until moistened—the batter should be lumpy and rough.

Fill greased muffin tins two-thirds full and bake at 400°F. for about 20 minutes.

Serve hot. They freeze well if you happen to have 1 or 2 left over.

Beat the eggs, molasses, honey, and butter until creamed. Combine the dry ingredients, figs, and nuts and blend into the creamed mixture, alternating with the milk and ending with the flour mixture.

Pour into buttered 9 × 5-inch loaf pan and let rest for 25 minutes. Then bake in a preheated oven at 350°F. for 1 hour or until bread tests done.

NOTE: If you do not care for bran, omit it and add 1 cup more of flour. For a fruitier flavor, you may use part freshly squeezed orange juice and substitute it for an equal part of milk.

Fig-Nut Bread

(1 loaf)

2 large eggs
¼ cup light molasses
½ cup honey
3 tablespoons melted butter
1 cup bran
2½ cups whole wheat flour
½ teaspoon baking soda
2 teaspoons baking powder
1 teaspoon salt (optional)
1 cup dried, chopped figs
½ cup chopped walnuts
1½ cups milk

Stir together the cornmeal and ½ cup *cold* milk. Bring another ½ cup of milk to boil, add the corn kernels and stir in the cornmeal mixture gradually. Add ½ teaspoon of salt and cook 5 minutes, stirring constantly.

Remove from heat and beat in the butter. Beat the egg yolks well and stir in the remaining milk (1 cup). Add to the corn mixture.

Beat the egg whites to soft peaks with ¼ teaspoon salt and the cream of tartar. Fold into the corn mixture lightly but thoroughly and pour into a buttered 6-cup casserole.

Bake at 325°F. for about 45 minutes and serve immediately.

Fresh Corn Spoon Bread

(1 loaf)

⅓ cup yellow cornmeal
2 cups milk, divided in half
1 cup cooked fresh corn kernels
½ teaspoon salt (optional)
¼ cup melted butter
2 large eggs, separated
¼ teaspoon salt (optional)
¼ teaspoon cream of tartar

Homegrown Crackers

(about 4 or 5 dozen crackers,
depending on size)

2 cups whole wheat flour
1 teaspoon salt (optional)
½ teaspoon baking powder
¼ cup butter
½ cup milk
1 large egg
coarse salt (optional)

Sift flour, salt, and baking powder into a bowl. Cut in the butter until very fine. Add milk and egg to make a stiff dough and knead thoroughly—about 5 minutes. On a lightly floured surface, roll out until very thin.

Sprinkle the tops with coarse salt, cut into squares or rounds of any size and place on a lightly buttered cookie sheet. Prick with a fork and bake at 400°F. for about 10 minutes or until very lightly browned.

They store well in airtight containers.

Orange Oatmeal Muffins

(about 1 dozen muffins)

1 egg
¼ cup light honey
3 tablespoons melted butter
1 cup milk
1 cup uncooked rolled oats
1 cup whole wheat flour
1 tablespoon baking powder
½ teaspoon salt (optional)
1 tablespoon freshly grated
orange peel

These are delicate muffins that need nothing on them but butter.

Beat egg, add honey and butter, blend well and then beat in the milk. Stir in oats and let mixture rest for 1 or 2 minutes. Sift all the dry ingredients and add to the milk mixture along with the orange peel. Mix just enough to blend. DO NOT BEAT.

Fill cupcake liners in muffin cups half full. Stir batter gently as you fill the cups.

Bake 20 to 25 minutes at 400°F. until nicely browned.

On an antique car tour (The Horseless Carriage Club), one of the meals was served by a lovely group of ladies from a little, historical church in Hyde County. One bread selection was something they called Pone Bread, which they assured me was a tradition in Hyde. This is the recipe they shared with me—dark, rich, heavy and delicious.

Sift cornmeal, flour, and salt. Pour in boiling water and mix thoroughly. Add the molasses, honey, and butter.

Bake in a round, greased 10-inch tube pan for 45 minutes at 325°F.

Pone Bread

(1 loaf)

1½ cups cornmeal
½ cup unbleached white flour
½ teaspoon salt (optional)
2½ cups boiling water
1 pint molasses
2 tablespoons honey
4 tablespoons melted butter

Combine the mashed potatoes, butter, honey, salt, and eggs and cream them well. Dissolve the yeast in the lukewarm water, add to the milk and then add to the potato mixture. Add enough flour to make a stiff dough. Turn out onto a lightly floured board and knead for about 8 minutes.

Put the dough in a large, greased bowl, cover and let rise to double in a warm place (about 1½ hours). Knead down lightly, rub the top with melted butter, cover tightly and place in the refrigerator until ready to bake.

About 1 hour before baking time, roll out on a floured surface, cut into shapes, place on greased cookie sheet, and let rise, lightly covered in a warm spot for about 45 minutes to 1 hour.

Bake at 375°F. for about 20 minutes or until done.

Refrigerator Rolls

(4 to 5 dozen rolls, depending on size)

1 cup mashed potatoes (2 medium-size potatoes)
⅔ cup butter
¼ cup honey
1 teaspoon salt (optional)
2 eggs
1 package dry yeast
½ cup warm water
1 cup milk, scalded and cooled to lukewarm
6 to 7 cups whole wheat flour
melted butter

Rice Muffins

(about 8 to 10 muffins)

1 egg
4 teaspoons honey
½ cup milk
1 tablespoon melted butter
¾ cup cooked brown rice, *not instant*
¾ cup whole wheat flour
2½ teaspoons baking powder
½ teaspoon salt (optional)
2 tablespoons wheat germ

These muffins are light and moist, with a nutty flavor.

Beat the egg, then beat in the honey, milk, and butter. Add the rice, separating with a fork, and blend well. Sift all dry ingredients and stir in. Batter will be stiff. DO NOT BEAT.

Fill cupcake liners in muffin tins two-thirds full and bake at 400°F. for 20 to 25 minutes.

Rye/Wheat Germ Batter Bread

(1 loaf)

1 package dry yeast
⅓ cup warm water
¼ cup thick, pure maple syrup
1½ cups hot water
¼ cup butter
2 teaspoons salt (optional)
2¼ cups rye flour
1½ cups wheat germ
1 tablespoon caraway seeds

This is a dark, hearty bread that should be made a day in advance and then sliced very thin.

Combine the yeast and warm water (at about 110°F.) and add the maple syrup. Let stand for about 10 minutes to soften.

Combine the hot water, butter, and salt and blend until the butter is dissolved and the water is cooled to lukewarm. Combine with the yeast mixture and add the rye flour. Beat well, stir in the wheat germ and caraway seeds and beat again. Cover and set in a warm place to rise (about 1½ hours).

When risen, beat down with a wooden spoon. Put into a well-buttered loaf pan and spread evenly. Cover and let rise until batter almost reaches the top of the pan. Put pan into an oven preheated at 300°F. and raise the setting to 350°F. Bake only 20 minutes, then lower heat to 325°F. and bake 25 minutes more. After baking for 45 minutes, turn off heat and let bread stay in oven 5 more minutes before turning out onto wire rack to cool.

This is an unusual bread, a delicious blend of honey, banana, and peanut butter.

Cream butter, add the peanut butter, and gradually add the honey, creaming until light and fluffy. Add the eggs, 1 at a time, beating well after each, then stir in the bananas.

Sift the dry ingredients and add alternately with the buttermilk, stirring to blend well. Spoon batter into a greased loaf pan 8 × 4 inches and bake at 350°F. for 1 hour or until the bread tests done.

Cool on wire rack.

Savannah Bread

(1 loaf)

⅓ cup softened butter
¾ cup chunk-style peanut butter
⅔ cup light honey
2 large eggs
1 cup mashed bananas (2 large bananas)
2 cups whole wheat flour
½ teaspoon salt (optional)
2½ teaspoons baking powder
¼ teaspoon baking soda
¼ cup buttermilk

Serve the first one warm, and freeze the other two.

Dissolve the yeast in warm water (about 110°F.) in a large bowl. Blend in the salt, eggs, and half the flour. Beat thoroughly for 2 minutes or more until the batter is smooth. Add the cheese, caraway seeds, and the remaining flour and beat until thoroughly blended. Cover and let rise in a warm spot until double, about 45 minutes.

Stir down and divide into 3 greased, 4 × 8-inch loaf pans, cover lightly and let rise until batter almost reaches the top of the pans.

Bake at 375°F. for 40 to 50 minutes; turn out onto wire rack and brush with melted butter while still hot.

Sharp Cheddar Batter Loaves

(3 loaves)

4 packages dry yeast
3 cups lukewarm water
1 tablespoon salt (optional)
4 large eggs
8 to 10 cups whole wheat flour
4 cups grated sharp cheddar cheese
⅓ cup caraway seeds (optional)
butter

Spicy Southern Cheese Bread

(1 loaf)

1 package dry yeast
¼ cup warm water
½ cup milk, scalded
½ cup cold water
1 tablespoon light honey
½ teaspoon salt (optional)
⅛ teaspoon dry mustard
⅛ teaspoon powdered mace
⅛ teaspoon powdered ginger
2 tablespoons melted butter
¾ cups grated sharp, natural
cheddar cheese
3 to 4 cups whole wheat flour

Bea says that this is a good "make-ahead" bread. It's excellent sliced thin and toasted, and it makes marvelous sandwiches.

Dissolve the yeast in warm water in a large mixing bowl and set aside. Scald milk, quickly remove from heat and add cold water. Let cool slightly. Blend honey, salt, mustard, mace, and ginger into the yeast mixture. Mix well and slowly add the cooled milk. Mix lightly, add the melted butter, cheese, and 1 cup of the flour. Beat by hand until the mixture is smooth. Set bowl aside and let rise in a warm place, covered, for about ½ hour.

Add the remaining flour and knead with hands until dough is stiff—a little more flour may be necessary. Cover bowl again and set in a warm spot to rise until double—about 1 hour.

When dough has doubled in bulk, turn out onto a lightly floured surface and knead *very lightly* until dough becomes shiny smooth—about 5 to 8 minutes. Shape into loaf and place into a large, greased 9 × 5-inch loaf pan; cover and let rise in a warm place for 45 minutes.

Bake at 375°F. about 40 minutes, or until loaf is golden in color. Remove and cool on rack while still in pan for about 20 minutes, then turn out loaf onto rack and completely cool.

Do not slice for at least 5 hours.

These buns are another Southern tradition. They're great served hot—and they can be easily reheated.

Soften yeast in the warm water. Add butter, honey, salt, and nutmeg to the scalded milk, stir until well blended and cool to lukewarm.

Add the cold, mashed sweet potatoes to the milk mixture, along with the yeast. Then add enough flour to make a stiff dough. Turn out onto a lightly floured surface and knead until smooth, about 8 minutes. Place in a greased bowl, turning to coat the top, cover and let rise in a warm spot until doubled in size (about 2 hours).

Punch down and shape into rolls. Place on greased cookie sheet, cover with towel and let rise in a warm spot until almost double in bulk. Bake at 400°F. for about 15 minutes, then turn temperature down to 350°F. and bake 10 minutes longer, or until browned.

NOTE: Whole wheat flour may be successfully substituted for unbleached white flour in this recipe.

Yummy Yam Buns

(2 to 3 dozen buns, depending on size)

1 package dry yeast
½ cup lukewarm water
2 tablespoons butter
¼ cup light honey
1 teaspoon salt (optional)
⅛ teaspoon nutmeg
½ cup milk, scalded
¾ cup cold, mashed
   sweet potatoes
2½ to 3½ cups unbleached
   white flour

Holiday Hospitality Loaf

(1 loaf)

1 cup buttermilk
⅓ cup light honey
1½ teaspoons salt (optional)
2 packages dry yeast
¼ cup warm water
4½ to 5 cups whole wheat flour
2 eggs
¼ cup softened butter

Filling:

½ cup light honey
¼ cup thick, pure maple syrup
1 scant tablespoon freshly
squeezed orange juice
⅓ cup raisins
1½ cups finely chopped nuts
1 tablespoon freshly grated
orange peel
1 teaspoon cinnamon
1 tablespoon melted butter

This is a superb treat with hot coffee as a touch of the well-known "Southern hospitality."

Heat the buttermilk to lukewarm, stirring constantly, being careful not to overheat as it will separate. Pour into a large bowl and add the honey and salt. Dissolve the yeast in warm water (110°F.).

Beat 1½ cups of the flour into the buttermilk mixture, add the yeast mixture and continue beating to blend well. Add eggs, butter, and more flour, a little at a time, blending until the dough begins to come away from the sides of the bowl. The dough will be soft.

Turn dough out onto lightly floured surface and knead until smooth and elastic—about 8 to 10 minutes. Shape into ball and place in lightly greased bowl, turning once to coat the top. Cover and let rise in a warm place about 1 hour or until doubled in bulk.

Meanwhile, prepare the filling by mixing together all the ingredients *except* butter.

When dough has doubled, punch it down, turn onto floured surface and divide into 2 parts. Keep 1 part covered with cloth and roll the other one out to a 10-inch square. Brush with butter and sprinkle with half the filling. Roll up like a jelly roll, pinching the edges of the dough into the roll. Roll the dough a few times to secure the edges, then cut into 1-inch pieces.

In a 10-inch greased tube pan, lay the slices around the bottom of the pan, with each one nearly touching the next one. The second group of 1-inch slices should be placed vertically around the edge of the pan. The third layer should be placed atop the first layer. Prepare the second half of the dough as you did the first and place the slices in the pan as before. Cover and let rise in a warm place until doubled (about 45 minutes).

Bake at 350°F. for 45 minutes to 1 hour. Carefully turn out onto wire rack to cool.

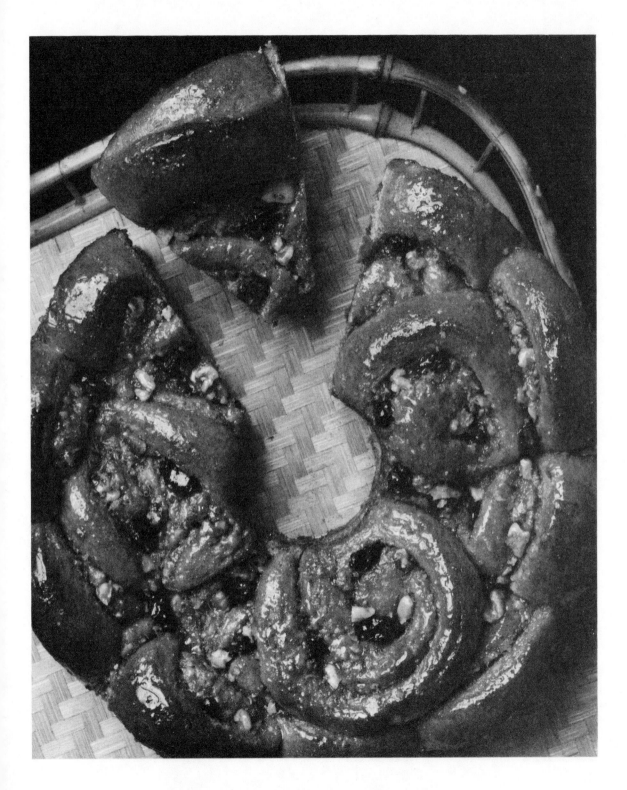

Holiday Hospitality Loaf (Bea Seal) page 202   *203*

204   Sourdough English-Style Muffins (Bea Seal) page 114

One of our wonderful, traditional celebrations on our Outer Banks is "Old Christmas," celebrated on the day of Epiphany (January 6) complete with "Old Buck," a legendary animal, with gifts for all the children. The feast consists of a fabulous oyster roast with all the trimmings. Hush puppies are always served, but a native "Outer Banker" gave me a recipe for this Old Christmas Bread, snowy white and unbeatable!

For the sponge—dissolve the yeast in water and thoroughly blend in the honey and the flours. Cover with a towel and let rise in a warm place for 4 hours.

For the dough—dissolve the yeast in warm water, blend in the salt, honey, and the flour. Blend thoroughly together with the sponge until pliable and smooth—the dough will pull away from the bowl when ready.

Put onto a lightly floured surface and knead for 5 minutes. Let rise for 10 minutes, then shape into a long or round loaf. Cut a cross in the center with a floured knife and place on a cornmeal-sprinkled pan. Cover lightly with a towel or plastic wrap and let rise in a warm place until almost doubled in bulk—about 1 hour.

Place a 9 × 12-inch pan half filled with boiling water on the bottom of the oven; place the bread on the middle shelf and set the temperature to 400°F. Bake for 45 minutes or until golden brown and done. While still hot, brush with butter and cool on wire rack.

Old Christmas Bread

(1 loaf)

For the Sponge:

1 package dry yeast
2 cups lukewarm water
2 tablespoons light honey
2 cups hard white flour (may use
    unbleached white flour)
2 cups whole wheat flour

For the Dough:

1 package dry yeast
1 cup lukewarm water
1 tablespoon salt*
2 tablespoons light honey
2 cups unbleached white flour

cornmeal
butter

---

*The salt, though traditional, may be eliminated if you choose to do so.

Bermuda
Tea Biscuits

(about 2 dozen biscuits, depending on size)

2 cups whole wheat flour, sifted
3 teaspoons baking powder
1 teaspoon salt (optional)
½ cup butter
¾ cup milk
1 large egg, beaten

A number of interesting and delicious bread recipes have been shared with me in my square dance vacation travels around the world. While in Bermuda, a delightful Briton came to our house each morning to prepare breakfast for us. My favorites were Bermuda Tea Biscuits, served with honey and lots of fresh strawberries. It took me three weeks to beg the recipe from her. They're feather light and delicious!

Sift flour, baking powder, and salt together. Cut in the butter until the dough appears like rough cornmeal. Add all the milk together with the beaten egg and stir until you have a smooth, light dough. Now place on a lightly floured surface and lightly knead the dough. Pat out to a thickness of ½ inch and cut with a small biscuit cutter. Place the biscuits on an ungreased cookie sheet.

Bake about 12 minutes in a very hot oven—450°F.

Caraway
Swiss Biscuits

(about 2 dozen biscuits, depending on size)

2 cups whole wheat flour, sifted
1 tablespoon baking powder
1 teaspoon salt (optional)
1 teaspoon butter
¾ cup milk
1 cup grated natural Swiss cheese
2 tablespoons caraway seeds

These are a cheese lover's delight and they come from Bea's Aunt Trudy.

Sift flour, baking powder, and salt together. Cut in the butter until the dough appears like rough cornmeal. Add milk, cheese, and caraway seeds and blend to smooth dough. (You may need a very little extra milk.)

Turn out onto lightly floured surface and knead lightly for just a few minutes. Pat out to a thickness of ½ inch and cut into rounds.

Place on ungreased cookie sheet and bake at 450°F. for 12 to 15 minutes or until golden.

A British friend of mine who knows I enjoy cooking came to visit us for vacation and brought me some delightful recipes.

Cream yeast with honey until syrupy; stir in butter, salt, milk, eggs, and 2 cups of the flour. Beat until smooth, then stir in remaining flour, sifted with cardamom. Turn out onto lightly floured board and knead dough until smooth, about 8 minutes. Place in greased bowl, turn once to coat top, cover and let rise to double in a warm spot.

Punch down and turn out onto a floured surface, roll out to a thickness of ½ inch, and cut with a floured biscuit cutter. Place on buttered cookie sheet about 1 inch apart, lightly cover and let rise to double, about 45 minutes. Brush tops with light cream or milk and bake at 350°F. for about 25 minutes.

Serve hot right from the oven.

Cornish Splits

(about 2 dozen biscuits)

1 package dry yeast
⅓ cup light honey
⅓ cup softened butter
½ teaspoon salt (optional)
⅔ cup milk, scalded and cooled
2 large eggs
3½ to 4 cups whole wheat flour
⅛ teaspoon crushed cardamom
light cream or milk

This is another delicious favorite that comes from Bermuda.

Combine flour, baking powder, and salt. Toss in oats and cut in butter with a pastry blender. When mixture is like coarse cornmeal, stir in milk and eggs. Dough should hold together and be kneadable.

Turn out onto a lightly floured surface and knead lightly—not more than 10 times. Roll or pat out to a thickness of ½ inch and cut into 2-inch rounds.

Bake on an ungreased cookie sheet at 450°F. for 12 to 15 minutes.

Egg Oatmeal Biscuits

(1 dozen biscuits)

1 cup whole wheat flour
3 teaspoons baking powder
½ teaspoon salt (optional)
1 cup uncooked rolled oats
¼ cup butter
⅓ cup milk
2 large eggs

Fruit-Nut-Butter Casserole Bread

(1 loaf)

Tennia, a school teacher in Barbados, invited us to a luncheon for several square dancing couples. She served a delicious buttery bread and told us that the recipe was given to her by a classmate while she was in teacher's college in Sweden. This is her recipe.

1 cup milk, scalded
½ cup sweet butter
¼ cup light honey
1 package dry yeast
¼ cup warm water
2 large eggs
freshly grated peel of
1 large lemon
1 teaspoon salt (optional)
2 teaspoons ground ginger
3 to 4 cups whole wheat flour
¼ cup slivered almonds
½ cup chopped walnuts or pecans
½ cup chopped raisins
cream
slivered almonds

Pour scalded milk over butter and honey, and let cool to lukewarm. Dissolve yeast in water and add to milk mixture. Stir in eggs, lemon peel, salt, ginger and half the flour. Beat thoroughly and then stir in remaining 2 cups of flour with nuts and raisins blended in. Beat until thoroughly blended, cover and let rise in a warm spot until doubled in bulk (about 1 hour).

Punch down and let rise again to double. After second rise, stir down and pour into well-buttered, 6-cup casserole. Let dough rise again until just doubled, then brush very lightly with cream and sprinkle with additional slivered almonds.

Bake at 350°F. for 30 to 40 minutes.

Texas Corn Bread

(1 to 1½ dozen squares)

This is a superb corn bread from another branch of our family in Texas. It just might destroy your taste for any other corn bread!

1 cup yellow cornmeal
½ cup whole wheat flour
1 teaspoon salt (optional)
1 cup buttermilk
1 egg
1 tablespoon baking powder
½ cup sweet milk
½ teaspoon baking soda
¼ cup melted butter

Thoroughly mix the cornmeal, flour, and salt. Then add the buttermilk, egg, baking powder, sweet milk, baking soda, and melted butter. Do not blend! Do not mix!

Grease an 8-inch-square cake pan, muffin tins, or cornstick molds and heat them in the oven. Stir the mixture very thoroughly and pour into the hot, prepared pans.

Bake at 450°F. until done (about 20 minutes). The bread will be light and moist and brown and crusty on the bottom.

We found a number of places in Mexico where we were permitted to try our hands at making tortillas. Of course, theirs were superior to anything we did. Here are their recipes for both cornmeal and flour tortillas.

Stir cornmeal into boiling water, add salt and shortening. Shape into extremely thin, flat cakes and bake on *hot,* ungreased griddle.

Blend flour with milk, salt, and butter. Knead very thoroughly and make small balls of dough. Roll balls until they are very very thin. Bake on *hot,* ungreased griddle.

NOTE: There is a flour available in some specialty shops called *Masa Harina* and it's specially blended for use in *tortillas.*

Tortillas

(Mexican)

(about 1 to 2 dozen *tortillas*)

Cornmeal Tortillas:

1 cup cornmeal
1 cup boiling water
1 teaspoon salt*
1 tablespoon shortening

Flour Tortillas:

2 cups flour
⅓ cup milk
½ teaspoon salt*
⅓ cup butter

*The salt, though traditional, may be eliminated if you choose to do so.

The Treat of
Triticale

In an earlier chapter about flours and grains, I mentioned that I had become fascinated with a fairly new cereal development called triticale (trit-i-*kay*-lee). For about two years I had been experimenting with the grain and, when I decided that there might be a book in my future, I began to research by mail and by telephone—to Shiloh Farms in Sulphur Springs, Arkansas; through Mark Sorrells at Cornell; with the United States Department of Agriculture; and the University of Nebraska. My best information and some of my most interesting conversations came when I discovered Ron Kershen, who grows triticale commercially in Canyon, Texas.

I suppose that I could have remained content that my breads were developing new tastes and new textures, that a new vista was opening in my bread-baking world. But I found, too, that much of the current information was vague, if I could find it at all. Some books and articles, in fact, were giving totally false information about triticale (calling it high gluten when it is, in fact, low gluten—high protein).

Triticale is the result of crossing wheat and rye—but when it accidentally occurs in nature, the resulting grains are sterile. This was overcome by scientists in the late 30s and, as a result, triticale is considered a man-made species, the first grain of its kind in the world. In fact, one of the most prominent people working with the grain, Dr. Charles Jenkins of Salinas, California, obtained 10 seeds in 1953 and has, since then, experimented with over three thousand varieties of triticale.

In terms of protein, triticale runs about three to four percent higher than other grains, and it's a much higher quality than other proteins because it has a better balance of essential amino acids. Because of its low gluten content, it is much better blended with unbleached white flour in your baking. Usually, a blend of one-third triticale and two-thirds white flour gives best results, though you can use 50 percent of each for a heavier loaf. In my earlier experiments I tried loaves using only triticale flour and though they were somewhat heavy (as expected), the taste still made them worthwhile.

Which gets me to the reason that I began this chapter in the first place—*the taste*. I'm afraid that all the protein information in the world would still not convince me to continue working with a flour or grain unless I could also present a bread at my dinner table that brought comments such as, "What *is* this? It's delicious!" The flavor has been described as "ryelike" and possibly that is a good description. I find that triticale has its own distinctive flavor and a natural, mild sweetness without being cloying.

It can now be found all over the country—as a flour, in flake form, and as a grain that can be sprouted in the same way that you sprout any other grain. In any recipe calling for whole grain, you can easily substitute triticale to get a new taste treat.

The recipes that follow are just a few examples of the ones I've tried. Let your own imagination expand the list.

The Breads:

Triticale Bread
Buttermilk Triticale Bread
Double Triticale Bread
Triticale Honey Bread
Pumpernickel Triticale Bread
Triticale Biscuits
Triticale Nut Bread
Triticale Muffins
Triticale Batter Bread

Triticale Bread

(2 loaves)

1 package dry yeast
¼ cup warm water
2 teaspoons honey
4 tablespoons oil
1 tablespoon salt (optional)
¼ cup honey
1 egg
1¾ cups milk
2 cups whole grain triticale flour
3½ cups unbleached white flour

This is a good beginning recipe for your triticale baking. It was sent to me by Ron Kershen and it makes loaves that are perfect for sandwiches or for toasting in the morning.

Mix the yeast in the ¼ cup warm water, add the 2 teaspoons of honey and set aside while getting the other ingredients ready.

In a large bowl, mix all the other ingredients except the flours and bring to room temperature. Add the yeast mixture, then the triticale flour and 2 cups of the white flour. Mix well. Add the remaining 1½ cups of unbleached white flour and make a fairly soft dough. Stir with a wooden spoon until smooth. Cover and let rise until almost triple in size (about 2 hours) in a warm spot.

Turn out onto a lightly floured board or surface and knead for about 8 minutes. Divide dough into 2 sections and place in greased 9 × 5-inch loaf pans. Cover lightly and place in warm spot to rise for about 1 hour, or until dough is slightly higher than the sides of the pans.

Bake at 350°F. for 45 minutes or until breads test done. (Preheating the oven to 450°F., then reducing the heat to 350°F. when the bread is put in the oven, helps make a lighter loaf of bread.)

Cool on wire racks.

NOTE: The testers at Rodale tried this one using only triticale (no unbleached white) flour, and pronounced it "perfection."

When my wife became interested in bread baking, she also became fascinated with triticale flour. This is her recipe and she calls it an "energy-saving" bread because she starts with a cold oven during the baking process. Professional jealousy keeps me from saying that the bread is delicious! (Which it is!)

Use an electric hand beater and a large bowl. Mix the yeast, honey, and 2 cups of the flour (1 triticale and 1 unbleached white).

Heat the buttermilk and the butter to about 115°F.—if it gets too hot, let it cool down—and then pour into the flour mixture and beat for about 2 minutes at medium speed.

To the remaining flour, add the salt and baking soda and stir in with a wooden spoon—then add the flour to the first mixture, stirring well.

Using your hands or a wooden spoon, knead for 1 or 2 minutes in the bowl to incorporate all ingredients, then turn out onto lightly floured surface and knead for 8 to 10 minutes, adding more unbleached white flour if the dough gets too sticky.

Place dough in a greased bowl, turn once to coat the top, cover and place in a cool oven (about 100°F.) for 1 hour. Punch down, divide into 2 pieces, knead for 1 or 2 minutes on a lightly floured surface, and place in 2 greased 8 × 4-inch loaf pans. Cover and place in oven again for 1 hour.

Remove cover and start oven with the breads inside. Raise the heat to 400°F. and bake about 25 to 30 minutes on a lower shelf or until breads test done.

Cool on wire racks.

Buttermilk Triticale Bread

(2 medium loaves)

1 package dry yeast
2 tablespoons honey
4½ cups unbleached white flour
2 cups triticale flour
2½ cups buttermilk
¼ cup butter
1 tablespoon salt (optional)
½ teaspoon baking soda

Double Triticale Bread

(2 medium loaves)

1 cup triticale grain
2 packages dry yeast
½ cup warm water
½ teaspoon honey
3 cups unbleached white flour
3 cups triticale flour
½ teaspoon salt (optional)
½ cup chopped, toasted
sunflower seeds
1 tablespoon honey
1½ cups water

I originally tried this one as a total triticale bread—no white flour at all. If you like, you can try it that way, though the bread will be dense and will rise very little. The taste is incredibly good, but you will probably prefer the use of some unbleached white for lightness. As a result, I've revised the recipe to include it. The sunflower seeds and the triticale grain add crunch.

Cook the triticale grain (as you would oats) for 15 to 20 minutes and, when cool, chop finely in blender or food processor. While the grain is cooking, put the yeast in the ½ cup of warm water, add the ½ teaspoon of honey, stir and put aside to proof.

In a large bowl, put the flours, chopped grain, yeast mixture, salt, sunflower seeds, honey, and water. The dough will be crumbly. Stir well or mix with your hands, then turn out onto lightly floured surface and knead for 8 to 10 minutes. The more triticale flour you use, the more dense the dough will feel.

Place in greased bowl, turn once to coat the top, then cover and place in a warm spot to double in size (about 1 hour).

Turn out onto floured surface, knead for 1 or 2 minutes and divide into 2 parts. Shape into loaves and place in well-greased, medium 8 × 4-inch loaf pans, cover and let rise in warm spot for about 45 minutes.

Bake in a 375°F. oven for 45 to 50 minutes or until loaves test done.

Cool on wire racks.

This recipe was given to me by a friend in California and it uses triticale flakes in the recipe. Just as triticale flour is becoming more available in natural foods stores around the country, the flakes and the whole grain are also beginning to appear.

In a bowl, pour the boiling water over the triticale flakes to soften them. Set aside and cool to lukewarm.

In a large bowl, put yeast and warm water, add ¼ cup of the honey and stir. Let stand for about 10 minutes, then add the remainder of the honey, the dry milk, oil, salt, the unbleached white flour, triticale flake mixture, and about a cup of the triticale flour. Mix with a wooden spoon and then, as dough becomes smoother, beat in the remainder of the triticale flour.

Turn out onto a lightly floured surface, knead for about 8 to 10 minutes. If the dough seems too sticky, add more white flour. The dough should be smooth and elastic when the kneading is finished. Place in a greased bowl, turn to coat the top, cover, and place in a warm spot for about 1 to 1½ hours, or until doubled in size.

Turn out onto lightly floured board, punch down and knead for 2 or 3 minutes. Divide dough into 2 parts, shape into loaves, and place in 2 well-greased, 8 × 4-inch loaf pans. Cover and place in warm spot to almost double in size—about 45 minutes.

When loaves have almost doubled, brush with egg yolk mixed with water, and sprinkle sesame or caraway seeds on top.

Bake at 350°F. for about 45 minutes, or until breads are golden brown and test done.

Cool on wire racks.

Triticale Honey Bread

(2 medium loaves)

2 cups boiling water
1 cup triticale flakes
1 package dry yeast
⅓ cup warm water
½ cup mild-flavored honey
½ cup nonfat dry milk
3 tablespoons oil
1 tablespoon salt (optional)
3 cups unbleached white flour
3 cups triticale flour

Glaze:

1 egg yolk
1 tablespoon water
¼ cup sesame or caraway seeds

Pumpernickel Triticale Bread

(2 round loaves)

2 packages dry yeast
1½ cups warm water
½ cup dark molasses
⅔ cup nonfat dry milk
3 tablespoons honey
2 teaspoons salt (optional)
1 cup wheat germ
3 cups unbleached white flour
3 cups triticale flour

Glaze:

1 egg yolk
1 tablespoon water

In a small bowl, put 2 packages of yeast in ½ cup of warm water, stir and set aside to proof (about 10 minutes).

In a large bowl, put molasses, dry milk, honey, and salt; then add the yeast mixture and balance of the water, stirring to make a smooth liquid. Add the wheat germ and stir, then the white flour, 1 cup at a time, stirring after each addition. Add the triticale flour 1 cup at a time, stirring as you do so. The dough should be fairly stiff.

Turn out onto a lightly floured surface, knead for about 8 to 10 minutes, adding more white flour if the dough seems too sticky. Place in a greased bowl, turn once to coat the top, cover, and place in a warm spot to double in size, about 1½ to 2 hours.

Turn out onto floured surface, punch down, and knead for 1 or 2 minutes. Shape into 2 free-form loaves, round or oval, place on a greased, baking sheet that has been lightly dusted with flour, cover, and let rise in a warm place for about 45 minutes, or until doubled in bulk.

When loaves have doubled in size, brush tops with the egg yolk beaten with water to glaze the breads, and bake at 350°F. for about 45 to 50 minutes or until loaves sound hollow when tapped on the bottom.

Cool on wire racks.

Triticale Biscuits

(12 to 15 biscuits)

½ cup triticale flour
2 cups unbleached white flour
5 teaspoons baking powder
1¼ teaspoons salt (optional)
6 tablespoons oil
⅓ cup buttermilk
½ cup water

Preheat the oven to 450°F.

In a large bowl, mix the dry ingredients, then blend in the oil, the buttermilk, and then the water. Mix.

Pat out dough to a thickness of ½ inch and cut into biscuits of the desired size and shape. Place on a greased pan with sides almost touching.

Bake for 10 to 11 minutes.

This is another recipe from Ron Kershen in Canyon, Texas, and it was given to him by Charles Hunter. And I, in turn, pass it on to you. It has a lovely crunch to it.

In a bowl, mix the dry ingredients—triticale flour, graham cracker crumbs, rolled oats, baking soda, baking powder, and salt. Stir in the chopped walnuts and then add the honey and the milk. Mix well with a wooden spoon or with your hands. If the dough seems too sticky, you can add some unbleached white flour to make it smoother.

Use 2 pans, 7⅜ × 3⅝ × 2¼ inches, and put wax paper on the bottom and along the sides. Grease the wax paper with oil and bake at 350°F. for 1 hour.

Cool on wire racks.

Triticale Nut Bread

(2 small loaves)

1 cup triticale flour
1 cup graham cracker crumbs
1 cup uncooked rolled oats
1½ teaspoons baking soda
1½ teaspoons baking powder
1 teaspoon salt (optional)
1 cup chopped walnuts
⅔ cup honey
2 cups milk

Mix dry ingredients in a bowl. Blend in the oil. Add the eggs, honey, and milk and mix well.

Fill greased muffin tins about two-thirds full. Preheat oven to 425°F. (450°F. at higher altitudes) and bake for 10 to 11 minutes.

Serve warm.

NOTE: The Rodale testers found this to be another triticale recipe that yields equally fine results if triticale flour is used in place of unbleached white flour.

Triticale Muffins

(about 12 muffins)

1 cup unbleached white flour
1 cup triticale flour
4 teaspoons baking soda
¾ teaspoon salt (optional)
4 tablespoons oil
2 eggs
3 tablespoons honey
1 cup milk

SHERYL LONDON

Sheryl's amazing power of invention and her talent as a cook are shown to their full advantage on page 313.

Triticale Batter Bread

(with herbs and vegetables)

(1 loaf)

2 cups whole wheat flour
1 package dry yeast
2 teaspoons salt (optional)
¼ cup light molasses
2 tablespoons oil
1 egg
1 cup hot water
1 cup triticale flour
1 tablespoon wheat germ
1 cup finely grated carrots
1 finely chopped medium onion
½ teaspoon celery seed
¼ teaspoon black pepper
¼ cup fresh, minced parsley
¼ teaspoon dried, crushed
rosemary (or ½ teaspoon fresh,
minced rosemary)
1 small clove garlic
2 tablespoons melted butter

Just a few months prior to the publication of this book, we sat in Bob Rodale's office and discussed the joys (as well as the problems) of baking with triticale. Its taste and nutritional values were superb, but we were both distressed over the fact that it frequently had to be blended with unbleached white flour in the standard yeast bread recipes in order to make the texture acceptable. He asked if there weren't some way that we might develop a whole grain triticale bread, and that weekend, my wife and I experimented on Fire Island. This is the superb result, ingeniously developed by Sheryl. In a batter bread, triticale does, indeed, work as a whole grain bread. This one is a no-knead bread, it's made in a casserole, it's foolproof, healthful and delicious. And, the aroma will drive you insane while the bread is baking!

Combine the 2 cups of whole wheat flour, yeast, and salt in a large mixing bowl. Add the molasses, oil, egg, and hot water. Beat with an electric mixer at low speed for about 30 seconds. Scrape the sides of the bowl and then beat at high speed for 3 minutes. Add the triticale flour and the wheat germ and mix well.

If you have a food processor, the two vegetables can be chopped together. If not, prepare them separately according to the directions in the list of ingredients. Add the vegetables, celery seed, pepper, and herbs to the batter and mix together with well-floured hands.

Butter a 2-quart souffle dish or casserole. Put the batter in and cover with plastic wrap and a towel. Keep in a warm place to rise for 1 hour and 15 minutes or until double in bulk.

Bake in a 350°F. oven for 1 hour. After 20 minutes, cover top loosely with aluminum foil and continue baking. Test with a cake tester in the center of the bread.

Remove from casserole at once, place on wire rack and pour melted butter slowly over the top. Let cool slightly before eating—if you can wait that long!

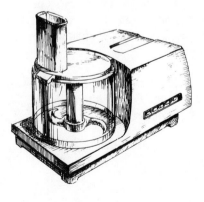

NATHAN ADLER

The Bread:

Granola Bread

When I asked Nathan Adler about the reactions to his first bread-baking experiences, he merely answered, "Happy!" He lives in Santa Fe, New Mexico, and he works as a computer systems analyst.

As for how I began baking, that's quite simple: I just enjoy the taste of homemade bread. But once I began, I found that the processes—the mixing, kneading, punching down, shaping, and especially the wonderful smell—are as soul-satisfying as the bread itself. In short, I'm hooked!

Since I am constantly hunting for new bread recipes and, thus, new bread-baking friends, Nathan was recommended to me by Eve Gentry, a long-time friend in Santa Fe. He, in turn, told us about Juliana James (see Index). And so a collection grows—both of recipes and of friends.

One of the most delightful things about Nathan Adler's Granola Bread is its simplicity. His own tips are very much in line with my own philosophy about baking bread—don't be uptight about it; enjoy it. Or, as he puts it:

Improvise! Let the bread rise as many times as possible—it improves the taste and the texture. Forget about things like proofing yeast, scalding the milk. They're just not necessary.

Here, then, is Nathan Adler's Granola Bread—it's great toasted for breakfast with honey—and it's as simple as A—B—C.

In large bowl, combine A.

Stir in B.

Knead for 8 to 10 minutes or until smooth. Cover and place in greased bowl, turn to coat top and let rise to double—about 45 minutes to 1 hour. Turn out onto a floured board, punch down, return to greased bowl, cover, and let rise until double again (about 1 hour).

After second rise, turn out onto floured board, punch down and knead for just a couple of minutes. Divide into 3 equal loaves and place in greased, medium-size baking pans (8½ × 4½ × 2½ inches).

Place the pans in a warm spot in the kitchen, cover and let rise until double (about 45 minutes to 1 hour). Preheat oven to 350°F.

When loaves are double in size, slash tops with a sharp floured knife and brush with C.

Bake for 45 to 50 minutes or until they test done. Turn out and cool on a wire rack.

Granola Bread

(3 medium-size loaves)

A

2 packages dry yeast
2 cups warm water
1 cup milk, warmed
½ cup oil (i.e., corn oil)
⅜ cup honey
1¼ teaspoons salt (optional)
4 cups whole wheat flour

B

½ cup granola
½ cup sunflower seeds
½ cup raisins
2 tablespoons freshly grated
   orange peel, cut in tiny slivers
4 cups whole wheat flour

C

1 egg, lightly beaten
1 tablespoon milk

HAVEN AND
MARGARET HOLSAPPLE

As a filmmaker, I sometimes get the impression that only I travel to unusual places. However, the last time I spoke with Haven and Margaret Holsapple, they had just returned to their home in Hamilton, Montana, from a trip up Mount McKinley!

Haven is a mountain guide and the director of Hondo Rast and Company of Hamilton, which specializes in mountaineering and wilderness expeditions. Margaret is also a mountain guide and general manager of Expeditions International, which manufactures high quality outdoor and expedition equipment. Together, this husband and wife team are two of the most exciting people I've met in a long time. Both began cooking and baking as youngsters and, as they began to discover the outdoors, the baking went right along with them.

With more and more people taking to the countryside for vacations and to escape big-city pollution, I think the tips that Haven and Margaret offer about bread baking over a campfire are invaluable. Thus, this chapter is theirs as they wrote it. I can sit back with my readers and enjoy a trip to the top of their snow-capped mountain.

The Breads:

Breads for Camping Trips, Backpacking and Mountain Climbing

Basic Yeast Bread
Basic Biscuit Mixture
Biscuits
Muffins
Pancakes
Pizza Crust
Flat Bread

We believe that one of the great joys of an outdoor experience is the ability to learn about all aspects of our environment and to function safely within that environment. This extends from understanding the physical world around us—including the ability to identify plants and animals and the knowledge of advance camping and cooking techniques. We think it's a pity that many of the people who enter the wilderness don't really appreciate what is around them. It's also a pity that people go camping or on an expedition carrying only "instant meals" to satisfy them.

Our Feelings
and
Philosophy

We enjoy and believe in teaching cooking and baking from basics. There's nothing more marvelous than fresh-baked muffins filled with ripe blueberries that you've picked along the trail —or a loaf of hot pan bread to take away a day's fatigue.

Cooking from basics becomes even more important on an extended expedition, where meals tend to become monotonous. Being able to create meals allows for flexibility in eating. It's especially important when you plan to be in the field for as much as four weeks!

Methods of Baking

Campers and expeditioners have two primary methods of baking available to them. The first is baking with live coals from a wood fire, and the second is stove-top baking.

Baking with wood-fire coals yields excellent loaves of bread, but fires are now prohibited in more and more ecologically fragile areas. Also, hordes of campers have stripped many areas of available wood, making stoves a necessity. However, in areas where wood is plentiful and the ecology will not be damaged, coal baking can be fun.

It just takes a little practice to bake with wood-fire coals under all situations (rain, snow, or cold), but the first time you sit back with a hot, fresh-baked muffin filled with just-picked berries, you'll be convinced it's worth it.

Building a Fire

At all costs, a fire scar must be avoided. To accomplish this, carefully remove the sod or forest cover, setting it aside to be replaced later. Next, dig your fire pit, setting aside the dirt and go down to the mineral soil (sand) to avoid starting a forest fire. Build your fire with only enough wood to get the job done— don't waste wood. Once the fire has burned down to the coals, take a small shovel and scrape enough coals aside to make a good bed on which to bake. To test the heat, hold your hand 10 inches above the coals. You should be able to do so for only 10 seconds. Then, place your pan of bread onto the coals and shovel coals onto the lid to cover it. Check the coals regularly and replace when necessary.

The best utensil for all-around outdoor baking is a fairly deep "no-stick" frying pan with a metal lid. (A plastic lid or handle will burn.) This one utensil can be used to make everything from pancakes to bread and, more important, you need only pack this one item for all of your cooking.

Utensils

This is a basic yeast bread that Margaret and Haven enjoy in the field. Though the recipe is given as it is baked over coals, many of today's campers use a small, lightweight gas stove for their backpacking and mountaineering. The bread can be made just as easily with this method.

Dissolve yeast in lukewarm water, add honey and salt and stir. Let stand in a warm place until bubbly (about 5 to 10 minutes).

Add half the flour and beat well to form a thick batter. Gradually add the rest of the flour to form a stiff dough. Turn out onto a floured surface (you can use your frying pan) and knead well, adding flour until you have a smooth ball (about 8 to 10 minutes). Shape into a flat, round loaf and place in a greased frying pan. Grease the top of the loaf and the lid of the pan. Let rise, covered, in a warm place for about 1 hour.

Punch down dough, cover and let rise again until almost doubled. Bake over coals for 40 to 50 minutes (as described in preceding instructions). Bread is done when it is golden brown and sounds hollow when thumped.

Basic Yeast Bread

(1 loaf)

1 package dry yeast
1¾ cups lukewarm water (110°F.)
2 tablespoons honey
2 teaspoons salt (optional)
4 cups unbleached white flour

Basic Biscuit Mixture

1½ cups unbleached white flour
3 teaspoons double-acting baking powder
½ teaspoon salt

The basic ingredient to the four recipes that follow is this basic biscuit mixture. It can be made at home and packaged in plastic bags for your outdoor trip. The beauty of this mix is that absolutely no adjustment is needed for altitude. It has worked well for Haven and Margaret both at 17,000 feet and right in their home kitchen.

Mix ingredients until thoroughly blended. Place in plastic bag and you're ready for your trip.

In other plastic bags, pack these other ingredients:
   nonfat dry milk
   powdered egg
   wheat flour
   honey

Just make sure you have enough to last you for the entire trip.

NOTE: Haven and Margaret tell me that you *must* use white flour for the basic mixture because of the high gluten content. Whole grains will not work in the starter at high altitudes.

Biscuits

(8 to 12 biscuits)

1 cup basic biscuit mix
½ cup whole wheat flour
¼ cup nonfat dry milk
water (enough to make a sticky dough)
corn oil or peanut oil for frying

Combine the basic biscuit mix with the flour, dry milk, and water. Heat the oil in a frying pan—about ¼ inch of oil to cover the surface. (Butter will burn and, in any case, it spoils quickly on an extended trip.)

Drop biscuit-size dough into the pan and fry until both sides are brown; then cover and cook over low heat until done (6 to 10 minutes) being careful not to burn the biscuits. If you're using a stove, rotate the frying pan over the heat to allow for even cooking.

Variations

Unbleached white flour, uncooked rolled oats, or dry wheat cereals may be added in place of whole wheat flour.

Garlic powder, soaked, dehydrated onion, or chopped cheese may be added for flavor.

These are excellent when eaten straight from the frying pan and covered with honey.

Blend the basic biscuit mix, flour, honey, and water into a sticky dough. Don't overmix or the batter will be lumpy. Fold in the berries, fruit, or nuts. Drop muffin-size pieces into the oil which has been heated in your frying pan.

Cover and bake over low heat, turning occasionally until the muffins are golden brown.

Muffins

(1 dozen muffins)

1 cup basic biscuit mix
¾ cup whole wheat flour
¼ cup honey
water (enough to make
   a sticky dough)
½ cup fresh berries, fruit or nuts
corn oil or peanut oil for frying

I suppose that pancakes are not technically "breads"—just as there is argument about pizza. However, whenever I think of camping, I think of pancakes and thus, have taken the author's liberty of including this recipe in Haven and Margaret's chapter.

Blend the biscuit mix, whole wheat flour, dry milk, powdered egg, and water to make a runny, pourable batter.

Heat oil and pour pancakes into frying pan. Fry uncovered over medium heat until the batter bubbles. Flip the pancakes and continue cooking until golden brown on both sides.

Fruit, nuts, berries, and cereals may be added for a real treat. Or—add potatoes or onions instead of flour for a different taste.

Pancakes

(1 dozen 4-inch pancakes)

1 cup basic biscuit mix
½ cup whole wheat flour
¼ cup nonfat dry milk
¼ cup powdered egg
water (enough to make
   a runny batter)
corn oil or peanut oil for frying

Variations

Pizza Crust

(1 pizza, 8 inches)

½ cup basic biscuit mix
½ cup unbleached white flour
water (enough to make
a moist dough)

Though a standard recipe for pizza is given in the chapter on George Meluso (see Index), this one is especially designed for outdoor cooking and, as a result, it's quite different. Imagine having pizza atop Mount McKinley!

Blend the biscuit mix, flour, and water until the dough is moist and workable, but not sticky. Pat out onto a lightly greased frying pan, toast lightly on one side. Flip dough and add tomato sauce or other toppings (cheese, onion, bacon bits, for example). Cover and bake over low heat until done.

Variation

For a cheesy crust, toast the first side of the pizza dough, then remove and place cheese slices in the pan, turn the crust onto the melting cheese and then add the topping. This method allows the cheese to bake into the crust and makes it extra crispy.

Flat Bread

(1½ dozen 5-inch breads)

1 cup unbleached white flour
½ cup cornmeal
pinch salt
water (enough to make
a moist dough)
corn oil or peanut oil for frying

Mix ingredients to make a moist, but not sticky dough. Press into thin patties (like *tortillas*). Heat a tablespoon of the oil in your frying pan and toast the patties until they are golden brown.

These are especially good if, just before removing them from the pan, you place a sliver of cheese on top and allow it to melt.

CATARINA STEFANOFF

I first met Catarina's grandson, Dennis, at a meeting of the National Institute of Cooperative Education in Bozeman, Montana—where I also had my first taste of buffalo meat (it tastes like pot roast). The Stefanoffs are fourth generation farmers from the Delta, Utah, area and, naturally, when I found out that Grandmother Catarina was a bread baker, the correspondence continued long after the meeting was over.

Though she is 76 years of age at this writing, she remains as active as the rest of the family—drives the pickup truck, gardens, sews, cooks, quilts. And she still makes the breads she learned to bake while still a child in Italy.

At the age of 8, I left home in Silvano D'Orba to work in the city of Genoa for the wealthy captain of a merchant ship. I cooked, washed dishes and baked for the family. They paid me two dollars a month.

She had to stand on a stool to reach the special bread-baking table:

. . . it was a special table that was used only for making bread and pasta dough and for nothing else . . . we were not allowed to use water on it. We had to scrape it with a knife and dry it with a cloth. . . .

The family came to the United States in 1919 and Catarina, then 17, went by train to Utah. She still remembers the trip and recalls how people stared at them when they carried their luggage on their heads, as everyone did in Italy.

Her breads are the ones that she baked as a child and she still uses the same recipes when she bakes for the frequent gatherings of the Stefanoff family. To Dennis, she is the best cook in the state of Utah (if not the world).

The Breads:

Common Bread
Fougassa **(Italian)**

Catarina tells a charming story about a friend of hers who was not allowed to eat any food with sweeteners, including bread, because of diabetes. In spite of it, he ate most of one loaf and she warned him that it might not be good for him:

He got up from the table, put a loaf of bread under each arm, walked to the door and said, "If I'm going to die, it's better to die with a stomach full of fresh-baked bread!"

Common Bread

(4 to 6 breads)

3 eggs
2 tablespoons butter
½ teaspoon salt*
3 pounds unbleached white flour
(approximately 9 cups)
2 packages dry yeast
3 cups warm water
butter

This bread uses a simple, basic dough, enriched by the addition of three eggs. The final shape can be free form, braided or rolled into the shape of a snail shell, as it is in parts of Italy.

In a bowl, combine the eggs, butter, salt, and flour. Gradually mix the dry yeast into the warm water, then add to the dough mix, stirring with a wooden spoon as you work it in slowly.

Turn the dough out onto a lightly floured surface and knead for 8 to 10 minutes or until the dough is smooth and elastic. Put in a greased bowl, turn to coat the top, cover and put in a warm spot for 1½ to 2 hours or until dough has doubled in bulk.

Punch down, turn out onto floured surface again and knead for 1 or 2 minutes. Return to greased bowl, cover and let rise again in a warm spot for 1 hour.

After second rise, turn out onto floured surface, punch down and divide the dough into as many breads as you wish to bake. Take 1 handful of the dough and roll it out to a length of approximately a foot. Then twist it into a braid or roll it into a snail-shell shape, curling it from the inside out. Place the breads on a greased cookie sheet and cover lightly. Place in a warm spot for about 1 hour.

Bake at 375°F. for 45 minutes to 1 hour, depending upon the size of the bread. It should be golden brown when done, and the bottoms should sound hollow when tapped.

After removing from the oven, grease the tops lightly with butter while the breads are still hot.

Cool on wire racks.

---

*The salt, though traditional, may be eliminated if you choose to do so.

This is a distinctive bread, a traditional Italian loaf that comes from Catarina's childhood. The finger holes in the top of the bread make it like no other that I know of. Note that the basic ingredients are very much the same as those used in the recipe for Common Bread. But then, most bread recipes are variations on a theme and it's your imagination that counts most.

In a bowl, combine the eggs, butter, salt, and flour. Mix the yeast with the warm water and then add to the flour mixture slowly, working it in continuously with a wooden spoon.

Turn dough out onto a lightly floured surface, knead for 8 to 10 minutes until smooth and elastic.

Take a baking pan that is at least 2 or 3 inches deep and approximately 12 × 15 inches in size. Coat the bottom with the olive oil.

Using floured hands and then a floured rolling pin, if you need it, work the dough down to a thickness of about 1 inch and just large enough to fit in the bottom of the pan. Place the dough into the pan, sprinkle the top with garlic powder.

At about 2-inch intervals, punch a finger hole into the dough about ½ inch deep. This will allow the cooking oil to stay on the dough while rising and baking.

Cover the top of the dough with olive oil or other cooking oil. Cover the pan and place in a warm spot to rise for about 45 minutes to 1 hour.

Bake at 375°F. until the top of the Fougassa is golden brown— about 45 to 50 minutes, or until a cake tester comes out clean.

To serve, cut into squares while still in pan or break off pieces as the bread is passed around the table.

Fougassa

(Italian)

(1 large loaf)

3 eggs
2 tablespoons butter
½ teaspoon salt*
3 pounds unbleached white flour
   (approximately 9 cups)
2 packages dry yeast
3 cups warm water
garlic powder
olive oil (or other cooking oil)

---

*The salt, though traditional, may be eliminated if you choose to do so.

ISABELLA GROBLEWSKI

The last letter I received from Isabella spoke of her return from the hospital to her home in Topsfield, Massachusetts. She's one of my favorite bread-story-tellers and this letter was no exception:

Some people aren't interested in bread. I wish I could confront the dietician of the hospital and ask her to explain hospital bread to me. All of the food was unappetizing, but the bread was the worst! It looked like bread but it quickly turned into Kleenex, no matter what spread I applied to it. English muffins, dinner rolls, toast—all looked their parts, but tasted and felt exactly the same. Whole wheat bread was never available. It was great to return to my house and find the bread I had made before my operation waiting in the freezer. I made a speedy recovery, but I can't help feeling that a longer stay in the hospital would have slowed down my progress!

Isabella is a potter and an artist and, in fact, she stores her flour in a jar that she made herself. The scoop was carved for her by a young wood-carver in exchange for some pots. Her kiln has been used for baking bread and, of course, as a potter she loves the feel of dough between her hands:

Art and bread are a way of life for me. I was caught up in both at an early age. Before The Depression, when we had a lot of help (my mother, in those days, knew little about cooking or rearing children), my sister and I would be bundled up and sent outdoors to play. There would be "nothing to do." Gray sky, sandbox full of tired toys—we would go around to the back door and Molly, our elegant Austrian cook, would give us each a piece of bread dough. We would shape and reshape them and the doughs would grow as gray as the sky and become very dry. We'd dampen them at the outside faucet and return our "breads" to Molly, who would bake them for us. Later, when

we tried to eat our "loaves," we were amazed to find them hard as stones.

A superb bread baker today, I thought Isabella might pass on some of her own tips:

- The more you bake bread, the easier it gets. Like riding a bicycle, you never forget how.

- You can knead a sticky dough right in the bowl in which it was mixed. However, it should always rise in a *greased* bowl.

- When mixing sticky dough, use only *one hand.* In that way, you have a clean, dry hand for scooping up more flour (or answering the telephone).

- Get good tools for bread making—a proper bowl, big measuring cups, wooden spoons, scoops, breadboard, etc., and take good care of them. (Isabella oils her breadboard once in a while with cooking oil, and it helps to keep the dough from sticking.)

Here are eight of Isabella's recipes—including a marvelous way to meet one of the bread baker's continuing problems: what to do with all that leftover bread.

Beaten Babka

(Polish)

(1 large loaf)

1 package dry yeast
5 tablespoons warm milk
1 teaspoon honey
7 tablespoons butter
2 egg yolks
1 whole egg
½ cup honey
½ cup milk
freshly grated peel of 1 lemon
1 teaspoon salt*
3½ to 4 cups unbleached
white flour
2½ tablespoons currants
or raisins (optional)

Our family is almost a League of Nations. My husband's forebears were all Poles. At Easter, Babka used to be served in every house. It is a wonderful yeast-raised bread, a little like French brioche. Most Babkas are frighteningly rich—one of my recipes calls for 20 eggs! Here is a beaten Babka that is better for us.

Mix yeast with 5 tablespoons of warm milk, add teaspoon of honey and set aside.

Cream butter, add the 2 egg yolks, the whole egg, and ½ cup of honey. Mix well and add ½ cup milk, grated peel of lemon, and salt. Then add the flour, 1 cup at a time. Beat with a wooden spoon until dough no longer sticks to spoon. Mix in the currants or raisins and place dough in a well-greased tube pan. Cover and let rise in a warm spot for about 1 hour.

When the dough has risen, bake in a 350°F. oven for about 45 minutes. Cool 15 minutes in the pan and then finish cooling on a rack.

---

*The salt, though traditional, may be eliminated if you choose to do so.

Here is another of those marvelous (and easy) recipes that does not detail the exact amount of an ingredient (in this case, the flour). It is typical of recipes that have been passed down through generations—but don't let it frighten you. The details are quite exact. Isabella writes:

Imagine a large summer house in the Adirondacks, bulging with cousins, aunts, uncles, grandparents, governesses, and servants. It has a large airy kitchen with a huge wood stove. Mrs. Beers, the blacksmith's wife, is chief cook and she bakes the best bread in the world. She is very stout and doughlike herself, and she is very kind to a small group of adoring children who love to watch her bake bread, and who are sometimes given pieces of dough to shape.

This is Mrs. Beers's bread and Isabella's sister, Anne Taylor, makes it. It takes most of the day, but it's worth it!

After scalded milk has cooled to lukewarm, add the honey, salt, butter, and the yeast mixed with the warm water and dissolved. Beat in only enough unbleached flour to make a mixture as thick as a pancake batter.

Cover and place in a warm spot to let rise to double in bulk (about 1 to 1½ hours). Beat it down with a wooden spoon and cover again to let it rise another hour.

Mix in enough unbleached flour to make a stiff dough, turn out onto a lightly floured surface and knead until smooth and elastic (about 8 to 10 minutes). Put in a greased bowl and cover. Let rise again (about 1 hour) and then turn out onto floured surface and knead until smooth (about 2 to 3 minutes).

This time, form into loaves or rolls, cover and let rise again for about 45 minutes. Bake about 45 minutes at 375°F. and then lower heat to 350°F. and bake until loaves are properly browned and the bottoms sound hollow when tapped.

Cool on wire racks.

NOTE: Isabella tells us that some whole wheat flour may be substituted for the white to make a brown bread. In that case, add a little more butter and honey to the sponge.

*The salt, though traditional, may be eliminated if you choose to do so.

Beautiful Bread

(3 loaves or many rolls)

1 pint milk (2 cups), scalded and
  cooled to lukewarm
1 teaspoon honey
½ teaspoon salt*
1 tablespoon butter
1 package dry yeast
½ cup warm water
unbleached white flour to follow
  directions below

Isabella's son-in-law is a native of India and she sends this recipe along from Jeet. I find that I can get *chapati* flour in the Indian food stores in New York; however, any fine whole wheat flour will serve as well.

Chapati

(Indian)

(8 breads)

1 cup whole wheat pastry flour
½ cup warm water
2 tablespoons yogurt
(or 1 tablespoon oil)

Place the whole wheat flour in a bowl. Add the warm water slowly and then stir in the yogurt (or oil). The quantities of flour and water may have to be adjusted—the dough should be soft but not sticky. Knead approximately 10 minutes on a lightly floured surface until the dough is smooth and elastic. Roll it into a ball, coat it lightly with oil and wrap it in plastic. Let the dough rest 12 to 24 hours.

Grease a cast-iron griddle or skillet and place over medium heat. Divide the dough into 8 round balls. Dip each one in flour. Roll out on a floured surface—the dough must not stick. The rounds should be 5 to 8 inches in diameter. Turn the rolled *chapati* one at a time onto the heated griddle. Within 1 minute, or when light brown spots appear, turn it over.

As the *chapati* cooks, spin it lightly with your hand. Press down on it carefully, protecting your hand with a pot holder or towel. The *chapati* will puff up, separating into layers. It should be completely cooked in a couple of minutes. Bits of *chapati* are torn off and used as scoops for the main dish and its accompaniments.

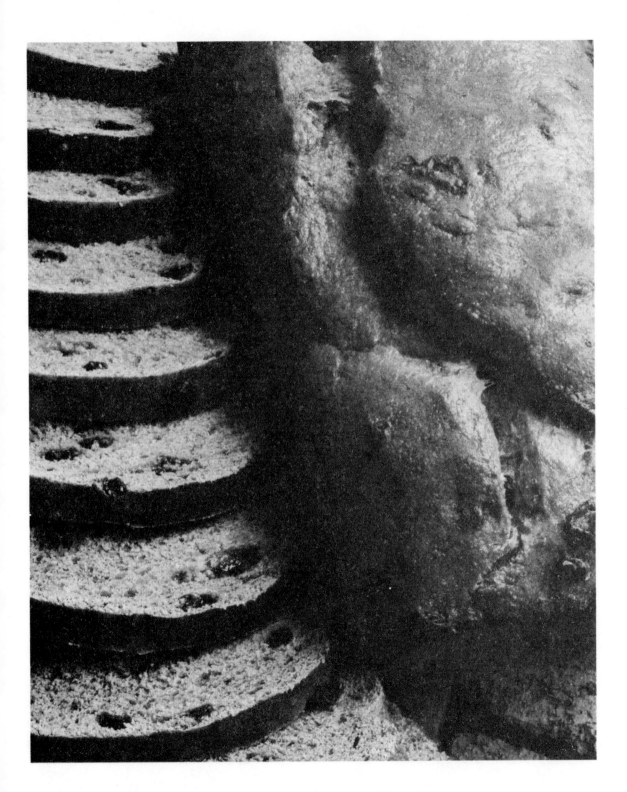

Cinnamon Raisin Bread (Vivian Hutchins) page 278   *237*

Isabella found this recipe in her grandmother's notebook. Those of us who bake often are constantly looking for new ways to use the leftovers. As Isabella writes, "After all, who wants to waste good bread!"

Scald the milk and pour it over the bread crumbs. Let stand until soft. Beat the 2 egg yolks mixed with the honey and add to the batter. Add the cinnamon and stir. Butter a 7-inch cake pan or a loaf pan and put the batter in to bake at 350°F. for 45 minutes. Cover the top with jam or jelly.

Beat the egg whites until they are stiff but not dry. Put the beaten egg whites on top of the loaf and return to the oven for only a few minutes, until the top browns.

This one brings back memories for Isabella:

The year four of us, 21-year-old school friends, won the battle with our parents and had an apartment in Cambridge, everyone was worried we wouldn't eat properly. The mother of one of our friends made this delicious bread for us. . . .

Pour boiling water over rolled oats. Add molasses, butter, and salt and mix well. Let stand for 1 hour.

Soften the yeast in the lukewarm water and add to the oats mixture. Gradually add the flour, 1 cup at a time, mixing it well with a wooden spoon.

Cover the bowl, let the dough rise in a warm spot until doubled in bulk (about 45 minutes to 1 hour). Turn out onto a floured surface, knead for 1 to 2 minutes. Divide into 2 pieces and place in medium-size, greased loaf pans. Cover and let rise until nearly doubled (about 45 minutes) and bake at 350°F. for 45 to 60 minutes or until breads test done. Turn out onto wire racks to cool.

Bread Pudding

(1 loaf)

1 pint (2 cups) milk, scalded
1 cup bread crumbs
2 eggs, separated
2 tablespoons honey
½ teaspoon cinnamon
your favorite jam or jelly

Oatmeal Bread

(2 loaves)

2 cups boiling water
1 cup uncooked rolled oats
½ cup molasses
1 tablespoon butter
2 teaspoons salt (optional)
1 package dry yeast
½ cup lukewarm water
5 cups whole wheat flour

Refrigerator Bread

(2 loaves)

5½ to 6½ cups whole wheat flour
2 packages dry yeast
1 tablespoon salt (optional)
2 tablespoons wheat germ
¼ cup soy flour
¼ cup honey
3 tablespoons softened butter
1 tablespoon freshly grated
lemon peel
2¼ cups hot water
oil

This is the bread that Isabella bakes in her kiln, but she quickly points out that the home oven is just as good. If you like, you may replace the honey with molasses.

Mix 2 cups whole wheat flour, yeast, and salt in a large bowl. Add the wheat germ and soy flour, then the honey, butter, lemon peel, and the hot water and mix well. If you like, you may also use an electric mixer for this first part of the recipe. Add 1 more cup flour and mix, then stir in another cup. Add enough of the remaining flour (about 1½ to 2½ cups) to make a soft dough. The dough should leave the sides of the bowl when the texture is correct.

Turn out onto a lightly floured surface and knead about 8 to 10 minutes until smooth and elastic. Let dough rest for 20 minutes. Punch down, shape into 2 loaves and put into greased medium-size (4 × 8-inch) loaf pans. Brush the tops of the loaves with oil.

Cover the pans loosely with wax paper or plastic wrap and then a towel and place them in the refrigerator for at least 4 hours, but for not more than 8 hours. This gives the best texture to the breads.

When ready to bake, remove the pans, uncover, and let stand while preheating the oven to 400°F. Bake for 30 minutes, or until done.

Turn out onto racks to cool.

NOTE: If it is more convenient for you, Isabella suggests that you can eliminate the refrigeration and just treat the bread as any other, letting it rise to double in a warm spot in the house, punching down and shaping before putting it into pans.

This is a most unusual bread, and another example of just how all kinds of leftover ingredients may be used in bread baking. The vegetable-fruit slurry gives this bread an appealing texture. Though Isabella uses pumpkin, carrots, and applesauce in her recipe, she suggests that almost any kind of fruit or vegetable might be used.

Warm in saucepan the pumpkin or squash, carrots, applesauce, plus enough water to make 3 cups. NOTE: Measurements are approximate and can be varied according to your own choice. Add the butter, honey or molasses, and the salt. Cook for a few minutes until every ingredient is blended and then remove from stove and cool to lukewarm.

To this mixture, add the yeast dissolved in the ¼ cup of warm water. Pour this slurry into a large bowl and add the wheat germ and the soy flour. Mix well. Add the whole wheat flour, 1 cup at a time, until the mixture is firm enough to be kneaded.

Turn out onto a lightly floured surface and knead for 8 to 10 minutes or until dough is smooth and elastic. If necessary, add more flour if dough becomes too sticky. Place in an oiled bowl, turn once to coat the dough and cover. Place in a warm spot to let the dough double in size (about 1 hour).

When doubled, turn out onto floured surface, punch down, and shape into 3 loaves. Butter a cookie sheet if you want free-form loaves—or 3 small loaf pans. Place the dough on the cookie sheet or in the loaf pans, cover lightly and let rise in a warm spot until almost double in size (about 45 minutes).

Bake at 375°F. for 35 to 40 minutes or until breads test done. Turn out onto wire racks to cool.

Slurry Bread

(3 loaves)

1 cup cooked pumpkin
    or squash, mashed
1 cup cooked carrots, mashed
½ cup applesauce
warm water
2 tablespoons butter
2 tablespoons honey or molasses
1 scant tablespoon salt (optional)
2 packages dry yeast
¼ cup warm water
5½ cups whole wheat flour
½ cup wheat germ
½ cup soy flour

Swiss Lemon Twist

(1 large or 2 small twists)

¾ cup milk, scalded
½ cup butter
⅓ cup honey
½ teaspoon salt (optional)
1 package dry yeast
½ cup warm water
2 eggs, beaten
juice and peel of ½ lemon
4½ cups whole wheat flour

Isabella's Swiss daughter-in-law says that she's tasted breads similar to this in her native country. However, Isabella has been making these Swiss Lemon Twists for many years, generally giving them for gifts at Christmas.

Scald the milk, stir in the butter, honey, and salt. Let cool to lukewarm. Soften the yeast in warm water. Add yeast mixture to milk mixture with the 2 eggs, well beaten. (Reserve a little bit of the egg to brush on bread as a glaze later on.) Add the grated peel and the juice of the half lemon. Mix well and add the flour, 1 cup at a time. Mix well, then turn out onto a floured surface and knead until smooth and elastic (about 8 to 10 minutes). Put in greased bowl, turning once to coat the top.

Cover and place in warm spot to let rise to double (about 1 hour). Turn out onto floured surface, punch down and knead for 1 to 2 minutes, then shape as in the photographs. Pay particular attention to putting butter on the underside of each flap. Place on buttered cookie sheet. Glaze with egg and let rise again, covered, until almost double in bulk (about 45 minutes).

Bake in a 325°F. oven for 10 minutes and then turn temperature up to 350°F. and bake for 30 to 35 minutes longer.

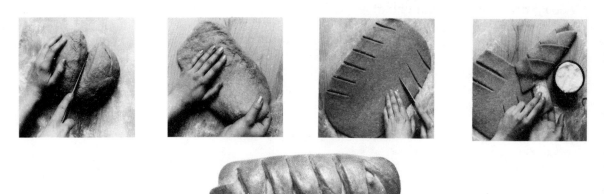

HOWARD AND
AGNES ARNS

The Breads:

100% Whole Wheat Bread
Whole Wheat Potato Bread
Whole Wheat Muffins
Whole Wheat Rolls
Johnny Cake
Banana Quick Bread
Zucchini Whole Wheat Bread

Typical of many Mormon families, Howard and Agnes Arns of Cedar City, Utah, keep a large supply of whole wheat grain on hand and then grind it as they need it for baking.

We feel very secure because we try to keep a two-year supply of wheat on hand. We fumigate it with dry ice. We also buy our honey in 60-pound cans. . . .

Though most of us buy and store in much smaller quantities, the basic reasons for baking homemade bread are very much the same for all of us and the Arns's are no exception. Aside from being aware of the nutritional value of home-baked products, Agnes also has vivid and fond memories of her childhood.

My great-grandparents crossed the plains and were among the first pioneers to settle in Utah. I grew up surrounded by the aroma of bread baking and the treat of hot bread and honey.

In 1970 the Arns's accepted an assignment to serve as missionaries for the Church of Jesus Christ of Latter Day Saints and they were sent to Australia. While there, they taught many women how to bake bread in their own kitchens, though yeast was not available in the stores and had to be purchased directly from the local baker.

Some of the recipes are the Arns's own; others have been adapted to their own tastes. All of them call for whole wheat flour as a base.

If you grind your own flour, select good clean wheat. The protein content should be at least 14 percent and the moisture content 9 percent or below. We use the hard winter wheat for all of our baking.

Howard and Agnes also recommend the use of shiny aluminum or stainless steel pans for baking, since the use of honey or molasses makes the bread more apt to burn at higher temperatures. Dark metal pans and glass baking dishes have a tendency to maintain a much hotter temperature.

NOTE: All recipes are given for electric bread mixer. If you are kneading by hand, merely follow standard instructions for mixing and kneading.

When they make this bread, the Arns's find that they can grind the flour, mix the dough, let it rise and have it baked in under two hours.

Dissolve honey in warm water. Sprinkle yeast on top. Do not stir. Set aside.

In mixer bowl, combine 7 cups of the flour with the salt, water, honey, and oil. Blend in mixer on low speed until thoroughly mixed. Add yeast mxiture.

Add the remaining 5 to 6 cups of flour 1 cup at a time until the dough is the consistency of cookie dough. Knead for 10 minutes on low speed.

Oil hands and mold dough into 4 loaves. (Lightly oil the counter top so dough doesn't stick.) Put into 4 large bread pans that have been greased with a solid shortening. Cover and let rise in warm place until the dough has increased by one-third in bulk. (Agnes tells me that by using the mixer, she only needs to increase the bulk by one-third instead of the usual doubling when kneading by hand.)

Preheat oven to 350°F.

When dough has increased its size by one-third, bake for 40 to 45 minutes or until loaves test done. If you live at an altitude of over 4,000 feet, as many of the Arns's friends do in Utah, bake the breads for 8 minutes at 425°F., then lower temperature to 350°F. and continue baking for 35 to 40 minutes longer.

Remove from pans and cool on wire racks.

100% Whole Wheat Bread

(4 large loaves)

1 tablespoon honey
½ cup warm water
2 packages dry yeast
12 to 13 cups whole wheat flour
2 tablespoons salt (optional)
5 cups hot water
½ cup honey
⅔ cup oil

Whole Wheat Potato Bread

(4 large loaves)

1 tablespoon honey
½ cup warm water
2 packages dry yeast
5½ cups hot water
⅔ cup oil
½ cup honey
2½ tablespoons salt (optional)
2 eggs, beaten
1 medium potato, boiled and mashed
⅔ cup nonfat dry milk
13 to 14 cups whole wheat flour, or more as needed

Dissolve honey in water. Sprinkle on dry yeast. Do not stir. Set aside.

Combine in mixer bowl, water, oil, honey, salt, eggs, mashed potato, dry milk, and 7 cups of flour (1 cup at a time). Blend thoroughly on low speed of mixer.

Add yeast mixture and blend.

One cup at a time, add 6 to 7 more cups of the flour until mixture is the consistency of cookie dough. Knead on low speed for 10 minutes.

Oil hands and turn dough out onto a lightly oiled counter. Divide dough into 4 portions, form them into loaf shapes and place in loaf tins that have been greased with solid shortening. Cover and let rise in a warm place until the dough is one-third larger in bulk.

Preheat oven to 400°F.

When dough has risen, bake in 400°F. oven for 15 minutes, then lower temperature to 350°F. for 30 minutes longer. When breads test done, remove from pans and cool on wire racks.

Whole Wheat Muffins

(12 large muffins)

2 eggs, beaten
⅓ cup yogurt
⅔ cup warm milk
⅓ cup honey
⅓ cup oil
2 cups whole wheat flour
¾ teaspoon salt (optional)
1 teaspoon baking soda

These are marvelous as breakfast muffins. If you like, you may add raisins to the dough or you may add chopped nuts for crunch.

In a mixing bowl, combine eggs, yogurt, and milk. Beat thoroughly with a wooden spoon, then add the honey and oil. Add the dry ingredients and blend thoroughly.

Pour into greased muffin tins. Bake at 425°F. for 15 minutes.

Dissolve honey in warm water. Sprinkle on dry yeast. Do not stir. Set aside.

In mixing bowl, combine milk, oil, honey, salt, and eggs. Add 5 cups of the whole wheat flour and knead on low speed until blended. Add the yeast mixture and blend again on low speed.

Add the remaining 4 cups of whole wheat flour and knead on low speed for 10 minutes. Place dough in a large, oiled bowl, turn once to coat the top, cover and let rise in a warm place until doubled in bulk.

When dough has doubled in size, turn out onto a lightly oiled counter. With a rolling pin, roll out dough to a thickness of about ½ inch.

Using a round cookie cutter or a thin wine glass, cut the dough into as many circles as the size will allow. When the maximum number of circles has been made, roll the dough again into a ½-inch thickness and cut it again with the cookie cutter. As noted in the beginning, the number of rolls will depend upon the size of the cookie cutter or glass that you're using. The rolls can be small or large, as you wish.

Brush each circle with melted butter, fold over once and place on a greased baking sheet. Cover lightly with wax paper and let rise to double in a warm spot in the kitchen.

Bake at 375°F. for 20 minutes. Serve warm.

One of the mainstay foods of the early Mormon pioneers was a corn bread called Johnny Cake (which evolved from the original description of the bread, Journey Cake). Agnes and Howard grind their own cornmeal as well as the whole wheat flour.

In a mixing bowl beat eggs, add buttermilk, honey, and oil. Combine dry ingredients and mix with liquid mixture. Pour into a well greased 9 × 9-inch baking pan.

Bake at 400°F. for 20 minutes.

Serve hot.

Whole Wheat Rolls

(yield will depend upon size of cookie cutter used; rolls can be made small or large)

1 tablespoon honey
½ cup warm water
2 packages dry yeast
4 cups warm milk
½ cup oil
⅔ cup honey
2 tablespoons salt (optional)
2 eggs, beaten
9 cups whole wheat flour
3 tablespoons melted butter

Johnny Cake

(1 to 1½ dozen squares)

2 eggs, beaten
1 cup buttermilk, room
    temperature
2 tablespoons honey
3 tablespoons oil
1 cup cornmeal
1 cup whole wheat flour
½ teaspoon salt (optional)
1 teaspoon baking soda
1 teaspoon baking powder

Banana Quick Bread

(2 large loaves)

1½ cups mashed bananas
½ cup yogurt
¾ cup softened butter
1 teaspoon pure vanilla extract
3 eggs, beaten
½ cup honey
3 cups whole wheat flour
2 teaspoons baking soda
½ teaspoon salt (optional)
1 cup chopped nuts (optional)

If you prefer, Agnes and Howard suggest that you can substitute applesauce for the mashed bananas in this recipe.

In a mixing bowl, combine mashed bananas, yogurt, butter, vanilla, eggs, and honey. Beat until smooth. Add the dry ingredients and blend thoroughly on low speed of mixer (or with wooden spoon). Stir in nuts, if desired.

Divide dough into 2 equal portions and place in 2 large well-greased loaf pans.

Bake at 350°F. for 20 minutes, then lower oven temperature to 300°F. and bake for 25 minutes longer or until breads test done.

Turn out and cool on wire racks.

Zucchini Whole Wheat Bread

(2 medium loaves)

3 cups whole wheat flour
1 cup honey
1 teaspoon salt (optional)
1 teaspoon cinnamon
1 teaspoon baking soda
½ teaspoon baking powder
2 eggs, beaten
1 cup oil
2 teaspoons pure vanilla extract
2 cups raw zucchini, unpeeled and shredded
nuts and raisins (optional)

This is a quick bread that helps utilize some of the surplus garden crop of zucchini.

Combine the whole wheat flour, honey, salt, and cinnamon in the mixing bowl. Add baking soda, baking powder, eggs, oil, vanilla, and zucchini. Blend all the ingredients thoroughly with the mixer. If you're using a wooden spoon, finish the job by using your hands to mix the dough while it's still in the bowl.

Add the nuts and raisins and blend well again.

Pour into 2 greased and floured medium-size loaf pans. Bake at 350°F. for 1 hour or until breads test done.

Turn out onto wire racks to cool.

JULIANA JAMES

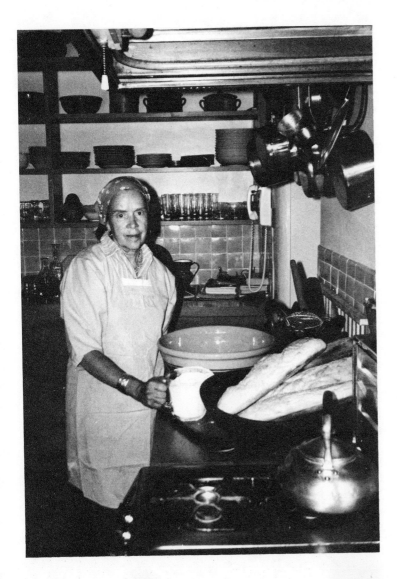

The Bread:

Multi-Grain French Bread

When I hear some of my students express their fears as they approach their first bread-baking attempt, I try to console them, give them a simple no-fail recipe and tell them that "even a child can do it." Of course there are failures—and my own breads have been no exception, but Juliana James of Santa Fe, New Mexico, strongly agrees that fearless children can also bake bread:

> When I was nine years old, my parents' best friends gave me a miniature set of Pyrex baking dishes for Christmas. My first venture in baking bread was so successful that I remember thinking it miraculous!

She still bakes her own bread, though she is now a full-time housewife, mother, new grandmother, part-time organic gardener, and occasional artist.

Since I live in a damp climate, I keep forgetting that some of us live in weather conditions that are quite the opposite. Santa Fe, for example—like most of New Mexico—is quite dry and Juliana suggests that bakers who live in areas such as this make certain they cover their rising dough with a damp cloth to keep the batter from drying out. She also likes to keep a mixing bowl filled with hot water while she kneads, so that the bowl will be warm when she returns the dough to it for rising.

Multi-Grain French Bread

(4 loaves)

2 packages dry yeast
⅔ cup tepid water
6 cups whole wheat flour
1 cup multi-grain flour
4½ teaspoons salt (optional)
2½ cups tepid water
white cornmeal

This is a variation of the standard French loaves, and Juliana uses multi-grain flour for an added taste. Multi-grains are sometimes premixed in natural foods stores or you can mix it yourself with a combination of wheat germ, triticale, rye or any combination of healthful whole grains.

Stir yeast into the ⅔ cup water and let it stand to dissolve.

In a large bowl, measure the flours, add the salt to the flour and then pour in the yeast mixture. Add the rest of the water, stirring with a wooden spoon as you do so.

Stir thoroughly, and then scrape the dough out onto a lightly floured surface and knead for about 10 minutes, until the dough is smooth and springy. Knead in more flour if you need it, since the dough might be quite sticky at first and a scraper will prove useful.

While the dough is being kneaded, leave the bowl full of hot water. When finished kneading, empty and wipe out the bowl and dry it. Lightly oil the bowl and return the dough to it, turning once to coat the top. Cover bowl with a damp towel and let the dough rise in a warm place until doubled in bulk (about 1 hour).

Scrape down the sides of the bowl with a rubber spatula, working it around the bowl twice and leave the dough, covered, to rise for a second time. This will take less time than the first rise—about 35 to 45 minutes.

Turn out onto the lightly floured surface, knead a little (about 1 or 2 minutes) and pinch out the bubbles. Cut the dough into 4 equal portions and roll each one between your hands, pulling it at the same time, until you have a long loaf.

Place the loaves on 2 lightly greased cookie sheets which have been sprinkled with white cornmeal, or use the specially shaped French bread pans, also sprinkled with cornmeal after a light greasing. Cover and let rise a third time—this should take only about 20 minutes.

Preheat the oven to 450°F.

With a sharp knife or old-fashioned straight razor, cut 3 diagonal slashes in the top of each loaf. Spray the loaves with water. (Juliana uses a small brass sprayer sold for spraying plants. I use a simple plastic plant sprayer.)

Place the loaves in the preheated oven and after about 5 minutes, spray again. Bake 25 minutes in all, spraying 6 or 7 times while baking. The loaves should be a light golden tan when done. Remove loaves from oven and pans and put on rack for cooling.

The bread freezes well when wrapped in plastic wrap or aluminum foil and it tastes best when warmed in a hot oven just before serving.

SUZANNE GOSAR

Suzanne and her family began growing wheat a decade ago on their ranch in Monte Vista, Colorado. Originally they sold it to the commercial mills, then:

> . . . we decided that the milling industry is ignoring a huge group of folks who don't want their kids to eat that "white junk" anymore and who are willing to make their own bread. . . .

So, the Gosar Ranch began grinding its own whole grain wheat, guaranteeing that the flour contained all the bran, wheat germ, and oils that nature had put there in the first place. Their brand, Mountain Mama Milling, has grown so rapidly that Suzanne has left her job as director of the Rio Grande Art Center to devote full time to the family business.

> I always used a hand grinder until this past spring when we acquired a beautiful old stone mill. We feel that ours is a pure endeavor—to grow, grind and deliver a healthful product to the consumer.

> A few years ago we built a sort of "Gringo" version of the traditional Spanish-Indian ovens of New Mexico. It's outside and made of a combination of cement and adobe—the baking floor is brick. You burn a fire in the oven for several hours, then remove all the wood, coal, and ashes, swab the bricks with a wet mop and put the bread inside directly on the bricks, seal the oven and later remove the loaves, perfectly baked, with a fabulous crust. We use ours for baking the Bolillos. We built the oven in 1975 during the first energy warnings—we wanted to eliminate as much as possible our dependency on fossil fuels and assure self-sufficiency. . . .

The Breads:

Bolillos (Mexican)
Mountain Mama's
 Whole Wheat Bread
Aunt Chana's
 Whole Wheat Pancakes

I find that as I correspond with my bread-baking friends and as I speak with them on the telephone, the stories in the files grow, the tips could make a book in themselves.

I smile warmly at the tales of Mormon grandparents who settled the West, of independent people who have found their own way of life, and I am in awe at the diversity that exists throughout the country. Suzanne writes of her grandmother:

> . . . she made sure that before she moved to greener pastures, she supplied each of her children with a hand grinder, and a year's supply of wheat berries, honey, salt, and powdered milk. The grinder she gave to my mother was the one I used until we installed the stone mill. There is an unexpected by-product from all of this hand grinding—I've developed an enviable pair of biceps!

Many of the great recipes used by Suzanne's grandparents and her other relatives were never written down, something I have found in my own family. Determined that this would not happen to her own children, Suzanne keeps a large file of the breads she bakes. Here are two of them plus a recipe for pancakes that I could not pass up.

These are the rolls that are famous in Mexico for their great crust.

In a pan, combine the water, honey, salt, and butter. Warm over low heat, stirring, to a temperature of between 105° and 115°F. Pour into a large bowl; stir in yeast until dissolved. With an electric mixer or (preferably) a heavy spoon, beat in 5 cups of flour to form a dough.

Turn the dough out onto a floured surface and knead in at least another ½ cup of the remaining flour (adding more if necessary) until the dough is smooth and velvety. Kneading time should be about 10 minutes.

Place the dough in a greased bowl, turn once to coat the top, cover and let rise in a warm place until almost doubled (about 1½ hours).

Punch down and squeeze down to release the air bubbles, then turn out onto a lightly floured board. Shape into a 16-inch roll, and divide into 16 equal pieces. Form each piece into a small ball by gently kneading. Shape each ball into an oblong by rolling it and gently pulling from the center to the ends until it is about 4 inches long (the center should be thicker than the ends). Place the rolls on greased baking sheets—you'll need 3 sheets approximately 12 × 15 inches in size.

Cover the rolls lightly and let rise in a warm spot for about 30 to 35 minutes.

In a pan, heat the cornstarch and water to boiling. Cool slightly. Brush each roll with the cornstarch mixture, then use a sharp knife or razor blade to cut a slash ¾ inch deep and about 2 inches long on the top of each roll.

Bake at 375°F. for 35 to 40 minutes or until they are golden brown and sound hollow when tapped.

Serve warm with butter.

NOTE: These rolls can be made using only whole wheat flour— about 5½ cups. The result is excellent.

Bolillos

(Mexican)

(16 rolls)

2 cups water
1½ teaspoons honey
1 tablespoon salt*
2 tablespoons butter
1 package dry yeast
3 cups unbleached white flour
3 cups stone-ground
   whole wheat flour

Glaze:

1 teaspoon cornstarch dissolved in
   ½ cup water

---

*The salt, though traditional, may be eliminated if you choose to do so.

Mountain Mama's Whole Wheat Bread

(4 loaves)

The Sponge:

6 cups lukewarm water
(85° to 105°F.)
2 packages dry yeast
½ cup honey or molasses
2 cups nonfat dry milk
6 to 8 cups whole wheat flour

The Dough:

2½ tablespoons salt (optional)
½ cup oil
8 to 11 cups whole wheat flour

The Glaze:

1 egg, beaten
¼ cup milk
sesame or poppy seeds

Suzanne is another bread baker who never washes her bread pans: ". . . the older and darker they get, the prettier the color of the bread will be. . . ."

She also suggests coating the bread with an egg wash before baking and then slashing the top in a variety of designs. That way the bread will come out of the oven with two shades of brown on top to emphasize the design.

Measure the water in a large bowl, sprinkle the yeast over the top and stir to dissolve. Add the sweetening and milk. Now, add the first quantity of whole wheat flour, 1 cup at a time, stirring briskly after each addition. The mixture will be quite thick, but still beatable, like thick mud. Now beat about 100 times until the batter is very smooth. Cover the bowl with a damp towel, set in a warm place, and let rise for an hour.

(As an intermission, I must tell the story about Suzanne's friend who, when the weather is bad, closes the curtains so the bread won't know the sun isn't shining while it rises. Suzanne says she doesn't go quite that far; she only recommends keeping the dough out of drafts.)

After the dough has risen, fold in the salt and the oil and then add the remaining flour a little at a time. The dough will become very thick and heavy, but don't be intimidated. Turn it out onto a floured board and begin kneading. It should be kneaded for 15 to 20 minutes—the longer the better. When it's nice and smooth and you're too exhausted to continue, oil a bowl and place the dough in it, turning once to coat the top. Cover with a damp cloth and set in a cozy place to rise. Let rise for an hour and then punch down 25 or 30 times, pushing your fist firmly and steadily into the dough. Cover and let rise again for about 40 minutes.

Knead the dough briefly and cut into 4 even pieces. Let them sit for 5 minutes. Shape into loaves, either for bread pans or in free-form shapes.

Place each in well-oiled loaf pans or on well-oiled baking sheets, allowing enough room between loaves for expansion.

Cut the tops with slits ½ inch deep in any design you choose and then brush the surface of the loaves with a wash made of a beaten egg and ¼ cup milk. Sprinkle with sesame or poppy seeds. Let rise for 20 minutes and bake at 350°F. for 50 to 70 minutes.

Remove from pans immediately after baking and place on wire racks to cool.

I could not resist! Again that inner voice says, "But pancakes are not breads!" How true—but using an author's prerogative, I just had to include Suzanne's recipe that originated with her Aunt Chana, a Mormon pioneer who lived in Salem, Utah, until she died at the age of 86. "Aunt Chana always said her pancakes would double as Frisbees, but once you've tried them, I guarantee they'll get your day off to a pleasant, nutritious start."

Here, then, in a book devoted to bread, is another pancake recipe. Purists may skip this page and move on to the next recipe.

Sift flour with baking powder and salt. In a separate bowl, beat the egg yolks, then beat into them the honey, milk, and oil. Beat the egg whites until stiff.

Combine the yolk mixture with the flour mixture until just blended. Add the nuts or seeds and then fold in the stiffly beaten egg whites.

Cook on a very hot, greased, griddle or frying pan.

Aunt Chana's Whole Wheat Pancakes

(4 to 6 pancakes)

2 cups whole wheat flour
3 teaspoons baking powder
1 teaspoon salt (optional)
3 eggs, separated
1 tablespoon honey
2 cups milk
½ cup oil
nuts, sesame or sunflower seeds
   (optional)

ELIZABETH VALASSIS

The first bread-baking experience for each of us has been a challenge, a curiosity, a yearning for the aromas that we read about, the yeasty smell throughout the house. For Elizabeth Valassis, there was one additional ingredient:

Of course I was curious and besides, I don't like store-bought bread. But, in addition, I had invested in an electric mixer with a dough hook attachment and my husband said I'd never use it. . . .

Now she loves her mixer and its dough hook attachment and in her Northville, Michigan, home a vast array of breads and rolls comes out of the oven. Elizabeth is a territory manager for a cosmetics company and, as a result of spending most of her day calling on department stores all over the state, she bakes mostly in the evenings and recommends that: "Everyone should try going to sleep with the just-baked aroma of bread lingering in the house. It's fantastic!"

Considering her expertise now, and the superb tips she passes on to beginning bread bakers (below), her first experience is all the more amusing:

All I can remember is how great the crust was and how terrible the crumb (inside) was—doughy and sticky. I just cut the crust off and sat there and ate it—and I threw the inside away.

My bread correspondence with Elizabeth has been large, and one envelope brought not only her recipes but some sage advice for the baker:

• I find that using nonfat dry milk in recipes simplifies making the dough, since the dry milk can be dissolved right in the yeast-water mixture. If the recipe calls for whole milk, one-third cup of nonfat dry milk and 1 cup water equals one cup milk. (If you use evaporated milk, one-half cup evaporated milk and one-half cup water equals one cup whole milk.)

• If a recipe calls for sugar, not only can you substitute honey or molasses, but malt powder may also be used.

• I stir whole grain flours before using in order to get a more accurate measurement. Don't bother to sift white flours in breads that are to be kneaded.

• I know that the dough is ready to knead by sprinkling a tablespoon or two of flour around the edges of the bowl and over the top of the dough. Then I stir the dough up and over to coat the underside. This "unsticks" the dough from the bowl. Next, I try to scoop up and lift all the dough in the bowl with a wooden spoon. If it holds together for a second or two before dropping back, it's ready for kneading.

• A dough that is to be rolled out with a rolling pin should be a bit stiffer than normal bread dough. I just add a bit more flour.

• I usually let dinner rolls rise once in the bowl and once on the baking sheet while I let breads rise twice in the bowl and one time in the pan to enhance the texture.

• I use shiny pans for light crusts, dark pans for dark crusts. My whole grain breads usually do better when baked in the smaller (8 × 4-inch) pans.

Dinner Rolls

(amount depends upon size of rolls)

1 package dry yeast
2 cups warm water
⅓ cup nonfat dry milk
(or 1 cup warm water
+ 1 cup fresh milk
or 1½ cups warm water
+ ½ cup evaporated milk)
2 tablespoons honey or 1
teaspoon malt
2 teaspoons salt (optional)
5½ to 6 cups whole wheat flour
pinch baking soda (only use if
dough is to be refrigerated)
1 egg
¼ cup softened butter

In electric mixer bowl, dissolve yeast in warm water (105° to 115°F.). Add milk, honey or malt, salt, and about half the flour mixed with the baking soda. Beat until mixed. Then add the egg and the butter; beat 2 minutes scraping bowl occasionally. Using a wooden spoon, gradually beat in enough of the remaining flour to make a soft dough.

Turn out onto a lightly floured surface and knead for 4 to 5 minutes. Place in a greased bowl, turning once to coat the entire surface. Cover tightly with plastic wrap and let rise in a warm place until doubled (about 45 minutes to 1 hour).

Turn out onto floured surface, punch down and knead for a minute or two. Shape the rolls as desired (you can make round shapes, twist them, braid them—use your imagination!), place them on a greased baking sheet, and cover with a clean cloth. Let rise in a warm spot until doubled in size (about 1 hour).

Bake the rolls at 375°F. for about 15 minutes.

To Use as a Refrigerator Dough

After kneading, cover tightly with plastic wrap and place in refrigerator until dough has doubled in size. Punch down and keep it in the refrigerator, using as desired. Every time the dough doubles in size, punch it down again. About 2 hours before baking, cut off pieces for rolls, shape, cover on a greased cookie sheet and let rise in a warm place.

Dinner Roll Variations

To the basic recipe, you can add one or more of the following in place of an equal amount of whole wheat flour: 1 cup rye flour, ½ cup soy flour, ¼ cup cracked wheat flour, wheat germ, or bran.

For Brown and Serve Rolls

Bake rolls at 275°F. for 20 to 25 minutes (until baked through but not browned). Store in refrigerator or freezer. To serve, brown at 400°F. or until color changes—about 10 minutes.

Dissolve yeast in water in a large mixing bowl; add dry milk and dissolve. Add the honey, the first amount of whole wheat flour (3 cups)—stirred before measuring—potatoes, and salt. Add the softened butter and enough flour to make a thick batter (about 1½ cups). Beat for 2 minutes with an electric mixer at medium-high speed. With a wooden spoon, mix in enough flour, a little at a time, to make a soft dough. Turn out onto a lightly floured surface and knead for 8 to 10 minutes.

Place dough in a lightly greased bowl, turning dough once to grease top. Cover and let rise in a warm place until doubled in size (about 1 hour). Punch down, turn out onto the floured surface and knead for 1 to 2 minutes. (For a second rise, dough may be returned to greased bowl, covered and then doubled once again.)

Divide dough into 3 parts, cover and let rest for 5 minutes. Shape into 3 loaves and place in greased, 9 × 5-inch loaf pans, cover and let rest until doubled (about 1 hour).

Bake in 375°F. oven for 40 minutes or until breads test done. Remove from pans and cool on wire racks.

Honey Whole Wheat Bread

(3 loaves)

2 packages dry yeast
4 cups warm water
½ cup nonfat dry milk
¼ cup honey
3 cups whole wheat flour
1 cup mashed potatoes
1 tablespoon salt (optional)
6 tablespoons softened butter
7 to 8 cups whole wheat flour

In the large bowl of the mixer, combine yeast, honey or malt, salt, sage, basil, nutmeg, and 1 cup of the flour. In a saucepan, heat the milk and butter to very warm—the butter does not need to melt. Gradually pour the warm liquid over the flour mixture and beat for 2 minutes at medium speed. Add the egg and enough flour to make a moderately soft dough.

Turn out onto a lightly floured surface and knead for 6 to 8 minutes. Place dough in a lightly greased bowl, turn once to coat all sides, cover and let rise in a warm place for about 1½ hours, or until doubled in bulk.

Punch down and let rest for 10 minutes, covered. Then shape dough into a round loaf and place it in a well-greased, 8- or 9-inch pie plate. Cover and let rise in a warm place until doubled (about 45 minutes). Bake at 400°F. for 35 minutes and cool on wire rack.

Herb Bread

(1 round loaf)

1 package dry yeast
2 tablespoons honey (or 1 teaspoon malt)
1½ teaspoons salt (optional)
1 teaspoon ground sage
¾ teaspoon crushed basil
¼ teaspoon nutmeg
2¾ to 3 cups whole wheat flour
1 cup milk (or 1 cup water + ⅓ cup nonfat dry milk)
2 tablespoons butter
1 egg

Swedish Rye Bread

(2 loaves)

¼ cup honey
¼ cup light molasses
1 tablespoon salt (optional)
2 tablespoons butter
3 tablespoons caraway seeds
1 cup boiling water
1 package dry yeast
¾ cup warm water
2 cups rye flour
3½ cups whole wheat flour
butter (optional)

Combine honey, molasses, salt, butter, and caraway seeds in small bowl; pour on the boiling water and stir until honey is dissolved. Cool to lukewarm.

Sprinkle yeast on the warm water and stir to dissolve. Add the cooled honey-molasses mixture. Stir in the rye flour and beat until smooth. Mix in enough whole wheat flour to make a thick batter and beat well. Add additional flour to make a dough that can be kneaded. Turn out onto a lightly floured surface and knead for 8 to 10 minutes.

Place dough in a lightly greased bowl, turning once to grease the top. Cover and let rise in a warm spot for about 1½ to 2 hours or until doubled in size.

Punch down, turn out onto floured surface, knead for about 1 to 2 minutes, shape into 2 loaves and place in greased 4 × 8-inch pans. Cover and let rise in a warm place until almost doubled in size (about 1½ hours).

Bake in 375°F. oven for 30 minutes, covering the tops with aluminum foil for the last 15 minutes if the loaves are browning too quickly.

Turn out onto wire racks to cool. If you like a softer crust, brush the loaves with butter while still warm.

Cracked Wheat Bread

(2 loaves)

1 package dry yeast
2¼ cups warm water
⅓ cup nonfat dry milk
1 cup rye flour
1 cup cracked wheat flour
1½ teaspoons salt (optional)
1½ tablespoons molasses
1½ tablespoons butter
4 to 4½ cups whole wheat flour
butter (optional)

Dissolve yeast in warm water in a large mixing bowl. Add dry milk, rye flour, cracked wheat, salt, molasses, butter, and about 1 cup whole wheat flour to make a thick batter. Beat with an electric mixer at medium-high speed for 2 minutes, scraping bowl occasionally. With a wooden spoon, stir in enough of the remaining flour to make a soft dough. Turn out onto a lightly floured board and knead for about 10 minutes.

Place dough in a lightly greased bowl, turn once to coat the top, cover and let rise in a warm spot until doubled in bulk (about 1 to 1½ hours).

Punch down, cover and let rise again in the bowl until doubled (about 45 minutes). Turn dough out onto floured surface, divide in half and shape into balls. Cover with a towel and let rest for 10 minutes. Shape into loaves and place them in 2 well-greased,

4 × 8-inch loaf pans. Cover, place in a warm spot and let rise until doubled (about 1 hour).

Bake in a 375°F. oven for 35 minutes, covering the tops with foil for the last 15 minutes if they begin to brown excessively. Cool on wire racks. Brush tops with butter while still warm, if you want a softer crust.

Potato Bread

(3 loaves)

2 packages dry yeast
3½ cups warm water
1 cup nonfat dry milk
3 tablespoons honey (or 2 teaspoons malt)
1 tablespoon salt (optional)
½ cup mashed potatoes
6 tablespoons butter
9 to 10 cups whole wheat flour
3 tablespoons cornmeal

Dissolve yeast in warm water in the large bowl of an electric mixer. Beat in the dry milk, honey or malt, salt, potatoes, butter, and enough of the flour to make a thick batter (about 3 cups). Beat 2 minutes with the electric mixer at medium-high speed, scraping bowl occasionally. Mix in enough of the remaining flour to make a soft dough.

Turn out onto a lightly floured surface and knead for about 10 minutes. Place dough in a greased bowl, turning once to coat the top. Cover and let rise in a warm place until doubled in bulk (about 1½ to 2 hours).

Punch down, cover and let rise again for about 45 minutes, or until doubled in bulk.

Turn out onto floured surface, divide into 3 parts, shape into balls, cover and let rest for 10 minutes. Grease 3 loaf pans (9 × 5 inches), sprinkle sides and bottom of pans with cornmeal (1 tablespoon per pan), and then shape dough into 3 loaves. Place in pans, cover and let rise in a warm spot until doubled in bulk (about 50 to 60 minutes).

Bake in 375°F. oven for 40 minutes or until loaves are richly browned and have a hollow sound when tapped on the bottom with your fingers. (Cover with foil for last 15 minutes.)

Remove from pans, place on wire racks and cool.

Cheese Bread

(2 loaves)

2 cups milk (or 2 cups water + ⅔ cup nonfat dry milk)
3 cups shredded cheddar cheese
2 tablespoons butter
5 to 6 cups whole wheat flour
1 package dry yeast
3 tablespoons honey (or 1 teaspoon malt)
2 teaspoons salt (optional)

Combine milk, 2 cups of the shredded cheese, and the butter in a saucepan. Heat and stir until the cheese melts. Cool to warm (about 120° to 130°F.).

In the large bowl of the mixer, combine 1¾ cups flour, yeast, honey or malt, and salt. Gradually add the lukewarm milk mixture to the dry ingredients and beat for 2 minutes at medium speed with the electric mixer, scraping bowl occasionally. Add the remaining 1 cup of cheese and enough of the remaining flour to make a soft dough. Turn out onto a lightly floured surface and knead for 8 to 10 minutes.

Place in a lightly greased bowl, turning once to coat the top. Cover and let rise in a warm spot until doubled in bulk (about 1 to 1½ hours). Punch down, turn out onto floured surface, divide into 2 balls, cover and let rest for about 10 minutes.

Shape into loaves and place in greased, 4 × 8-inch loaf pans, cover and let rise until almost doubled in bulk (about 45 minutes).

Bake in a 375°F. oven for about 40 minutes or until loaves test done. As with the other breads, if these seem to be browning too quickly, cover the tops with aluminum foil for the last 15 minutes of the baking time.

Turn out onto wire racks to cool.

Red Star Golden Granola Loaf

(1 large loaf)

1 package dry yeast
1 cup warm water
3 tablespoons honey
1½ teaspoons salt (optional)
2 tablespoons oil
1 egg
1 cup granola, crushed in blender
3 cups whole wheat flour
butter

In a mixer bowl, dissolve yeast in warm water. Add honey. Then add salt, oil, egg, and granola. Blend. Add enough flour to make a thick batter and beat well. Gradually stir in additional flour to make a dough that can be kneaded. Turn out onto a lightly floured surface and knead for 6 to 8 minutes. Place dough in a greased bowl, turning once to coat all sides. Cover, let rise in a warm place for about 1 hour, or until doubled in bulk.

Punch down dough, then turn out onto lightly floured surface. Roll or pat the dough into a rectangle about 15 × 9 inches. Then, starting with the shorter side, roll up tightly as with a jelly roll, pressing dough into the roll at each turn. Press each end with the side of your hand to seal and fold the ends under the loaf.

Place the seam-side down in a well-greased, 9 × 5 × 3-inch loaf pan and brush the top with butter.

Cover and let rise in a warm spot until light and doubled (about 1 hour).

Bake at 375°F. for 30 to 35 minutes or until golden brown and loaf sounds hollow when tapped on the bottom.

Remove from pan, brush loaf with butter while still warm and cool on wire rack.

Crunchy Whole Wheat Bread

(2 small loaves or 1 large loaf)

Dissolve the yeast in the warm water. Add 2 cups of the whole wheat flour and stir; then add 2 tablespoons of the honey. Let the mixture stand in a warm place for about 20 minutes.

Meanwhile, combine the hot water, salt, remainder of the honey, and the butter. Mix and let cool to lukewarm. Add to the yeast mixture in a bowl.

Add the rye flour (or variation), and enough of the remaining whole wheat flour to make a medium dough suitable for kneading. Knead on a floured surface for about 10 minutes and then place in a greased bowl, turning once to coat the top. Cover and let rise until doubled (about 1½ hours).

Punch down, turn out onto floured surface and knead for 1 to 2 minutes.

Shape into 2 loaves and place in well-greased baking pans, cover and let rise to double in a warm spot (about 45 minutes).

Bake at 350°F. for 35 minutes or until loaves test done when tapped on the bottom. Remove and cool on wire racks.

Brush with butter while still hot if you like a soft crust.

1 package dry yeast
1½ cups warm water
3½ to 4 cups whole wheat flour
¼ cup honey
½ cup hot water
1 tablespoon salt (optional)
3 tablespoons butter
2 cups whole wheat flour
½ cup rye flour (or ½ cup whole wheat graham flour or ¼ cup wheat germ + ¼ cup bran)
butter (optional)

Dilly Casserole Bread

(1 loaf)

1 package dry yeast
¼ cup warm water
1 cup creamed cottage cheese,
heated to lukewarm
2 tablespoons honey
1 tablespoon minced onion
1 tablespoon butter
2 teaspoons dill seed
1 teaspoon salt (optional)
¼ teaspoon baking soda
1 egg, unbeaten
2 to 2¼ cups whole wheat flour
softened butter and salt (optional)

This one is Elizabeth's contribution for those busy days—a no-knead bread with a delicious taste.

In a measuring cup, soften the yeast in the warm water.

In a mixing bowl, combine the cottage cheese, honey, onion, butter, dill seed, salt, baking soda, egg, and the softened yeast mixture. Add enough flour to form a medium dough, beating well after each addition. (For first addition of flour, use the mixer on low speed; then use a wooden spoon as dough becomes firmer.) Cover the bowl, let rise in a warm place until doubled in size (about 1½ to 2 hours).

Stir dough down. Turn into a well-greased, 8-inch round (1- to 1½-quart) casserole. Cover and let rise in a warm place until texture is light (about 30 to 40 minutes). Bake at 350°F. for 35 to 40 minutes until golden brown. Brush with softened butter and sprinkle with salt while still warm.

Cool on wire rack.

JOAN MOENCH

The most exciting thing about my friends all over the country is that they seem to find time to bake bread in spite of the busy lives they lead. Joan Moench is a greenhouse and flower specialist who lives in Lafayette, New York, and who wrote in her last letter:

. . . I don't know if I'm on foot or horseback half the time. This place constantly jumps. The house was struck by lightning, Bill's father and his spouse were here for two weeks. Susan's been home with a house guest and I'm expecting seven guests for the Apple Festival weekend. Must run—I've got to bake bread for the gang arriving on Friday!

There is an incongruity to Joan's bread baking. She uses a modern electric mixer with a dough hook attachment but she bakes her breads in an old-fashioned brick oven heated by wild-apple wood coals. "I found that before getting my dough hook attachment, it was like stirring quick-setting cement. . . .

As to testing the temperature of her brick oven, Joan has a simple solution:

The way you tell if the brick oven is the right temperature is to hold your hand inside for exactly a slow 10 seconds. If you can't hold it for that time, it's too hot—if you can hold it there longer, add more coals.

The Bread:

All Protein Bread

All Protein Bread

(6 small or 3 large loaves)

1 package dry yeast
4 cups lukewarm water
1½ cups nonfat dry milk
¼ cup honey
¼ cup molasses
9 to 9½ cups whole wheat flour
¾ cup sunflower seeds
½ cup sesame seeds
2 eggs
¾ teaspoon salt (optional)
½ cup olive oil

Dissolve the yeast in ¼ cup of the warm water. In a separate bowl, mix the dry milk with 1¾ cups of the warm water. This may be hard to dissolve, so I beat it with a whisk. Add the honey and molasses and then the rest of the water (2 cups). Mix in 5 cups of the flour, 1 cup at a time. Cover with a damp cloth and let rise in a warm spot for 45 minutes to make a sponge.

Add ¾ cup of sunflower seeds and the ½ cup of sesame seeds. Mix and let stand for 10 minutes so that the seeds absorb the moisture. Mix in the 2 eggs, salt, and the olive oil. Knead in enough of the balance of the whole wheat flour to make a dough that barely sticks to your fingers. (This will take about 4 to 4½ more cups.)

Place in well-greased loaf pans. Cover the pans and place in a warm spot to rise about 1 hour or until you don't "hear" it rise any longer.

Place in 325°F. oven for 45 minutes or until brown on top and it thumps well on the bottom.

Cool on wire racks.

SALLY GOBLE

Sally lives in an adobe-style house in Alamosa, Colorado, and thus it stays cool all the time:

Since there's no really warm place for bread to rise in our house, I put the bowl in our solar food dryer and I close the vents so that it won't get too hot. It works pretty well. . . .

Sally is a receptionist at the local newspaper, the *Valley Courier*, and she raises hybrid earthworms on the side.

They're Hybrid Red Wigglers and they'll eat anything biodegradable, and the success of my organic garden depends largely upon the rich castings of the worms. They make the best natural fertilizer in the world!

I've chosen three interesting recipes from Sally's large collection and you'll notice that she uses only whole wheat flour and that there is no salt in any of the breads. Again, we have the marvelous flexibility of bread baking—a craft in which everyone bakes for individual taste or reasons of health:

I don't use salt in my recipes—I don't believe it adds to the flavor. I believe that salt only adds to the salt addiction that many people have and to the problems of high blood pressure. . . .

Sally, like many of us, was raised on store-bought bread ("gross," she says). It was after she married that she discovered that "you are what you eat," and that only good healthy food can produce a good healthy body. She's been a confirmed bread baker ever since.

The Breads:

Spice Bread
Whole Wheat English Muffins
Mexican Corn Bread

Spice Bread

(2 loaves or 12 buns)

1 package dry yeast
½ cup warm water
½ cup mashed potatoes
¼ cup honey
1 cup milk
5 cups whole wheat flour
⅔ cup unsulphured molasses
½ teaspoon allspice
2 teaspoons anise seed
2 eggs, beaten
½ teaspoon cloves

Don't expect whole grain bread to be light, soft and fluffy as store-bought bread. Whole grain breads are by nature a little heavier and coarser.

Dissolve the yeast in the warm water. Let stand for a few minutes, then add the mashed potatoes, honey, and milk. Add 3 cups of the flour, 1 cup at a time, stirring after each addition. Cover the bowl and let rise in a warm place for 1 hour.

Then add the molasses, allspice, anise seed, and the 2 beaten eggs. Add the cloves and then beat together, gradually adding more flour as needed, up to 2 additional cups. Mix well, cover and let rise in a warm spot for 1 hour.

When dough has risen, turn out onto a lightly floured board and shape into 2 loaves or 12 buns. Place on a greased baking sheet, cover lightly and let rest for 15 minutes.

Bake for 30 minutes at 350°F. or until breads test done.

Cool on wire racks.

Italian Sesame Twist (George Meluso) page 54 *271*

272   **Sally Lunn (Betty and Branson Hobbs) page 299**

This is a recipe that uses mashed potatoes. Sally says that it makes the muffins a little firmer and more cohesive. You'll find that mashed potatoes also make a marvelous addition to many of your other breads.

Dissolve yeast with honey in ¼ cup of the water and wait 5 to 10 minutes until it's bubbly.

Add the remaining water and the other ingredients. Mix well and turn dough out onto a lightly floured surface. Knead 8 to 10 minutes or until dough is smooth and elastic. Divide the dough into about a dozen parts and press each part into a circle about 2 to 3 inches in diameter. Place on baking sheet dusted with cornmeal, cover lightly and let rise in a warm spot for 1 to 1½ hours.

Bake 6 to 8 minutes at 375°F.

Whole Wheat English Muffins

(about 1 dozen muffins)

1 package dry yeast
¼ teaspoon honey
1¼ cups warm water
3 to 4 cups whole wheat flour
1 small red potato, boiled and
   mashed
cornmeal

Mix ingredients together in a large bowl. Grease a 9 × 9-inch baking pan and pour batter into it.

Bake for 1 hour at 350°F.

Mexican Corn Bread

(1 to 1½ dozen squares)

1 cup yellow cornmeal
½ teaspoon baking soda
1 cup milk
2 eggs
1 small jar pimentos
1 8 to 10-ounce can corn (or 1
   cup cooked corn kernels)
1 large chopped onion
2 cloves garlic, finely chopped
1 cup grated cheddar cheese (or
   other sharp cheese)
1 small can green chilies

VIVIAN HUTCHINS

In her last letter from Pensacola, Florida, Vivian—a free-lance editor who (naturally) bakes bread—wrote:

> . . . *one favor I'd like to ask: please leave "receipt" as typed. I tried to change my thinking to "recipe" years ago, but it never felt natural, so I returned to the word I learned from my mother and aunts. Just a bit old-fashioned, I guess. . . .*

The receipts that follow reflect an interesting method of bread baking, a way to take the mystique out of it by giving one basic method and merely changing the ingredients. I would suggest that our readers try some basic receipts with specific instructions before attempting these—but once you get the "feel" of it, it's really quite easy. As Vivian explains it:

> *Three years ago I joined a bread-baking class at the high school in Tully, New York—and it turned out to be the most imaginative, interesting, and fulfilling adult-education class I ever took. Don Snyder, our teacher, had a new, practical, and challenging approach to bread baking.*

> *Bread making should be fun as well as producing an edible product, and the great point of the system is that you don't use exact measurements. You can start with a cup, a quart, or a dollop, and add all the other ingredients by sight, smell, feel, taste to achieve your loaf of bread. This is creativity at work. To those of us brought up on exact measurements, it's a bit scary at first—but look at any old cookbook with its "butter the size of an egg" or "a teacupful of flour." Our great-grandmothers never had any problem with this and neither should we.*

The theory behind this method, of course, is that the basic bread ingredients are generally liquid, sweetening, shortening, salt, yeast, eggs (sometimes), and flour. These can be varied in endless combinations:

Liquid can be anything wet—water, milk, buttermilk, tea, or beer. Flours are of all kinds—oatmeal and wheat germ are useful too. Butter for the shortening, honey or maple syrup for sweetening and yeast is yeast—absolutely essential. Measurements are not measured and the fun is in experimenting.

Vivian's teacher believes (and thus, so do his students) that part of the challenge is in learning that if you use rolled oats you don't need quite as much flour, since the rolled oats are extremely heavy and absorbent. Dark honey goes with dark breads, pale honey with light. Darker flours such as rye and buckwheat go a long way when they're added for extra interest. Some loaves will not come out too well if too much of an ingredient is used—for example, tea and beer are bases where caution is advisable.

So, here is a challenging attempt to take still more of the mystique out of bread baking while allowing for your own inventiveness to be unshackled. As a final note, Vivian writes: "I wonder what avocado-lemon bread would taste like. . . .

Here are her receipts.

Basic Instructions

Maple Whole Grain Bread

(4 loaves)

1 quart buttermilk
¼ pound (½ cup) butter
½ cup pure maple syrup
1 teaspoon salt (optional)
2 packages dry yeast
2 eggs
12 cups unbleached white flour
(or 10 to 12 cups whole
wheat flour)

Pumpkin Cider Bread

(4 loaves)

1 quart cider
¼ pound (½ cup) butter
½ cup maple syrup
1 cup pumpkin
1 teaspoon salt (optional)
2 packages dry yeast
1 cup whole wheat flour
1 cup white cornmeal
10 cups unbleached white flour
(or 9 to 10 cups whole
wheat flour)

These instructions apply to all the bread receipts that follow:

• Warm the liquid, butter, sweetening, pumpkin (where called for), and salt in a large pot (five quarts or so) until the butter melts. If you are going to add raisins or currants, put them in right away—they plump up nicely. Remove from stove and cool to lukewarm.

• Sprinkle the yeast over the surface of the liquid and let it get used to its new environment for a few minutes. Then, using a large wooden spoon, stir it in gently. Yeast does not like to be hurried at this stage. It has to wake up and start expanding.

• If you're using eggs, beat them thoroughly in a separate bowl. Then add a cupful of flour to the liquid and yeast and stir it in before adding the eggs. Mix thoroughly.

• Stir in the flour, a cup or two at a time, and cornmeal, rolled oats, or caraway seeds (when called for) until the dough is thick and very sticky. When your arm won't stir it any longer, it's time to knead. Vivian uses a breadboard three feet long, but she claims that she's a messy baker.

• Flour your hands and turn the mixture out onto a floured surface. Keep working extra flour into the dough until you feel the firmness and the dough stops sticking to the board and to your hands. When the dough is smooth and firm and elastic (about 10 minutes later) and it springs back when you apply pressure, place it in a greased bowl, turn to coat top, cover and let it rise for about one hour.

• Punch down, knead for one or two minutes, and shape into loaves. The receipts that follow will make four standard-size loaves. Place loaves in greased bread pans, cover again and let rise for about 45 minutes.

• Bake in a preheated 350°F. oven for approximately one hour. Bread should sound hollow when tapped on the bottom.

• Turn out onto racks and cool thoroughly before wrapping in foil or plastic.

NOTE: Vivian suggests staying with unbleached white flour for the Oatmeal Currant Bread, the Lemon Bread, and the Coconut Milk Bread because of the delicate flavors of the ingredients. However, all the other breads can be made either with unbleached white flour or whole wheat flour. We have tested them both ways and they work well.

Follow the Basic Instructions (page 276).

Oatmeal Currant Bread

(4 loaves)

1 quart buttermilk
⅛ pound (4 tablespoons) butter
1 cup medium honey
1 teaspoon salt (optional)
1 10-ounce box currants
2 packages dry yeast
2 eggs
1 cup graham flour
8 cups unbleached white flour
1 cup uncooked rolled oats

This bread also makes a good "cocktail" rye if baked in small loaves or long loaves. Bake them on a cookie sheet and cut down the baking time if you decide to do it this way.

Follow the Basic Instructions (page 276).

Sour Rye Bread

(4 loaves)

1 12-ounce can beer
2½ cups water
¼ pound (½ cup) butter
1 cup dark honey
1 teaspoon salt (optional)
2 packages dry yeast
2 eggs
4 cups rye flour
6 to 8 cups whole wheat flour
1 tablespoon caraway seeds
   (optional)

Cinnamon Raisin Bread

(4 loaves)

1 quart buttermilk
¼ pound (½ cup) butter
1 cup light honey
1 teaspoon salt (optional)
2 cups raisins
2 packages dry yeast
2 eggs
12 cups unbleached white flour
(or 12 cups whole wheat flour)
cinnamon

Follow the Basic Instructions (page 276).

When making this bread, add the raisins to the liquid mix and knead in generous amounts of cinnamon when kneading the dough.

Vivian suggests that the two receipts that follow will make *two* braided breads: "The first time I tried it, I only made one large braid. While baking, it overflowed and practically filled the oven!"

Lemon Bread

(2 braided breads)

1 quart buttermilk
¼ cup freshly squeezed
lemon juice
¼ pound (½ cup) butter
1 cup light honey
1 teaspoon salt (optional)
2 cups white raisins
4 packages dry yeast
4 eggs
12 cups unbleached white flour

Follow the Basic Instructions (page 276) to the first rise. Then Vivian goes on:

After the first rise, divide the dough into 2 uneven pieces—about two-thirds and one-third. Divide the larger piece into 3—roll these out in long rolls with your hands and place them side by side. Pinch them together at one end and braid them. Pinch the other end together and slide the braid onto a greased cookie sheet. Braid the smaller piece in the same way and place it atop the first braid. This will give you a 6-braided bread.

Cover and let rise, then bake at 350°F. for at least ½ hour. Braids need to be watched as they seem to vary in baking time to a surprising degree—smaller ones take about ½ hour, larger ones sometimes an hour or more.

This was Vivian's first attempt at a braid, and also is her favorite bread.

Blend the water and the coconut and let stand overnight in the refrigerator.

Follow the Basic Instructions (page 276) to the first rise. Then continue as with Lemon Bread on preceding page.

Coconut Milk Bread

(2 braided breads)

½ quart (2 cups) water
1½ cups shredded coconut
½ quart (2 cups) water
¼ pound (½ cup) butter
1 cup light honey
1 teaspoon salt (optional)
1 cup white raisins
2 packages dry yeast
2 eggs
12 cups unbleached white flour

JOYCE SLINDEN

The Breads:

Selbu Region *Lefse* **(Norwegian)**
Kake Bröd **(Swedish)**

One of the joys of my film life is the travel and, thus, the people I meet on the way. As a part of a film about family farming, I spent some time in Grove City, Minnesota, with the Slinden family—four generations who still farm the same land that their grandfather settled. Aside from producing the film, partaking of bountiful meals, home-grown on the farm, and even attempting to drive Don Slinden's truck while the combine harvested the corn, I also managed to find some time to speak with Joyce Slinden and to acquire two superb and unusual recipes for the book.

Don's family came from the Selbu region of Norway in 1866 and the *Lefse* was a special treat made by Grandmother Helga at Christmas only, since it was necessary to keep the *Lefse* cold:

Don's grandma had a large crock on the front porch where she stored them. It was sort of her "deep freezer," since the winters are cold in Minnesota and the temperature is generally well below the freezing point.

Grandma baked her *Lefse* on the top surface of the wood cook stove and they were much larger than the ones made by Joyce.

> . . . in fact, they took up the entire surface of the stove—they were about 18 inches in diameter. We don't serve them to just anyone, since they're very special and they're time-consuming to make. But during the Christmas holidays, we have them for breakfast as a special treat or with afternoon coffee or tea when the family drops by. . . .

Before leaving Minnesota, my wife insisted that we stop at the general store, so that she might buy a special rolling pin and *Lefse* stick. However, a regular rolling pin and a dowel or wooden spoon handle or spatula may be used if you want to try the recipe in your own home.

Selbu Region
Lefse

(Norwegian)

(about 28 *Lefse*)

4 cups unbleached white flour
1 teaspoon salt*
¼ cup lard
1 quart raw milk (using raw milk is
important because of butterfat
content—available in natural
foods stores)
1 cup unbleached white flour
and 1 cup graham flour,
mixed together

Filling:

2 cups milk
2 cups heavy cream
1 pound softened sweet butter
8 tablespoons mild honey
1 teaspoon salt*

My wife and I tested this recipe one rainy weekend and found it great fun as well as a challenge. It takes some time until you get the knack of rolling the dough and placing it on the hot griddle. I would also strongly suggest that, unless you have a huge family or you can round up some people to help you make them (because of the time involved), it might be wise to cut the recipe in half and make only 14 *Lefse*.

In a bowl, mix the 4 cups unbleached flour, salt, and lard. Bring milk to a boil and pour over flour mixture; beat with a wooden spoon until well mixed. Cool to ice cold in the refrigerator for 2 to 3 hours.

Put dough on a floured board. Mix together the cup of white flour with the cup of graham flour and then blend into the dough, kneading for about 8 to 10 minutes or until dough is no longer sticky. Dough must be soft. Let rest, covered, for about 10 minutes.

Divide the dough into balls the size of golf balls and roll each one into very thin rounds about ⅛ inch thick. They should fit comfortably on a 12-inch griddle. Roll them from the center outward for about 4 to 5 strokes, then turn the dough over and roll again on the other side. Keep turning and rolling until they are the right thickness.

Heat an ungreased griddle on the top of the stove (keep the griddle at about medium heat—too hot and the *Lefse* smoke) and place the *Lefse* one at a time on top, baking only until the top bubbles, just as in making pancakes. With a spatula or a wooden spoon handle in one hand, and using the fingers of your other hand, turn the *Lefse* carefully over to the other side and bake quickly until the underside is slightly dappled with brown.

Fold the *Lefse* quickly over the spoon handle to remove from the griddle and unfold onto a damp kitchen towel covered with wax paper. Cover each *Lefse* with another sheet of wax paper as you place them on the pile. Cover the top with a damp kitchen towel so they don't dry out. As you bake each one, lift the top towel, place the *Lefse* on wax paper and again replace the towel. When all the *Lefse* are finished, keep them covered with the damp towel while you prepare the filling.

---

*The salt, though traditional, may be eliminated if you choose to do so.

Heat the milk and cream to lukewarm (about body temperature). To test, put your finger in and count to 5—grandma had no thermometer. If you can't keep your finger in the mixture, it's too hot! It is important for the butter not to be melted, so cream the butter using an electric mixer or beater and, a little at a time, add the warmed milk-cream mixture, beating as you combine the ingredients until they solidify again. Then add a little more of the warm milk-cream mixture. When all the liquid is incorporated, add honey and salt and beat again. Chill in refrigerator for 15 minutes until slightly firm. If liquid forms, pour it off. Then spread filling generously over half of each *Lefse*. Fold over and cut into wedges to serve.

NOTE: The *Lefse* are generally made in advance, then frozen and defrosted before serving. Because they're so thin, they defrost quickly at room temperature. In my last letter to Joyce, I asked her whether or not the frozen *Lefse* should be reheated when thawed. She answered:

Do not warm the Lefse—thaw at room temperature. Warming will melt the filling and destroy it. Just remove the Lefse from the freezer, place them on a serving plate, cover them with foil or plastic and let them stand for about 20 minutes before serving.

Kake Bröd

(Swedish flat bread)

(2 breads)

1 package dry yeast
¼ cup lukewarm water
1⅓ cups lukewarm milk
1 tablespoon honey
2 teaspoons salt*
2 tablespoons softened butter
4 to 5 cups unbleached white flour
butter

Though Don's family came from Norway, Joyce traces her own line back to Sweden. During the filming, Joyce's mother dropped by, a youthful, active woman who looked more like Joyce's sister. This recipe was the result of our talk. Luckily, my film crews are quite used to my habit of writing down recipes during production.

Sprinkle yeast on the warm water and set aside. In a large bowl, mix the warm milk, honey, salt, butter, and 2 cups of the flour. Beat with an electric mixer or wooden spoon until smooth. Gradually add the rest of the flour. (If dough is too stiff to mix with the electric mixer, finish by hand.) Turn dough onto a floured board and knead until all the flour is used and the dough is not sticky. Invert mixing bowl over dough and let rest for 10 minutes.

Knead for 8 to 10 minutes until dough is smooth and elastic. Grease the dough, cover with a damp cloth and let it rise until doubled in bulk (about 1 hour).

Divide the dough into 2 parts. Butter a large, round pizza pan or a rectangular jelly-roll pan. Roll dough with a floured rolling pin to fit the pan. Place the dough on the pan and then press the edges with your finger to make it fit the pan. Prick all over with a fork.

Cover with a damp cloth and let rise until doubled in thickness (about 30 minutes). Then bake in a 350°F. oven for about 10 to 15 minutes until golden brown. Butter the top generously with melted butter as soon as it is removed from the oven.

Cool slightly on a wire rack before serving.

*The salt, though traditional, may be eliminated if you choose to do so.

EDWIN WILLIAMS

The Bread:

Tomato Quick Bread

Ed is a tax accountant who lives in Manlius, New York, and who started baking bread about 10 or 12 years ago—very much for the same reasons that most of us began:

. . . because I guess I just got fed up with the soft, spongy stuff that most commercial bakeries turn out. But I really began

cooking when I was still living at home, thanks to my mother who felt that it was ridiculous for a man not to be able to do a reasonable amount of cooking. . . .

Ed sent two recipes along, but I've placed one in the section on Salt Rising Bread variations (see Index). The other is included here and it's called Tomato Quick Bread. You may serve it hot or cold and it makes a deliciously different toast and it's great for sandwiches. In fact, if you take two slices, add some meat, a slice of cheese, some lettuce and fresh tomato, the results could easily be called a "pizza sandwich."

Tomato Quick Bread

(1 loaf)

2½ cups whole wheat flour
1 tablespoon baking powder
pinch baking soda
1 teaspoon salt (optional)
1 teaspoon garlic powder
1 teaspoon crushed oregano
1 teaspoon basil
½ cup shredded mozzarella cheese
¼ cup grated Parmesan cheese
1½ cups peeled, chopped fresh tomatoes (about 1 pound)
⅓ to ½ cup milk
2 eggs
¼ cup oil
1 tablespoon honey

Mix the flour, baking powder, baking soda, salt, spices, and cheeses together in a bowl. Drain the liquid from the chopped tomatoes and reserve the tomatoes. Add enough milk to the tomato liquid to make ⅔ cup. Blend the liquid with the eggs, oil, and honey, then stir into the flour mixture just until thoroughly moistened. Add the reserved tomatoes. Pour the batter into a well-greased, 4 × 8-inch loaf pan.

Bake in a preheated oven at 350°F. for 60 to 70 minutes. If the bread is brown before the baking time is complete, cover the top with a foil tent and continue baking until it tests done and the bottom sounds hollow when tapped.

Cool for 10 minutes in the pan and then turn out onto a wire rack to cool thoroughly before slicing. The bread keeps well in the refrigerator or may be frozen.

NANCY FUERSTENBERG

I have a tendency to forget time zones when I call my bread-baker friends. I assume they are all awake and busily taking fresh loaves from the oven. Unfortunately, Nancy Fuerstenberg lives in Anchorage, Alaska—six hours earlier than New York and her last letter reminded me that noon for me is rather early for her:

> . . . I was not fully awake when you called the other morning, but after hanging up and thinking about the call, I can't remember if I had thanked you for wanting to use my recipes. . . .

Since Haven and Margaret Holsapple (see Index) travel to Alaska quite frequently for their climbs up Mt. McKinley, they got to know Nancy and, in turn, suggested that I contact her. Though her mother often baked bread, Nancy didn't get involved until her move to Alaska:

> . . . up here nearly everyone bakes bread at home because it's so expensive to buy. I experimented at first and made mostly white or sourdough bread. After running a child care center and then having children of my own, I found out just how much the children enjoyed homemade bread and I began to try other breads and to bake more frequently. . . .

Nancy's recipes are simple to make—and Atomic Bread is an original and funny bread. It literally "blows its top!"

The Breads:

Atomic Bread
Quick Raisin Bran Bread
Spicy Banana Bread
Oatmeal-Molasses Bread
Pineapple-Orange Bread

Atomic Bread

(1 large loaf)

1 package dry yeast
½ cup warm water
⅛ teaspoon ground ginger
2 tablespoons honey
1 13-ounce can evaporated milk
1 teaspoon salt (optional)
2 tablespoons oil
4 to 4½ cups whole wheat flour
butter

A friend of mine, Mary Boyle, and I were interested in the ad for the local bakery for "flintstone bread." It was round-shaped at the bottom and it had a puffy top like a mushroom. We accomplished the same thing by using coffee cans. My children think it's great to get "round" sandwiches in their lunches. . . .

Dissolve yeast in the warm water in large mixing bowl. Blend in the ginger and 1 tablespoon of the honey. Let stand in a warm place until the mixture is bubbly (about 15 minutes). Stir in the remaining honey, and the milk, salt, and oil. With mixer on low speed (or with a wooden spoon) beat in the flour 1 cup at a time, mixing well after each addition. If you are using a mixer, beat in the last cup of flour with a wooden spoon. The dough should be heavy but too sticky to knead.

Place dough in a 2-pound, *well-greased* coffee can. Cover with greased plastic lid. At this point, you may freeze the dough if you want to and bake it at a later time.

To bake, let stand, covered in a warm place until the dough rises and pops off the lid. This will take 1 to 1½ hours. Discard the lid and bake at 350°F. for 1 hour. The crust will be very brown. Brush the top lightly with butter.

Let the entire bread and can cool for 5 to 10 minutes on a wire rack, then loosen the crust around the edge of the can with a thin knife and slide the bread from the can. Cool it in an upright position on the wire rack.

*For a Special Occasion
Atomic Bread*

Add to the yeast mixture 1 teaspoon cinnamon and ½ teaspoon nutmeg. With the final addition of flour, add ½ cup raisins and ½ cup chopped walnuts.

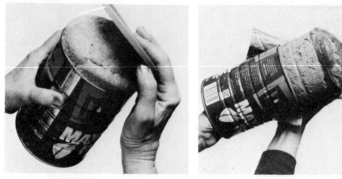

Sift the flour, salt, and baking powder together, stir in whole bran and raisins. Beat the eggs, milk, and honey together and stir into the batter only until mixed. This will make a fairly stiff batter.

Pour into a large nonstick or greased loaf pan and bake in a preheated oven at 375°F. for 50 minutes.

When loaf tests done, turn out onto a wire rack to cool.

Quick Raisin Bran Bread

(1 large loaf)

3 cups whole wheat flour
1 teaspoon salt (optional)
4 teaspoons baking powder
1 cup whole bran
6 tablespoons raisins
2 eggs
1 cup skim milk
4 tablespoons honey

In a large mixing bowl, sift the dry ingredients. Add butter, buttermilk, honey, and bananas; mix until flour is dampened. Beat at low speed with electric mixer for 2 minutes. Then add the eggs and beat 2 minutes longer. Stir in nuts, if desired.

Place in 2 well-greased and floured 4 × 8-inch bread pans. Bake at 350°F. for approximately 45 minutes or until toothpick inserted comes out clean. Cool on wire rack.

This bread has the texture of cake and is equally good with or without the chopped nuts.

Spicy Banana Bread

(2 large loaves)

2½ cups whole wheat flour, sifted
1¼ teaspoons baking powder
3 teaspoons baking soda
1 teaspoon salt (optional)
1½ teaspoons cinnamon
¾ teaspoon nutmeg
½ teaspoon ground cloves
⅔ cup butter
⅔ cup buttermilk
1 cup honey
1½ cups mashed bananas
2 eggs
½ cup chopped nuts (optional)

Oatmeal-Molasses Bread

(2 large loaves)

2 packages dry yeast
½ cup warm water
1½ cups boiling water
1 cup uncooked rolled oats
½ cup butter
1 cup molasses
3 teaspoons salt (optional)
2 eggs, beaten
6 cups whole wheat flour, sifted

Soften yeast in warm water and set aside. In a large bowl, combine the boiling water, oats, butter, molasses, and salt. Cool to lukewarm. Add the softened yeast mixture and blend well.

Blend in eggs, add flour 1 cup at a time and mix thoroughly after each addition. This is softer than kneaded dough. Place in a well-greased bowl, turning to coat the top, cover and place in refrigerator for at least 2 hours.

On a floured board, divide dough into 2 loaves and place in 2 well-greased, 9 × 5-inch loaf pans. Cover with a towel or plastic wrap and let rise in a warm place until doubled in size—about 2 hours.

Bake at 350°F. for 1 hour or until loaves test done. Turn out onto wire rack to cool.

Pineapple-Orange Bread

(1 large loaf)

2 cups whole wheat flour, sifted
1½ teaspoons baking powder
1 teaspoon salt (optional)
½ teaspoon baking soda
1 cup crushed pineapple, well drained
½ cup chopped walnuts
2 teaspoons freshly grated orange peel
1 egg, beaten
½ cup honey
¾ cup freshly squeezed orange juice
2 tablespoons oil

In a mixing bowl, sift dry ingredients together. Stir in the pineapple, nuts, and orange peel. In another bowl, combine the egg, honey, orange juice, and oil; then add to the dry ingredients, stirring only until moistened.

Bake in a greased 9 × 5-inch loaf pan at 350°F. for 50 minutes or until bread tests done. Remove from pan and cool on wire rack. This bread tastes better if you let it sit at least overnight.

RICHARD HENTGES

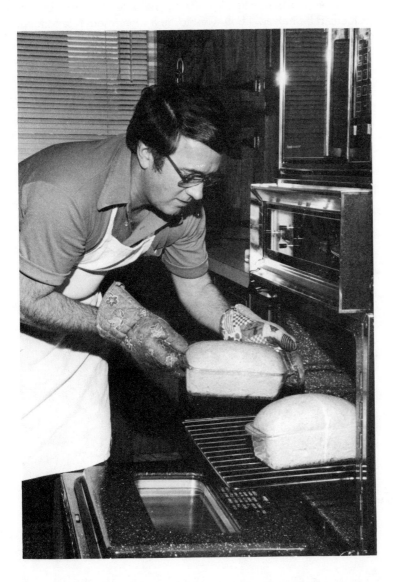

The Bread:

Honey Wheat Bread

The local public broadcasting television station was having its annual week-long TV auction for fund raising. All week long it had been advertising that the mayor would bake bread and sell it on the last night. It went well and we auctioned off about six loaves for a total of $70. The highest bid was $25 for one loaf.

"The mayor" was Richard Hentges and his Honey Wheat Bread was the prize. Now a real estate developer in Fargo, North Dakota, Dick served one term as mayor of that city and three terms in the North Dakota House of Representatives.

Dick likes to bake eight breads at one time (as I do), but his recipe can be halved if you want to try a more moderate amount or if your freezer is not large enough to hold the yield. In fact, Dick considers himself a "nonstop" baker:

While the loaves rise, I usually make rolls in between. One Saturday a few years ago, when my wife was out of town and I was in charge of our three children, I started a nonstop baking spree by rising and baking, rising and baking double and triple recipes of Honey Wheat Bread, white bread, rye bread, white rolls, and cinnamon rolls. They all turned out well, much to the surprise of my children. . . .

The test report that came back from the Rodale Test Kitchens reads: "Very good basic bread." I agree.

Heat 9 cups of milk to 110°F. (Dick always uses a thermometer, he tells me.) Pour milk into a very large mixing bowl, add the salt and mix. Then mix molasses and honey, and add to bowl. Stir well.

Melt the butter and add to the milk mixture. Using the same cup in which you mixed the molasses and honey, add the 3 packages of dry yeast to 1 cup of 110°F. water. Set aside to let the yeast proof.

When yeast has bubbled, add to the mixture in the bowl, add the wheat germ and stir.

Add 8 cups of the whole wheat flour and mix. Then add 8 more cups of the flour and mix again. Add 4 more cups, 1 at a time, mixing well after each addition. Then add the balance of the flour (2 to 4 cups) until the dough reaches the proper consistency for kneading.

Turn out onto a lightly floured board and knead for 8 to 10 minutes, adding more flour if needed. Clean and grease the mixing bowl to use as a rising place. Roll the dough into a large ball and put it topside down in the bowl, roll it around to grease all sides, cover and allow it to rise in a warm spot for 1½ to 2 hours, or until doubled in size.

Thoroughly grease 6 to 8 bread pans, 9 × 5 inches. When the dough has risen, punch it down and knead again for 2 to 3 minutes to remove the air.

Divide into 6 or 8 pieces. Cover with a towel and let rest for about 5 minutes and then shape the dough into loaves. Place in pans. Cover and let rise in a warm spot for 1 hour. Before baking, brush tops of loaves with beaten egg mixture and sprinkle with sesame seeds (optional).

Bake in a 350°F. oven for 35 to 40 minutes. After about 20 to 25 minutes, check for brownness and cover the tops with aluminum foil if they seem to be browning too quickly though the bread is not yet baked through.

When loaves test done, turn out onto wire racks to cool.

Honey Wheat Bread

(6 to 8 loaves)

9 cups milk
2 tablespoons salt (optional)
½ cup molasses
½ cup honey
¾ cup butter
3 packages dry yeast
1 cup warm water
½ cup wheat germ
22 to 24 cups whole wheat flour

Glaze:

1 egg, beaten
1 teaspoon water
sesame seeds (optional)

You may take off a portion of the dough that has been prepared for bread, make it up into little round cakes or rolls, and bake them for breakfast or tea.

BRAN BREAD.—Sift into a pan three quarts of unbolted wheat meal. Stir a jill of strong yeast, and a jill of molasses into a quart of soft water, (which must be warm but not hot,) and add a small tea-spoonful of pearl-ash, or sal-aratus. Make a hole in the heap of flour, pour in the liquid, and proceed in the usual manner of making bread. This quantity may be made into two loaves. Bran bread is considered very wholesome; and is recommended to persons afflicted with dyspepsia.

RYE AND INDIAN BREAD.—Sift two quarts of rye, and two quarts of Indian meal, and mix them well together. Boil three pints of milk; pour it boiling hot upon the meal; add two tea-spoonfuls of salt, and stir the whole very hard. Let it stand till it becomes of only a lukewarm heat, and then stir in half a pint of good fresh yeast; if from the brewery and quite fresh, a smaller quantity will suffice. Knead the mixture into a stiff dough, and set it to rise in a pan. Cover it with a thick cloth that has been previously warmed, and set it near the fire. When it is quite light, and has cracked all over the top, make it into two loaves, put them into a moderate oven, and bake them two hours and a half.

COMMON YEAST.—Put a large handful of hops into two quarts of boiling water, which must then be set on the fire again, and boiled twenty minutes with the hops. Have ready in a pan three pints of sifted flour; strain the liquid, and pour half of it on the flour. Let the other half stand till it becomes

32*

BETTY AND BRANSON HOBBS

The Breads:

Grandmother Ruffin's Biscuits
Mary's Quick Breakfast Puffs
Cornmeal Muffins
Banker's Rolls
Joicey's Spoon Bread
Sally Lunn
Hush Puppies
A Hush Puppy Variation

I doubt that I could have found more perfect people to provide some traditional southern recipes than Betty and Branson. They live in Rocky Mount, North Carolina, and the family dates back to 1619 as settlers in Virginia. My correspondence with them has reached voluminous proportions and not only am I the proud possessor of some of Grandmother Ruffin's original recipes, but I have been inundated and charmed by tales of the Old South, local news from North Carolina, and marvelous Civil War stories:

. . . Branson's great-grandmother brought food to the troops fighting at Ft. Fisher during the Civil War—and along with the food, she brought in matches to fire the guns. . . .

Branson is a banker and Betty is a genealogist who teaches and conducts private classes. She remembers her first bread-baking experience while standing on a stool in the kitchen to help her mother.

Of course, there's an old southern tradition of never measuring anything—a pinch of this and a dash of that—so sometimes things work and sometimes they don't. . . .

Betty claims that Branson is the cook of the family, a reflection of his mother who was the best cook in Chapel Hill, ". . . and when Papa died, all Branson wanted was his cast-iron chicken cooker. . . ."

Here are seven of the Hobbs family recipes, plus a variation of the Hush Puppies that I found one day while traveling through Tennessee.

Grandmother Ruffin's Biscuits

(1 dozen biscuits)

½ pound (1 cup) butter
2 cups warm milk
1 teaspoon soda
½ cup honey
6 cups unbleached white flour

The original recipe (naturally) gave no oven temperature or time for baking. It was just as Betty describes the old recipes—a pinch and a dash. We've worked it out together to translate it into more modern terms, but it wouldn't surprise me if grandmother's were even better!

Melt the butter in the milk and when lukewarm, add the soda and the honey.

In a large bowl, sift the flour and make a well in the center, pouring the liquid into the well. With floured fingers, pull the flour toward the center until the dough forms a ball. Flour the surface and knead the dough for 10 minutes, adding more flour if it seems too sticky.

Roll out the dough with a floured rolling pin to a thickness of about ½ inch. Using a small wine glass or round cookie cutter, cut out the biscuits and place them on a greased and floured cookie sheet. Prick the tops with a fork several times.

Bake in a 425°F. oven for 8 to 10 minutes or until golden brown.

You may also add leftover baked and mashed sweet potatoes to the dough to make sweet potato biscuits. The last time I spoke with Betty she told me that she also will bake these occasionally in tiny, sterling silver, whiskey jiggers and she serves them at cocktail parties with "real sho-nuff Smithfield Ham."

Mary Hobbs was Branson's mother and this is her recipe. It's still used by the Hobbs family.

Beat the eggs and add the milk and the butter. In a separate bowl, sift the flour, salt, and baking powder twice and then add the liquid ingredients. Beat for 2 minutes.

Pour in hot greased muffin tins and bake in a hot oven (450°F.) for 20 minutes.

NOTE: These puffs can be made using whole wheat flour and they are delicious.

Mary's Quick Breakfast Puffs

(1 dozen puffs)

2 eggs
1 cup milk
1 tablespoon melted butter
1½ cups unbleached white flour, sifted
½ teaspoon salt*
3 teaspoons baking powder

Sift together cornmeal, flour, baking powder, and salt. Add the honey, milk, egg, and butter. Mix well.

Bake in hot greased muffin tins for 20 to 25 minutes at 450°F.

Cornmeal Muffins

(1 dozen muffins)

1 cup cornmeal
1 cup whole wheat flour, sifted
4 teaspoons baking powder
1 teaspoon salt (optional)
2 tablespoons honey
1 cup milk
1 egg, beaten
1 tablespoon melted butter

*The salt, though traditional, may be eliminated if you choose to do so.

Banker's Rolls

(5 to 6 dozen rolls or 4 loaves)

1 package dry yeast
½ cup lukewarm water
1 cup warm mashed potatoes
(about 3 medium potatoes,
diced, and boiled in
salted water)
2 eggs, well beaten
⅔ cup butter
¼ cup honey
1 cup milk, scalded and cooled to
lukewarm
2 teaspoons salt (optional)
5½ to 6 cups whole wheat flour

This was another one of the recipes in which amounts were given in nonspecific terms ("a little of this and a bit of that") but I called Branson and asked him to bake them again—which he did. He called back the next day with the detailed amounts and said, "I hadn't baked these in some time. I'd forgotten just how good they were!"

Mix the yeast with the lukewarm water and set aside to proof.

In a large bowl, mix the mashed potatoes with the eggs, add the butter, honey, lukewarm milk, and salt. Then add yeast mixture. Mix well after each addition. Add the flour 1 cup at a time until the dough is fairly stiff. This may take about 5 cups—reserve the rest for addition when kneading.

Turn out onto a lightly floured surface and knead for 8 to 10 minutes or until dough is smooth and elastic.

Place in a greased bowl, turn once to coat the top and cover. Place in a warm spot and let rise for 1½ to 2 hours or until doubled in bulk.

Turn out onto floured surface and knead again for 1 or 2 minutes. Form into rolls—they can be round, braided, twists, or any shape that suits your fancy at the moment. Place them on a greased baking sheet and cover lightly with a towel or plastic wrap. Let rise in a warm spot for about 1½ hours.

Bake at 425°F. for 10 minutes or until the rolls are done.

Branson says the recipe will work just as well for loaves—it will make 4. The baking time should be increased accordingly to about 45 minutes or until loaves test done when tapped on the bottom.

This recipe comes from Betty's sister, Joicey, and it's an old Virginia dish, very much like a souffle. The children like to put butter and syrup on it.

In a saucepan, put the cornmeal, salt, and honey and add the 2 cups of water. Boil until thick. Add the butter. Cool.

Add the beaten eggs and the milk and continue cooking slowly until the mixture has the consistency of custard.

Add the baking powder and put the entire mixture into a greased, 2-quart souffle dish and bake at 400°F. for about 45 to 50 minutes or until a silver knife inserted into the center comes out clean. The finished bread will fill about two-thirds of the souffle dish.

Joicey's Spoon Bread

(6 servings)

1 cup white stone-ground cornmeal
2 teaspoons salt (optional)
1 teaspoon honey
2 cups water
1 tablespoon butter
2 eggs, beaten
1 cup milk
2 teaspoons baking powder

This is another of those traditional breads that carry various tales as to their origins. Grandmother Ruffin's cookbook says it was named after its creator. When my wife was doing research for a series of recipes she was testing, she found another story—that the name came from medieval Europe, where it was hawked on the streets as *soleil et lune* (sun and moon). Whatever the derivation, it is a bread that has been around a long long time and this one is Betty and Branson's recipe for it.

Heat the milk in a saucepan, add the butter and the water. Cool to lukewarm. Pour the mixture into a bowl and add the flour, salt, beaten eggs, honey, dry yeast, and the flavorings. Beat with a mixer for 3 minutes or mix with floured hands or a wooden spoon until all ingredients are well blended. Cover and place in a warm spot to rise for about 1 hour.

Mix down and put in a greased 9- or 10-inch tube pan. Bake at 350°F. for 50 minutes.

Sally Lunn

(6 to 8 servings)

1 cup milk
½ cup butter
¼ cup water
3½ cups unbleached white flour
2 teaspoons salt*
3 eggs, beaten
½ cup honey
2 packages dry yeast
1 teaspoon pure vanilla extract
½ teaspoon pure almond extract

*The salt, though traditional, may be eliminated if you choose to do so.

Hush Puppies

(6 to 8 servings)

2 cups stone-ground cornmeal
1 teaspoon baking soda
2 teaspoons salt (optional)
8 tablespoons grated onions
2 tablespoons flour
1 tablespoon baking powder
1 egg
2 cups buttermilk
red pepper to taste
oil for cooking

Hush Puppies are the mainstay of the South. They're served with all kinds of seafood, and they're especially well known as an accompaniment to catfish dinners. They're probably also the first dog pacifiers on record—the cooks used to throw them to yelping, hungry puppies to quiet them down, calling "Hush puppy!"

Mix all the ingredients in a bowl. Drop the batter by the teaspoonful into boiling oil. They will be crisp and they'll float when they're done.

Drain on paper and serve hot.

A Hush Puppy Variation

(6 servings)

½ cup whole wheat flour
1½ cups white stone-ground cornmeal
2 teaspoons baking powder
1 teaspoon salt (optional)
1 teaspoon baking soda
¼ teaspoon black pepper
1 egg, beaten
½ cup beer
½ cup buttermilk
1 large grated onion
oil for frying

Using the author's prerogative, I just couldn't resist adding this small addendum to the Hush Puppy recipe. Some years ago, long before I even knew how to bake bread, I traveled frequently to Tennessee and on each trip I cajoled my friends, Bill and Kay Womack, into taking a trip to the Shelby Motel north of Memphis. They didn't like catfish—but this Yankee loved them. At that time they served all the catfish you could eat for just a dollar or two—and the accompaniment was a platter of the most delicious hush puppies I had ever tasted. Naturally, I questioned the chef about his secret, and I learned that the difference was *beer*. It gave an added lightness to the hush puppies. Here's the variation on the recipe which I've had in my files all this time.

Sift all the dry ingredients. Heat the oil for deep-fat frying to about 375°F. and heat the oven to 400°F. to keep the hush puppies warm while making the rest of the batter.

Beat the egg and add the beer and buttermilk. Combine with the dry ingredients, add the grated onion and mix. The batter should be slightly stiff—if it is not, add a bit more flour.

Drop the batter by the teaspoonful into the oil and fry the hush puppies 3 or 4 at a time so that the temperature of the oil is maintained. They will float to the top when they're brown and done.

Lift out with a slotted spoon, drain on paper and keep hot in the oven.

LINDA WAGGY

We live in a cabin in the woods. We have a telephone and a propane refrigerator, but no electricity or other utilities. We carry our water from a nearby stream. All of our cooking and baking is done on an Economy wood stove and, of course, we heat with wood. I've found bread baking with the wood stove to be a joy.

Linda Waggy, her husband Barry and their two children, Benjamin and Joshua, live in a cabin in Goose Hollow in upstate New York.

We built the cabin ourselves just a few years ago entirely of recycled wood—mostly from barns. After one and a half years, we find that we don't miss much except a stereo and a freezer. Someday we hope to generate our own electricity—probably with wind power, since we live in an area along the southern shore of Lake Erie and there is almost constant wind.

The most fascinating thing about Linda and Barry is that they did what so many of us have dreamed of doing—escaping to a hollow near a stream and turning our backs on the cities. And, more important, the family is ecstatic about their life.

Linda is a full-time artist-in-the-community for the Chautauqua County Association for the Arts. She works mainly in the six day-care centers as an arts coordinator and creative dramatics teacher. The Seneca Indian Nation is near their home and she is developing a special day-care program in conjunction with the Indian officials. In addition to developing the house and the land, teaching, and bringing up two children, she has started a seat-weaving business, doing cane, rush, splint, and wicker repair—and she is involved in the early stages of writing a children's book about Goose Hollow!

Added to all of this, of course, she bakes marvelous breads.

The Breads:

Brown Bread
Linda's Whole Wheat Bread
Swedish Coffee Bread

I find that I bake bread more often during the heating season because of the wood cookstove. It's easier when the stove is already going. I find bread baking extremely satisfying—the process itself is enriching—watching the dough develop in your hands, the warmth, the smells. It's all so real and alive! In the growing world of plastics, it's great to be in touch with the earth!

This Brown Bread recipe came from Linda's grandfather who lived in central Pennsylvania.

I've tried others but found this to be my favorite recipe. I like to keep it in the refrigerator because it's so moist. My favorite way of eating it is to spread a slice with cream cheese.

Mix flour, soda, and salt in a large bowl. Combine the milk, honey, and molasses, then add mixture to the dry ingredients. Pour into 2 well-greased, 9 × 5-inch bread pans.

Bake at 350°F. for 50 to 60 minutes.

Brown Bread

(2 loaves)

5½ cups graham or whole
    wheat flour
4 teaspoons baking soda
2 teaspoons salt (optional)
1 quart buttermilk or sour cream
½ cup honey
⅔ cup molasses

Dissolve the yeast and teaspoon of honey in the warm water. Put aside to proof.

In a large bowl, put butter or oil, honey or molasses, and salt. Add the boiling water and stir. Let cool to lukewarm. Add the yeast mixture, dry milk, eggs, and 4 cups of flour. Beat with a whisk, spoon, or mixer. Add enough flour to make a soft, workable dough. Turn out onto a lightly floured surface and knead for 10 minutes.

Place the dough in a greased bowl, turn once to cover top, cover and place in a warm spot to rise to double in bulk (about 1 hour).

Turn out onto floured surface, punch down, and knead for a minute or 2. Cover with bowl and let rest for 10 minutes. Then divide in half and form 2 loaves. Place in greased bread pans, cover with a towel, and let rise in a warm place until almost doubled (about 45 minutes).

Bake at 400°F. for 35 minutes or until done. (Cover with foil the last 10 minutes to prevent burning.) Bread will sound hollow when tapped with fingers.

Turn out onto wire racks to cool.

Linda's Whole Wheat Bread

(2 very large loaves or 3 medium loaves)

2 packages dry yeast
1 teaspoon honey
1 cup warm water
¼ cup butter or oil
⅓ cup honey or molasses
1½ tablespoons salt (optional)
2 cups boiling water
1 cup nonfat dry milk
2 eggs
8¾ cups whole wheat flour

Swedish Coffee Bread

(2 breads)

2 packages dry yeast
½ cup warm water
2 cups milk
⅔ cup butter
2 eggs
⅓ cup honey
¾ teaspoon ground cardamom
1 teaspoon salt*
6½ to 7 cups unbleached
white flour

Filling:

½ cup butter
¼ cup honey
¼ to ½ cup chopped raisins,
chopped dates, or
dried apricots (optional)
cinnamon

My maternal grandmother came from Sweden all by herself when she was 16. She worked as a cook in logging camps. My grandmother taught me this recipe and it's my favorite. It's a traditional Swedish bread served on holidays, especially on Christmas.

Dissolve yeast in warm water and set aside to proof. Heat milk in a saucepan until just below boiling. Add butter. In a big bowl, beat eggs, honey, and cardamom until well blended. Add salt. Pour hot milk with butter over mixture while beating. Add 2 cups of flour and mix well. Let cool to lukewarm.

Add dissolved yeast and enough flour to make a soft dough. (Linda says, "I find it difficult to measure or to follow any recipe exactly—it satisfies my creative urge! Of course, sometimes it would have been better to measure!")

Turn out onto a lightly floured board and knead until elastic (about 8 to 10 minutes). Return to a greased bowl, turn dough to coat the top, cover and place in a warm spot to rise until doubled in bulk (about 1 hour).

When dough has doubled, punch down, knead for 2 to 3 minutes and return to bowl, cover and let rise to double again.

Turn out onto a lightly floured board, punch down and divide the dough in half. With a floured rolling pin, roll out each half into an oval shape about ¼ inch thick.

Melt the butter in a small pan and add the honey. Remove from heat and add the raisins, dates, or dried apricots, if desired. Stir until cool and spreadable. Spread the mixture evenly over the dough. Sprinkle with cinnamon and roll up dough lengthwise, pinching the seams closed with your fingers. Place both breads on a greased, large cookie sheet, seams down. Place in a warm spot, cover with a towel and let rise for about 20 to 30 minutes.

Bake in a 375°F. oven for 25 to 30 minutes or until breads test done.

*The salt, though traditional, may be eliminated if you choose to do so.

Prepare dough the same method as for bread, then cut into 1-inch-long pieces and place on greased cookie sheet with filling side up. Let rise, covered, and then bake at 375°F. for 10 to 20 minutes.

For Rolls

Fill the dough as described for the bread, and then, on a greased cookie sheet, form the roll into a circle. Using a pair of scissors, cut almost through the dough at 1-inch intervals to reveal the filling inside. Turn the sections sideways to expose the center and then let rise, covered, for about 20 to 30 minutes. Bake at 375°F. for 20 to 30 minutes.

For Coffee Cake

NOTE: This recipe works very well using whole wheat flour in place of unbleached white flour.

The Great Salt-Rising Bread Mystery

The Breads:

Salt-Rising Bread
Potato Salt-Rising Bread

It is, without any doubt in anyone's mind, the most stubborn, the most difficult, the most frustrating, and the most delicious bread—*if* it works.

I baked my first salt-rising bread a few years ago. I had been warned by the experts that it was tricky, that it smelled just awful while it was rising, that the temperature of the oven had to be perfect, that no drafts could ever penetrate the area in which the bread was rising. I felt like a surgeon about to begin a delicate brain operation.

Carefully, I followed the instructions, watched the temperatures, even used thermometers to be certain, and the dough rose—and it smelled as they said it would. Delicately, it was placed in two pans—the same dough mixed at the same time—put in the same oven. While the two jewels baked, the smell changed from pungent to cheeselike, a strange aroma quite different from the usual yeast breads that permeate our house.

The time was up—I opened the oven door. *One had risen. The other had not!*

Through these years, then, the saga of salt-rising bread has been a constant delight of mine. And I have heard stories from bread bakers all across the country—the tips and the failures, the successes, the hints and the "do's" as well as the "do-nots"—and I have tested most of them. Some work sometimes. Others do not. The only solace I get from all of this is that I am not alone!

In an article by Barbara Gibbs Ostmann, food editor of the *St. Louis Post-Dispatch,* she tells of a recipe she tested which worked perfectly each time it was made—until picture-taking day, when it was a total flop! The rest of the article ("Salt-Rising Bread." *St. Louis Post-Dispatch,* 6 October 1976.) has some excellent information for those of us who are adventurous enough to try baking the bread:

Salt-rising bread, also known as lightnin' bread, was popular when homemade yeasts were unreliable. The name "salt-rising" refers to the old kitchen practice of keeping the bowl of starter nested overnight in a bed of warm salt, which retained the heat nicely. It does not refer to the bread's peculiar taste.

. . . most people either love it or can't stand it. This is largely because of the smell. Frankly, this bread smells to high heaven while being prepared. An old saying is that the more sour it smells while baking, the sweeter it will taste after baking. The smell is not unlike a soft, ripe cheese. It is here that lovers of salt-rising bread are sorted out from those who are not. To the former, it is a glorious aroma; to the latter, an unpleasant smell. Once you get past the odor, however, the bread itself is delicious. . . .

Although no two people will agree on the exact recipe, there are some basic processes that almost everyone will agree on. The important thing to remember is that once you start making the bread, each process has to follow the previous one, for the dough waits for no one. The times given in the recipes for fermenting and rising are only guides and may vary considerably depending upon heat, humidity, and ingredients.

One old-fashioned "receipt" begins "it must be made on a clear day and kept at a warm temperature." Do not attempt this bread in damp, cold weather unless the house is heated and the batter is well protected from drafts.

The starter is a true starter. No yeast is used. (Some versions use potatoes and yeast, but are not considered true salt-rising bread.) The starter is temperamental, however, and if it doesn't bubble up during the night to produce the oddly sweet odor and become light and fluffy, then don't be patient and wait. It is useless to proceed, as the bread will not rise properly. Just toss it out and start a new starter, but put it together in another way. Use different milk or another kind of cornmeal. There is no reason why one combination works and another doesn't, but it happens. As one old "receipt" said: "Salt-rising bread is as changeable as a woman's mind."

Remember that salt-rising bread loves warmth. Warm everything it comes in contact with—spoons, cups, bowls. Don't let it chill. The ideal place for the starter to ferment should range from 90° to 95°F. This might be in a pan of water over a pilot light in a gas oven, or maybe on a shelf near the hot water heater. One woman uses a heating pad set on "low" (as does Edwin Williams, whose recipe is on page 310). The sponge and dough are not as temperamental as the starter and demand less heat and attention as the bacteria grow stronger. Be careful during the second rise to not let it overrise, or the dough can sour.

As for ingredients, water-ground cornmeal is the best to use, but commercial white cornmeal can also be used successfully. Use pasteurized whole milk. Nonfat dry milk works sometimes, but not always. Hard wheat or whole wheat flours may be used, but we did not like the combination of whole wheat and salt-rising flavors. The measurements for flour should always be read as "about" because the amount always varies, depending upon the flour.

. . . be prepared for some ups and downs. If at first you don't succeed, try again, because sometimes it works and sometimes it doesn't. In any event, be prepared for the odor while baking, and for the great taste after it's finished.

The two recipes that follow are variations on salt-rising bread. One uses the traditional cornmeal starter, the other adds potatoes.

Salt-Rising Bread

(3 loaves)

For the Starter:

1 cup milk, scalded
½ cup cornmeal
1 teaspoon honey

For the Dough:

3 cups milk
1 tablespoon honey
1 tablespoon salt (optional)
1 teaspoon baking soda
3 tablespoons melted butter
9 to 11 cups whole wheat flour

There are some of us who claim that no real bread baker would ever use potatoes in Salt-Rising Bread. The traditional recipe calls only for cornmeal. However, this bread is a bit trickier to handle than the one that uses potatoes. But, in any case, remember that this recipe (as all other salt-rising recipes) requires consistent warmth. The bread makes marvelous toast.

To make the starter, scald the cup of milk and pour it over the cornmeal, then add the teaspoon of honey. Mix lightly and place the container or bowl in a pan of warm water. This can be placed on a heating pad set on "low" or in the oven with the pilot light on. Cover tightly and let it stand for at least 24 hours, or until the mixture ferments. You will know by its smell whether or not you are succeeding.

When the mixture has fermented and there is a bubbly foam over the surface, scald the additional 3 cups of milk and pour it into a mixing bowl. Add the tablespoon of honey, the salt, and the baking soda. Add the melted butter and stir the mixture to dissolve the ingredients. Set aside to cool to lukewarm.

When the batter is lukewarm, add about 5 to 6 cups of the flour, 1 cup at a time, stirring as you do so. Add the cornmeal starter and beat with a wooden spoon for about 4 to 5 minutes.

Place the bowl in warm water again and then on the heating pad set to "low." Cover and let stand for 2 to 3 hours. The batter should be bubbly and should have increased in bulk. The smell, at this point, should begin to match the descriptions written in this chapter and in every other book or article devoted to salt-rising bread. I happen to love it, for it notifies everyone in the family that I am baking this most unusual of treats.

Add about 4 to 5 cups of flour and mix to make a soft dough. Turn out onto a floured surface and knead until the dough is smooth and elastic—about 10 minutes. Shape the dough into 3 loaves. Place in greased, 9 × 5-inch bread pans and cover lightly.

Place the covered pans in a warm place for the second rising— either back in the oven with the pilot light on, or in warm water atop the heating pad set to "low." The dough should double in about 50 minutes to 1 hour. The dough will fill only about one-third of the pan when you first place the loaves in them and the batter will rise to fill about two-thirds of the pan when it has risen.

Preheat the oven to 375°F. and bake for 45 to 50 minutes. When the loaves test done by tapping on the bottom and getting a hollow sound, turn them out at once onto wire racks to cool.

EDWIN WILLIAMS

Turn to page 285 for another sample of Ed Williams's unique ability.

Potato Salt-Rising Bread

(3 loaves)

2½ cups new nonmealy potatoes, pared and sliced thinly
1 tablespoon salt (optional)
2 tablespoons cornmeal
4 cups boiling water
1 teaspoon baking soda
1½ teaspoons salt (optional)
11 cups hard wheat flour
1 cup milk, scalded
1 teaspoon honey
1½ tablespoons butter

This salt-rising bread uses potatoes as well as the cornmeal. Its aroma is milder than that of the previous recipe.

Place the potatoes in a bowl and sprinkle salt and cornmeal over them. Add the boiling water and stir until the salt is dissolved. Place the bowl on a heating pad set to "low" and cover the bowl and wrap it with a towel. (You can also use the oven with the pilot light on.) It is important to maintain a temperature at a constant 115°F. After standing 15 to 20 hours, the mixture should be quite bubbly. Squeeze out the potatoes and discard them. Drain the liquid into a large bowl and add baking soda, salt, and 5 cups of the flour.

Beat the mixture thoroughly with a wooden spoon for several minutes or use an electric mixer, set on medium speed, and beat for 2 minutes. Return the bowl to the heating pad, cover with a towel, and let the mixture rise until it has increased in volume by about one-third. This will take 1½ to 2 hours.

Then scald 1 cup of milk. After it has cooled to lukewarm, add the honey and butter. Add this mixture to the potato sponge along with the remaining 6 cups of flour.

Turn out onto lightly floured surface and knead for 10 minutes or until dough is smooth and elastic.

Shape into 3 loaves, place them in well-greased, 9 × 5-inch loaf pans, cover and let the dough rise until light and nearly double in bulk. Here again, keep the temperature constant, either in the oven or on the heating pad—and beware of drafts!

Bake in a preheated oven at 350°F. for 1 hour. When loaves test done, turn out onto wire racks to cool.

ROBERT RODALE

The manuscript for this book was almost ready. There were the discussions and the meetings and the testings, the decisions to make about size, photographs, the agony of dropping recipes while replacing them with others for balance and nutrition. And it was another of those chilly prewinter days when Bob Rodale had the fire going in the office wood stove. Our discussion, as always, had been about the balance in the book, and where to allow the use of unbleached white flour—only for purposes of tradition or where the whole grain flour would not work well for rising, by itself, because of its lesser gluten content.

The talk turned to the bread-baker friends who had contributed to this book, and Bob smiled and said modestly, "Oh, I bake bread too!"

All of us turned and laughed. My wife muttered, "How would you like to be in Mel's book?" Bob said, "I was kind of hoping you'd ask," and gave me this recipe.

And so, my own publisher joins the other friends from around the country, and I am most delighted.

These corn flat breads appeal most to people who have an unfulfilled urge for more primitive food in their diets. This bread is as far as you can possibly get from white bread. I find that almost everyone likes them once they adjust to the chewiness. Numerous times I have watched people eat these and almost always they must chew each mouthful 40 times before swallowing. The delicate sweetness that is naturally present in cornmeal is fully extracted by the saliva during that chewing.

The breads are especially valuable for hikers and for traveling, because they keep well, don't require slicing and can be eaten with almost any kind of spread, such as peanut butter, or with an apple, banana or other fruit topping. As to the chewiness, Bob states, properly:

The Bread:

Corn Flat Bread

A hard job of chewing, I believe, signals the appetite to be satisfied more quickly. In other words, you eat less yet feel more satisfied.

Corn Flat Bread

(4 to 6 servings)

1½ to 2 cups boiling water
(amount will depend upon
desired dryness of bread)
3 cups white cornmeal
1 cup uncooked rolled oats
¼ cup sesame seeds (optional)
⅓ cup corn oil

Put water on to boil. While water is heating, mix dry ingredients in a bowl, then pour boiling water on the mixture and add the corn oil. Mix with wooden spoon. Add less water than you think is necessary and then add more until you achieve the desired moistness. The dough should be dry enough to be handled easily after it cools—dryer than the mortar used for laying bricks. Trial and error will teach you a few lessons.

Put the dough aside to cool for about half an hour. Preheat oven to 375°F. Shape the dough into patties, using your hands (it's a good idea to oil your hands first). The size of each patty can depend upon personal preference, the size of your hands, or your expected appetite. Mine start out as a piece of dough the size of a golf ball or slightly larger. Place the patties on an oiled cookie sheet.

Bake the patties for about 1 hour. They should be turning a nice golden color and even be somewhat brown around the edges, when finished. I like my breads dry, so I turn off the oven after an hour and then let them dry out for about 15 more minutes with the oven fan turned on.

SHERYL LONDON

She is a writer and has had her own books published. She is a superb cook, a painter, has traveled extensively and has over 20 film credits. She lives with me in New York and Fire Island. She is my wife and my most recent convert to the joy of baking bread.

I've always baked since I was a little girl—pies, cakes, cookies, and pastries—never bread. Somehow, if I failed with a cake or pie, it didn't matter. They were, after all, luxuries. Bread was a thing to respect, the staff of life. . . .

She felt that she was intimidated by the mystique of something so secretive that it had to be "baked while you slept," as one manufacturer's slogan proclaimed when she was a child.

Then, one rainy day, while looking through the typed manuscript of this book, reading about all the people around the country and how they started to bake bread, I decided to try it. If I failed, I was alone and there were hungry birds outside. . . .

As with all of us who love to bake bread, she now speaks of the dough as it came alive under her fingers, like sculptor's clay, the magic of doubling in size, the sensuality, the rewards, the drama that unfolds:

. . . I put the breads in the oven and turned on the light so I could watch through the glass door. What I discovered was comparable to viewing a television screen—only a much better show! And no violence either!

And so, I have created a competitor within my own household. With her superb gourmet sense of cooking, she will soon surpass me in my craft and I will graciously yield my crown to lie back and

The Breads:

Onion Poppy Seed Diamonds
Monkey Bread
Three Wheat Marble Loaf
Never Fail Popovers

enjoy the fruits of her efforts. For she, too, has discovered ". . . man does not live by cake alone, once he/she has baked bread."

Onion Poppy Seed Diamonds

(approximately 4 dozen diamonds)

2¼ to 2½ cups whole wheat flour
2 teaspoons baking powder
2 teaspoons salt (optional)
½ teaspoon black pepper
scant ½ cup poppy seeds
4 to 5 finely chopped
medium-size onions
2 eggs, beaten
½ cup corn oil
3 tablespoons ice water
(if needed)

These marvelous, crisp little breads make a fine accompaniment for soups, stews or *hors d'oeuvres*. The original recipe came from Sheryl's grandmother who used to make 8 to 12 dozen at one time. The reason for so many, we discovered, was that every visitor to grandma's house took a box of these home as a gift.

The day before baking prepare the dough. Put all the dry ingredients in a large bowl. Stir and make a well in the center. Add the onions, eggs, and corn oil. Mix or knead with a floured hand to incorporate all the dry ingredients. If dough seems too dry, add the ice water. If dough seems soft and smooth, the water is not necessary. When the dough forms a ball, wrap in plastic and chill overnight in the refrigerator.

Next morning, divide dough into 3 parts and roll each part with a floured rolling pin until thin. Fold dough and roll again to ¼-inch thickness. Cut with a knife into diamond shapes about 4 inches long by 1½ inches wide.

Place on oiled baking sheets and puncture breads in several spots with a fork. Bake in a slow oven—about 300°F.—until light brown, about 40 to 45 minutes. Turn the pans frequently to prevent burning.

After cooling, the Onion Poppy Seed Diamonds keep well in a plastic bag.

Sheryl calls this "tear-off-a-piece-of-bread bread" because it consists of ropelike pieces that separate easily. I was quite impressed with it the first time I saw it—and, after tasting it, I was even more impressed!

In a large bowl, mix 1½ cups flour, yeast, honey, and salt and set aside. Heat the milk and ⅓ cup butter to 110°F. and pour over the flour-yeast mixture. Add the egg and, using a hand beater, beat 3 minutes at medium speed. Add another cup of flour and beat 3 minutes longer. Stir in remaining flour and mix with a wooden spoon until completely blended. Place in a greased bowl, turn to coat dough, and cover. Place in a warm spot to rise for about 30 minutes.

Turn out onto a lightly floured surface and knead for 10 minutes. Cover lightly and let rest for 10 minutes.

Divide the dough into 2 equal parts. Roll out each piece into a 12 × 18-inch rectangle. Cut into ¾-inch strips and then divide each strip into 3-inch pieces. Using a large bowl or a deep saucepan, dip each of the strips into the melted, cooled butter and then toss them (haphazardly) into a 10-inch tubed angel food cake pan. Cover and place in your unheated oven and allow it to rise for about 1½ hours. The pilot light will provide just enough heat to keep the rising temperature at about 100°F.

Remove covering towel or wrap (don't forget this, or you'll incinerate it), then turn the heat up to a setting of 425°F. Bake on bottom rack for 30 to 40 minutes or until golden brown. If top begins to burn before bread is done, cover lightly with aluminum foil and continue baking.

Turn out on rack to cool slightly. Serve warm by tearing it off, piece by delicious piece. Remember, it has already been buttered!

Monkey Bread

(1 large loaf)

4 to 5 cups whole wheat flour
3 packages dry yeast
2 tablespoons honey
1 tablespoon salt (optional)
1½ cups milk
⅓ cup softened butter
1 egg
¾ cup melted butter, cooled to
  room temperature

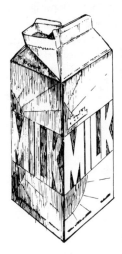

Three Wheat Marble Loaf

(1 large loaf)

3½ to 4 cups unbleached white flour
1 package dry yeast
1½ cups buttermilk
2 tablespoons honey
4 tablespoons butter
2 teaspoons salt (optional)
1 tablespoon wheat germ
2 tablespoons dark molasses
½ teaspoon baking soda
½ cup cracked wheat flour
1½ cups stone-ground whole wheat flour
¼ cup warm water

After a trip to Minnesota, Sheryl came home carrying stone-ground whole wheat flour and a large bag of cracked wheat flour (in addition to a *Lefse* stick and two pounds of Minnesota wild rice). The first weekend back at Fire Island, this bread was baked—a large, marbled loaf of superb texture and color. The cracked wheat makes it slightly crunchy.

In a large mixing bowl, combine 1½ cups of the white flour with the dry yeast. In a saucepan, heat the buttermilk, honey, and butter until warm. Add the salt to the liquid and then pour into the dry mixture in the bowl. Beat at low speed with an electric hand mixer for 1 minute, then beat at high speed for 3 minutes. Add wheat germ and stir with a wooden spoon. Divide the dough in half (it will be soft) and put one-half in another bowl.

In the first bowl, add another cup of white flour (more if necessary) to make a stiff dough. Turn out onto a floured board and knead for 10 minutes. Shape into a ball and place in a well-oiled bowl, turning once to coat the entire surface. Cover with a cloth and let rest while preparing the other part of the dough.

In the second bowl, add the molasses, baking soda, cracked wheat flour, and whole wheat flour. Add the remaining 1 to 1½ cups of white flour and the warm water. Mix with a wooden spoon. Turn out onto a floured board and knead for 10 minutes. Lightly coat the dough with oil and place it in the same bowl as the first half. Cover with a cloth and let rise in the oven with only the pilot light on (about 90° to 100°F. for 1½ hours).

Punch individual dough down separately and let rest for 10 minutes, covered. Butter a large 9 × 5 × 3-inch loaf pan and then roll out each piece of dough into a rectangle about 8 × 12 inches in size. Place the darker dough on top of the lighter one and roll them both up together, starting at the narrow end. Place in loaf pan and cover with a cloth. Return to the cold oven for a second time. Let rise for about 45 minutes or until doubled in bulk.

Remove the cloth and turn on heat in oven to 375°F. (Do not preheat oven.) Bake for about 40 to 45 minutes or until bread tests done by tapping bottom and hearing a hollow sound. If, after 30 minutes, you find that the top is browning too fast, cover with aluminum foil and continue baking.

Remove from pan and place on a wire rack to cool.

This bread is delicious served slightly warm and covered with butter.

Butter 4 large custard cups (or 6 small ones). Sift flour and salt together. In a separate bowl, beat eggs lightly, and add milk and melted butter. Stir mixture into flour. Stir well until smooth.

Ladle mixture into cups and fill a little more than half-way. Put cups on a baking sheet and put in *cold* oven. This is quite important—do not preheat the oven.

Bake 50 minutes, letting oven reach 400°F.

Serve immediately or the popovers will collapse since it's heated air that puffs them up, rather than leavening.

Never Fail Popovers

(4 large or 6 small popovers)

1 cup whole wheat flour, sifted
1 teaspoon salt (optional)
2 eggs
1 cup milk
1 tablespoon melted butter, cooled

AND NOW
IT'S MY TURN...

Though several of my own recipes are scattered through the book (in the Triticale and Sourdough sections), there are some other breads that I love to bake. Several were the Christmas gifts that I baked for my island neighbors, others just happened to find their way into my overflowing files after I tested them for a dinner party or for my own delight. Here are 10, ranging from flat breads to quick breads to traditional breads—all of them easy, and all of them delicious. The first—Bagels—holds a special place in my heart. Read on and you will soon know why.

The *New York Times* called them unsweetened doughnuts with *rigor mortis,* and though they began as a distinctive part of the Jewish culture, especially in New York, bagels are now found almost anywhere in the United States. They are unusual in that they are first simmered in water before baking and thus are sometimes called "water bagels" or, as in the recipe I've given, "egg bagels."

Among my own students, the bagel has become a strange mark of accomplishment—and there are mornings when two or three or more people come over to the house to show me plastic bags filled with the round doughnut-shaped breads, proudly holding them up to the light in a triumphant gesture.

One of my best students is a pathologist, a man who began to bake quite late in life. Determined, precise, Norman Cooper baked his first bagels and made his way into the garden, where I was busy harvesting some lovely tomatoes. I looked at the bagels in awe. Each and every one was a perfect circle—the same size, same weight. I asked about the perfection of size, for home-baked breads seldom achieve it. Normally, one bagel is larger than another—or smaller—it doesn't really matter, for they all taste magnificent, especially with cream cheese and smoked salmon.

Norman told me that when he had gotten my recipe, I had told him just how long each strand of dough had to be before making a circle, but he had not remembered the *width* of the strands.

The Breads:

Bagels
Buttermilk Rye/Whole
   Wheat Bread
Dill-Onion Bread
Hiivaleipa **(Finnish Sour Rye)**
Irish Soda Bread
Irish Brown Bread
Soaked-Wheat Bread
   (Unleavened)
Jalapeno **Corn Bread**
   with Cheese
Pita **(Middle Eastern)**
Zucchini Parmesan Bread

Being a scientist, he knew that the recipe made 15 bagels, and that each one was to be 7 inches long before making a circle. So he rolled out the dough to *105 inches in length* and, using a ruler, cut it into 15 equal parts, each one identical, each one the exact same size. Therefore, his finished bagels were all exactly alike—certainly better than those of his teacher.

Bagels

(14 or 15 bagels)

1 medium potato, boiled
2 cups water
1 package dry yeast
1 tablespoon honey
4 cups unbleached white flour, sifted
1 tablespoon salt (optional)
1 whole egg
1 egg separated; reserve yolk for glaze
3 tablespoons oil
3 quarts water

Glaze:

1 egg yolk
1 teaspoon cold water
coarse salt, poppy or sesame seeds (optional)

Peel 1 medium-size potato and cut it into fairly thick slices. Put the slices in a saucepan and cover the potatoes with water, making certain that you use at least 2 cups of water, since some will evaporate with the cooking. Boil the potato slices about 15 minutes or until soft. Measure out 1 cup of the water. The potatoes can be put aside and used for dinner. Let the cup of potato water cool to about 90°F.

Proof yeast in ½ the potato water with ½ teaspoon of the honey. Sift the flour into a large bowl and add the salt. Stir the yeast mixture into the flour and add the whole egg, the remaining egg white, balance of the potato water, remaining honey, and oil. Blend with flour to make a firm dough, adding more flour if necessary.

Turn out onto a floured board or counter and knead for 8 to 10 minutes, or until dough springs back when touched. Place dough in an oiled bowl, coat top with a small amount of oil to keep from drying out and cover with a towel. Place bowl in a warm, draft-free place and let the dough rise to double (about 1½ hours). Dough is ready when you push down with 2 fingers and the indentations remain. If they spring back, let it rise a bit longer.

Preheat the oven to 425°F.

Boil the 3 quarts of water in a large pot.

Punch down the dough and knead for about 2 or 3 minutes. Pull off or cut dough into about 14 or 15 pieces. Roll each piece between floured hands until it is about 7 inches in length and ¾ inches thick. Coil each length into a ring, moistening the ends so that they stick when turned onto each other. Let the rings stand about 10 minutes on an oiled board or pan.

Using a slotted spoon, slide each bagel into the pot of boiling water, being careful not to crowd them too much. They will float.

Boil 2 minutes on each side. Remove with the slotted spoon and place them on oiled cookie sheets. They will be very slippery.

Mix the remaining egg yolk with the 1 teaspoon of water and glaze each bagel with a pastry brush. Sprinkle with coarse salt, and poppy or sesame seeds, if desired.

Bake 20 to 25 minutes until golden brown. Place on a wire rack to cool.

NOTE: Beautiful bagels can be made using whole wheat flour in place of the unbleached white flour. They're great that way too—just different from what grandma used to make.

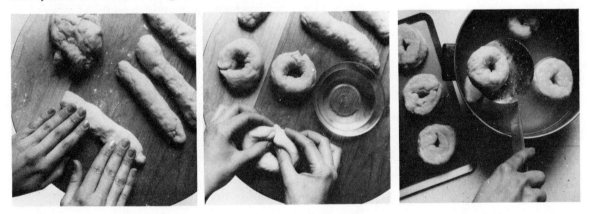

Buttermilk Rye/Whole Wheat Bread

(3 medium loaves)

3½ cups rye flour (or
pumpernickel or triticale)
4 cups whole wheat flour
1½ tablespoons salt (optional)
1½ teaspoons baking soda
2 tablespoons baking powder
½ cup caraway seeds
1 quart buttermilk,
room temperature

When I found that Irish-style breads were easy to make and marvelous to look at (not to mention how they taste), it occurred to me that the use of buttermilk could be extended to other breads as well. The cookbooks seem to avoid them for some reason, yet they are healthful, simple to prepare, and the results always bring some appreciative comment from guests. I began to experiment some years ago and I found that a whole range of healthful breads could be baked—with rye, whole wheat, and later, with triticale flour.

In a large bowl, mix the dry ingredients, then add the buttermilk to make a sticky dough. Mix with a wooden spoon or with floured hands. (Though this is technically a no-knead bread, I like to get my hands in there and blend the ingredients thoroughly.) If the dough seems too sticky, add more flour.

Form the dough into any of the basic shapes—long, oblong, oval, or round. Shape the breads smoothly with your hands and place them on a buttered and floured cookie sheet, leaving room between them for expansion. With a floured knife, cut a design in the top. Do it deeply—a cross, star, anything that will allow the bread to expand evenly instead of bursting open at the seams.

Dust the tops with flour, then blow off the excess.

Bake at 425°F. for about 50 minutes. The tops will brown nicely and the bottoms should sound hollow when tapped.

Cool on wire racks.

I make frequent trips to Atlanta for business reasons and, over the years, I've gotten to know many of my clients socially. At a dinner party in Dee Jackson's home one evening, I was introduced to another bread baker—Patsy Wagner, who then lived in Norcross, Georgia. Of course, the conversation turned to breads and she promised to send a favorite recipe to me. It has been one of my standbys for seven years now.

Dissolve the yeast in the warm water and stir in the teaspoon of honey. Set aside to proof.

In a large bowl, combine the cottage cheese, additional honey, onion, butter, dill seed, salt, and baking soda. Add the yeast mixture and stir. Then add the eggs and stir again.

Add enough flour to make a stiff dough, beating well after each addition. Turn the dough out onto a lightly floured surface and knead for 8 to 10 minutes or until dough is smooth and elastic. If the dough seems too sticky, add more flour.

Place in a greased bowl, turn once to coat the top, cover and place in a warm spot to rise to double (about 1 hour).

Stir down, knead gently for 1 or 2 minutes and shape into 3 loaves. Place in buttered, medium-size (8 × 4 inches) loaf pans. Cover and let rise to double in a warm spot (about 45 minutes).

Bake at 350°F. for 40 to 50 minutes or until loaves test done.

Cool on wire racks.

Dill-Onion Bread

(3 medium loaves)

2 packages dry yeast
¼ cup warm water
1 teaspoon honey
2 cups large-curd cottage cheese
3 tablespoons honey
6 teaspoons grated fresh onion
4 tablespoons melted butter
4 teaspoons dill seed
3 teaspoons salt (optional)
½ teaspoon baking soda
2 eggs, unbeaten
4 to 4½ cups whole wheat flour

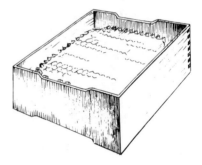

Hiivaleipa (Finnish Sour Rye)

(2 loaves)

3½ cups rye flour
3 cups flat beer (or buttermilk or potato water)
2 packages dry yeast
½ cup warm water
1 teaspoon honey
2 tablespoons salt*
4 cups unbleached white flour

Glaze:

1 egg
1 tablespoon water

My friend, Helena D'Avino, originally comes from Finland, and her stories of lonely nights in the Arctic taking care of an isolated weather station have always intrigued me. One evening, knowing that I baked bread, she turned and said, "You know what I haven't tasted since coming from Finland—a *Hiivaleipa!*" The word sounded Greek, but I knew that it had to be Finnish in origin, so I went home and looked in my files. A few days later, I tried my first bread, brought it to Helena's house and watched as she carefully tasted it. Looking up in surprise, she exclaimed, "Why, it's a *Hiivaleipa!*" Which is what I thought I had baked. I was very very proud.

The pronunciation, by the way, is Heé-va-lay-pa.

Begin the recipe 4 days before baking. Make a starter by combining 1 cup of the rye flour with 1 cup flat beer and cover the bowl loosely with a towel or with plastic wrap.

Put the bowl in a warm place. Stir the mixture once a day—on the fourth day it should be bubbling.

When you are ready to bake, mix the yeast in ½ cup of the warm water, add the honey, stir and set aside to proof. Put the starter in a large bowl, add 2 more cups of the beer, add the yeast mixture, the salt, and 2½ more cups of the rye flour. Stir it well with a wooden spoon, then add—1 cup at a time—the 4 cups of unbleached white flour. The dough should not be too sticky. If it is, add more flour.

Then, turn the dough out onto a lightly floured surface, knead for about 10 minutes, adding more flour if necessary. The dough should be smooth and velvety when finished. Place the dough in a greased bowl, turn once to coat the top, cover and place in a warm spot to double in bulk (about 1 to 1½ hours).

Turn out onto floured surface, knead for 1 or 2 minutes and divide the dough in half. Form each half into a large doughnut-shaped ring and place on a greased baking sheet. Cover lightly with plastic wrap and let rise to double in a warm place (about 45 minutes to 1 hour).

Bake at 400°F. for 45 to 50 minutes. About 10 to 15 minutes before breads are finished, mix 1 egg with 1 tablespoon of water and brush on breads. Cool on wire racks.

---

*The salt, though traditional, may be eliminated if you choose to do so.

This is a "quick bread"—it uses no yeast and it's a traditional Irish bread, thus the use of unbleached white flour in the recipe. However, the recipe that follows it (Irish Brown Bread) was developed for those of us who prefer whole grains in our baking. Both are delicious. Irish breads make marvelous toast and, when sliced thinly and covered with jam or marmalade, it's a mouth-watering breakfast treat.

One of my friends on the island, Paul Connelly, is a secret lover of the bread and he asked me for a loaf the next time I baked it. I gave him one, then forgot about it for some months. One day he met me on one of our island walks and I asked if he had liked it. *Liked it!!??* He still had it! He kept it hidden in the freezer and each week he took it out and sawed off a frozen piece, let it thaw, and then ate it in secret, away from his family. He just wasn't going to share his favorite bread with anyone! I have since baked another loaf for him.

Preheat the oven to 375°F.

In a medium-size bowl, combine the buttermilk, eggs, and the baking soda. Stir vigorously with a wooden spoon.

In a second large bowl, combine the flour, raisins, honey, caraway seeds, baking powder, and salt, stirring with a wooden spoon after each ingredient is added. Pour the buttermilk mixture into the flour mixture and stir well until everything is blended. If you like, flour your hands and then complete the mixing. The bread does not require kneading, however. If the dough seems too damp, add more flour.

Divide the batter into 2 equal parts and place in 2 buttered and floured loaf pans (9 × 5 inches)—or place in small, round ceramic bowls, buttered and floured. Bake 1 hour and 15 minutes or until well browned and a cake tester comes out clean. Let the loaves cool in the pans for 15 minutes, then turn out onto wire racks. Cool thoroughly before freezing.

Irish Soda Bread

(2 loaves)

4 cups buttermilk,
    room temperature
2 eggs
½ teaspoon baking soda
7 to 8 cups unbleached white flour
2 cups black raisins
3 tablespoons honey
½ cup caraway seeds
2 tablespoons plus 2 teaspoons
    baking powder
1 tablespoon salt*

---

*The salt, though traditional, may be eliminated if you choose to do so.

Irish Brown Bread

(2 loaves)

8 cups stone-ground
whole wheat flour
2 teaspoons salt (optional)
½ teaspoon baking soda
2 tablespoons baking powder
½ cup white raisins
½ cup caraway seeds
1 tablespoon honey
4 cups buttermilk,
room temperature

This is basically the Irish Soda Bread recipe, but is made with whole grain flour.

In a large bowl, mix the flour, salt, baking soda, and baking powder. Add the raisins and stir to coat them thoroughly. Add the caraway seeds and stir. Add the honey and then pour the buttermilk slowly into the bowl, mixing as you add it. The dough should be sticky, but easy to handle. However, if it feels too sticky, add more flour.

Using floured hands (or a wooden spoon if you don't like to get dough between your fingers), mix thoroughly while still in the bowl. Divide the dough into 2 parts and form free-form shapes—oval or round or long—and place on buttered and floured cookie sheet. Cut deeply into the dough with a floured knife—in the shape of a cross—then dust lightly with flour and blow off excess.

Bake 40 minutes at 425°F. Cool before slicing.

Soaked-Wheat Bread (Unleavened)

(2 loaves)

¼ cup oil
3¼ cups water
½ teaspoon salt (optional)
4 cups stone-ground
whole wheat flour
2 cups whole wheat kernels

This is a chewy, healthful, unleavened bread. Actually, the whole wheat kernels can be added to any bread for nutrition.

In a bowl, mix the oil, 1¼ cups of the water, and the salt; then add the whole wheat flour, 1 cup at a time, stirring after each addition. The dough should be stiff. Turn it out onto a lightly floured surface and knead only until smooth. Place in a lightly greased bowl, turn once to coat the top and cover. Place in a warm spot for 24 to 36 hours.

Soak the whole wheat kernels in the remaining 2 cups of water and leave for 24 hours. Then drain the water and chop the soaked kernels coarsely by hand or in a blender or food processor. When chopped, mix with the dough, divide into 2 loaves and set on a greased and floured baking sheet, covered, for about 30 minutes.

Bake at 325°F. for 1 hour and 15 minutes or until breads test done.

Cool on wire racks.

This bread was my Christmas gift a few years ago—delivered by wagon, as usual, and given with a mild warning that this bread was quite different from any I had baked before. It has a chili-pepper tang to it—not too hot, but very evident nevertheless.

In a bowl, stir in the cornmeal, flour, honey, salt, baking powder, and baking soda.

In a separate bowl, beat the 3 eggs lightly and then stir in the buttermilk, oil, and add the liquid to the first bowl. Stir.

Stir in the can of cream-style corn, add the *jalapeno* peppers (make sure you've taken the seeds out and chopped the peppers), and then add the cheddar cheese and the grated onion. Mix after each addition, using a wooden spoon.

Pour the batter into 3 well-oiled, medium-size (8 × 4-inch) loaf pans and bake at 425°F. for 35 to 40 minutes or until a cake tester comes out clean and dry.

Let the breads stand for 10 to 15 minutes in the pans before turning them out onto wire racks to cool.

Jalapeno Corn Bread with Cheese

(3 medium loaves)

2½ cups yellow cornmeal
1 cup stone-ground
    whole wheat flour
1 tablespoon honey
1 tablespoon salt*
4 teaspoons baking powder
1 teaspoon baking soda
3 eggs
1½ cups buttermilk,
    room temperature
½ cup oil
1 1-pound can cream-style corn
6 *jalapeno* chili-peppers, seeded
    and chopped
2½ cups grated sharp
    cheddar cheese
1 large grated onion

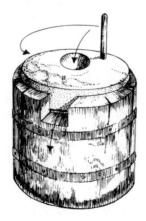

*The salt, though traditional, may be eliminated if you choose to do so.

Pita

(Middle Eastern)

(8 to 10 breads)

2 packages dry yeast
2 cups warm water
½ teaspoon honey
¼ cup olive oil
1 tablespoon salt (optional)
5 to 6 cups whole wheat flour
cornmeal

This bread is marvelously versatile. It originated in the Middle East and sometimes is known as "pocket bread." The breads come out flat, but with a hollow center so that they can be filled with all kinds of marvelous things. They're fun to make because they puff up in the oven as they're baking, giving everyone a great show through the oven window. I suppose that I was most flattered when, one day, one of our Lebanese neighbors asked *me* to show *her* how to bake *Pita!*

Mix the yeast in ½ cup of the warm water, add the honey, stir and set aside to proof.

In a large mixing bowl, add the remaining 1½ cups of water, the oil, salt, and the yeast mixture. Then stir in 5 cups of the flour, 1 cup at a time, mixing vigorously with each addition. Turn out onto a lightly floured board and knead for 10 minutes, adding the additional cup of flour if the dough gets too sticky. When the kneading is finished, the dough should be smooth and elastic. Shape into a ball, place in a greased bowl, turning once to coat the top, cover and let rise to double in a warm spot for about 1½ to 2 hours.

Punch down on floured surface, let the dough rest for about 10 minutes and then divide it into 8 to 10 pieces, shaping each piece into a ball. Knead each ball for 1 or 2 minutes, cover and let rest for about 30 minutes.

Using a floured rolling pin, flatten each ball into a circle about 8 inches in diameter and about ⅛ inch thick. Dust 2 baking sheets with cornmeal, place 2 of the circles on each sheet, cover, and let rest for about 30 minutes. Let the remaining circles stay on the floured surface—when you have baked the first breads and the cookie sheets are empty, you will bake the remaining *Pita*. (Each time you place new breads on the cookie sheets, dust them with cornmeal again.)

The oven is set for 500°F.—very hot for these little breads, and therein lies the secret. Place 1 sheet on the lowest rack for 5 minutes. *Do not open the oven* during this first baking. After 5 minutes, transfer the sheet to a higher shelf and let it bake for 3 to 5 more minutes. The breads will puff up and be lightly browned when they're ready.

When done, remove from oven, place the next tray on the bottom for its 5-minute, high-heat baking and remove the first ones to a wire rack to cool.

Continue the process until all the breads are baked. Let them cool—rewarm them for serving, or freeze them for future use.

Actually, I stole this recipe. (I cannot tell a lie.) It originally appeared in my wife's cookbook *Eggplant and Squash: A Versatile Feast* (New York: Atheneum, 1976) and I now have it firmly ensconced in my own files. Of course, if she ever wants to use it again, I think I would graciously allow her to.

Preheat oven to 350°F.

Butter a 9 × 5-inch loaf pan. In a bowl, mix the flour, cheese, baking powder, baking soda, salt, and shredded zucchini.

In a separate bowl, mix the buttermilk, honey, melted butter, eggs, and onion until smooth. Then add the liquid mixture to the dry ingredients all at once and mix until just blended.

The batter should be somewhat dry. Spread in the loaf pan and bake for about 1 hour, or until a toothpick inserted in the center comes out clean and the bread pulls away from the sides of the pan.

Turn out onto wire rack to cool. Let cool thoroughly before slicing.

Zucchini Parmesan Bread

(1 loaf)

3 cups whole wheat flour
4 tablespoons grated
   Parmesan cheese
5 teaspoons baking powder
½ teaspoon baking soda
1½ teaspoons salt (optional)
1 medium zucchini, unpeeled and
   shredded (about ½
   to ¾ pound)
1 cup buttermilk,
   room temperature
4 tablespoons honey
6 tablespoons melted butter
2 eggs, beaten
3 tablespoons grated onion

8 What If . . .

Frankly, not too many things can go wrong when you bake your own bread. You are dealing with only a few constants—flour, liquid, and a leavener and, in addition, an oven. Generally, one or the other has been used incorrectly and, with practice, you should be able to bake a perfect loaf every time. However, there are some common (and a few not-so-common) things that seem to happen to bread bakers. Your problem is probably included in this short addendum:

What if . . . the dough doesn't rise at all? The chances are that the problem lies with the yeast. When you use dry yeast, make certain to check the date of expiration. With compressed yeast, the reason for proofing (see Index) is to prevent just such an occurrence. Another reason might be that you used a too-cold liquid, thus not activating the yeast. Also you might have used a liquid that was too hot, thus killing the yeast. Another possibility is that one or more of the other ingredients was too cold—the flour, for example. Remember to have all your ingredients at room temperature.

What if . . . you live in a high altitude area? Does it affect your bread baking? It certainly does — but to no great extent. Dough will rise faster at an altitude over one mile — and you may want to decrease the amount of yeast you use by 50 percent. Another result of baking bread in lofty places like Denver or Mexico City may be that the dough does not rise to exactly double in bulk. When you think the rising time is sufficient, just check it by putting two fingers into the dough and, if the indentations remain, it is ready for the next step. Two of our bakers, Margaret and Haven Holsapple (see Index) have answered many of these questions.

What if . . . you don't have enough bread pans and you have, as the author suggested, doubled your recipe? First off, I suggest that you buy some inexpensive extra pans next time you're out shopping. My cabinet has 14, ready and able to do service. However, for that moment, either bake them free form on a cookie sheet or place them, shaped, side by side in a large roasting pan with plenty of space between them to allow for expansion. Remember, with no loaf pan to hold them, they will expand outward as well as upward.

What if . . . an emergency comes up and you can't complete the bread? Since cold will not harm the dough—and, in fact, some recipes require that you hold dough overnight—merely wrap it in plastic and pop it in the refrigerator. The cold will retard the rising. Dough can be kept for one or two days in this way.

What if . . . you have no time to allow the bread to rise twice but you'd like to finish the bread? No harm, the bread will just have a coarser texture. Remember that the number of rises determines the texture of your bread—the more rises, the finer the texture. You might also want to try *three* rises in a recipe that calls for only two. Quite all right.

What if . . . the bread is too heavy? Chances are that you used too much flour, or that the dough did not rise sufficiently before you put it in the oven. It all comes back to getting the "feel" of the dough, not a very difficult achievement, as you will no doubt find out.

What if . . . the loaf has hard lumps in it? This may happen more often in quick breads than in yeast breads, though both are subject to this not-very-serious condition. Try mixing your dough more thoroughly next time. Also, you might try adding your flour in smaller amounts as you mix. The "hard lump" syndrome is one of the reasons that I still like to turn out quick breads onto a floured counter and complete the mixing with my hands. Though this is not technically "kneading," it accomplishes the smoothing-out of the dough in much the same way.

What if . . . your free-form loaves spread outward too much? Of course, they should also go "upward" and sculpt a lovely shape in your oven, but if the loaves seem to flatten out, they may not have enough flour in them. The dough may be too soft. If you're in doubt, try baking them in loaf pans next time until you get the texture worked out.

What if . . . the breads come out of the oven in uneven loaves? Chances are they'll taste great, but you may be having a problem with your oven temperature. Ovens are notorious for having different temperatures at different parts of the baking area—hotter near the top or in some corners than directly in the middle. And yet, *every* bread can't be placed right smack in the middle of the oven. Space your pans or your free-form breads, then turn them and move them in the oven as the dough begins to set. I always know that the bread in the upper right portion of my oven will begin to brown near the back at least 10 minutes before the others do. You can also turn the cookie sheet around if you're baking free-form breads. Just do it quickly so that the oven temperature doesn't drop too much. (And use pot holders or gloves!)

What if . . . the bread bursts in the oven? The second rise was probably too long and the dough burst on contact with the oven heat. This is a common mistake. Don't let the dough rise too much after it's been shaped. Remember that it expands yet again during baking.

What if . . . the loaf is cracked along the sides or near the edges? That's why many recipes call for cutting the tops of loaves with either a razor blade or a knife right before baking. The slashes allow the bread to expand evenly. Another reason might well be that the oven was too hot and the loaves expanded too quickly.

What if . . . the loaf breaks away from the crust at the bottom? Again you might be having a temperature problem in the oven and when the bread comes into contact with the heat, the bottom is baked quickly while the top breaks away and expands too much. Watch the temperature—it may be too hot. In any case, the bread will probably taste just fine. It just won't look too professional.

What if . . . the bread feels too damp after baking? It probably didn't bake long enough. Change the baking time in your recipes. Also, you might add a bit more flour to your dough the next time you bake that bread. Many whole grain breads create this problem because, by its very nature, the mixed dough of these breads is more moist than dough in other breads.

What if . . . the bread is filled with air bubbles? The dough may have risen too fast (too warm a room or too much yeast)—or you may have let the dough rise too long. Again, there is no harm done to the taste of the bread.

What if . . . the bread seems to dry out quickly? You'll find this to be true of all your homemade breads, since no preservatives are used. Commercial loaves may last longer, but they can't compete in any other way. To moisten a dried-out loaf, simply sprinkle the bread with water and put it in your oven at 300°F. for about 10 to 15 minutes. If you want to keep the loaf moist, wrap it in aluminum foil. On the other hand, if you want the crust to be crisp, keep it unwrapped during the warming time and serve it at once.

9 Mail-Order Sources

Of course, the basic flours are always available to most of us—unbleached white, some stone-ground whole wheat, and possibly rye. Natural foods stores are springing up all over the country and by searching them out, I have been able to obtain triticale, dark rye, and high gluten flour in Montana, Louisiana, and Kentucky. The standard bread pans are also easily obtainable in supermarkets and hardware stores.

But some of us have other requirements, aside from not living near enough to supply resources. Possibly the family is larger now, and you'd like to use oversize loaf pans when you bake. French loaf pans are fun to work with but not so easy to find in smaller communities. And—in keeping with the trend toward more nutritious breads (thus, home baked)—some of us have begun grinding our own grain into flour.

Whatever the potential problem, I thought it might help if I listed some mail-order sources around the country, with some indication as to just what it is they supply. Some offer catalogs. Others are retail stores. All are happy to supply the needs of far-flung bread bakers who require their services.

Flour and Grains

EDWARDS MILL, THE SCHOOL OF THE OZARKS, POINT LOOKOUT, MO 65726   This mail-order resource was recommended to me by bread-baker Suzanne Corbett (see Index). She buys all her stone-ground flour from them. They carry cornmeal, whole wheat flour, wheat germ, unbleached flour, rye, and cracked wheat. Send for their order blank to get a complete list. They accept orders for as little as 1½ pounds and go up to 25-pound bags.

GREAT VALLEY MILLS, QUAKERTOWN, BUCKS COUNTY, PA 18951   They carry a choice of whole grain flours, pumpernickel, rye meal, brown rice flour, and graham flour. The catalog is free.

GROVER COMPANY, 2111 S. INDUSTRIAL PARK AVE., TEMPE, AZ 85282   They carry a whole range of mail-order products, including first-grade whole grains packed in buckets for storage. Everything is stone ground. You'll find rye, triticale, hard red wheat, buckwheat, corn, millet, legumes, honey, long grain brown rice (gluten free), rice flour for special diets, nonfat dry milk, sprouting seeds, and yeast. They have a catalog available. TELEPHONE TOLL-FREE: (800) 528-1406

LETOBA FARMS, BOX 180, RTE 3, LYONS, KS 67554   Whole grain wheat, rye, and other flours are available, as well as corn and millet. A catalog is available.

THE NAUVOO MILLING COMPANY, NAUVOO, IL 62354   The town of Nauvoo is worth a side trip if you're ever in the area. I discovered it while filming for the Lincoln Heritage Trail. Nauvoo was the jumping-off place for the Mormons when they went West. The Nauvoo Milling Company grinds all of its whole grain on a stone mill. They have finely ground whole wheat flours and high protein hard wheat flour. They'll send a list with prices if you request it.

SHILOH FARMS, BOX 97, HIGHWAY 59, SULPHUR SPRINGS, AR 72768. BRANCH OFFICE: WHITE OAK RD., MARTINDALE, PA 17549   Shiloh played an important role in my search for the triticale story so that I might include the recipes you'll find in this book. I first spotted the name on the package of triticale flour that I'd purchased in my local store. I telephoned and the people there were most gracious and helpful. Through Shiloh, I first met Ron Kershen of Canyon, Texas, who provided much of the information in the section on triticale flours and recipes. Though Shiloh is well-known through its products distributed in natural foods stores, Shiloh also mails a variety of grains and flours to customers all over the country. Naturally, triticale is included in the Shiloh list, as well as rye grain, hard-berry wheat, sunflower meal, rice flour, and barley. The catalog is free.

VERMONT COUNTRY STORE, WESTON, VT 05161   Their specialties include oat flour, ground oatmeal flour, and graham flour. Their catalog is 25¢.

WILSON MILLING COMPANY, P.O. BOX 481, LA CROSSE, KS 67548   Their organically grown wheat is high gluten, high protein winter wheat. Wilson also sells whole wheat berries, stone-ground whole wheat flour, cracked wheat and whole soy beans. They'll send a price list upon request.

Maple Syrup

Though honey is now available in most every supermarket and grocery store around the country, I have found that maple syrup—the pure, unblemished, untainted kind—is sometimes difficult to locate. (I recently read the label of a commercial "maple pancake syrup" and found that it contained only 4 percent maple syrup!) I thought it wise, therefore, to include three mail-order sources in case you can't get pure maple syrup in your neighborhood.

The producers generally grade the syrup as either A, B or C. For those of us brought up on the theory that we must always buy and eat the best, the term Grade A seemed to cover that requirement. Here is one case, however, where I strongly recommend you select Grade B or Grade C when buying maple syrup. Grade A is the most refined of the syrups and thus the extended boiling removes much of the nutrition. I suggest that you order Grade B for your bread-baking needs (and for your pancakes). It's much healthier.

BROOKMAN FARMS, BOX 157, R.R. 2, SOUTH DAYTON, NY 14138   For many years I thought that Vermont was the only place to buy pure maple syrup. I later discovered New Hampshire—and then found that New York State is the largest producer of this fine, characteristically American product. The Brookmans have syrup available in pints, quarts, half-gallons, and gallons and they'll send a price list if you request it.

BROOKSIDE FARM (HENRY AND CORNELIA SWAYZE), TUNBRIDGE, VT 05077   As with many of the better-run maple syrup producers, Brookside is a family farm. The Swayzes sell both Grade A and Grade B syrups in pints, quarts, or gallon sizes. A free price list is available.

CLARK HILL SUGARY, CANAAN, NH 03741   Their syrup is available in pints, quarts, and half-gallons. A free brochure is available.

Equipment and Utensils

I realize that most of the standard items are available locally. However, when it comes to special baking projects, you may find it difficult to get the item you need. The suppliers listed below all have catalogs available and each of them carries a large stock of the hard-to-get equipment.

Though the normal recipes are geared to loaf pans that measure either 9¾ × 5¾ × 2¾ inches or 8½ × 5¾ × 2¾ inches, larger loaf pans are available in 10, 12, 14, 16 and 18-inch sizes. Two-bread French loaf pans (16 × 6 inches) and Italian loaf pans (16 × 9 inches) are also available by mail order. My own pride and joy is my five-loaf black steel French loaf pan that I purchased from H. Roth and Son (address below), allowing me to make five sourdoughs all at the same time.

Some bakers feel that black steel gives a better crust to their breads—and there are mail-order suppliers who handcraft their own utensils for shipment around the country. So, whether you need a special *brioche* mold, cookie sheets, cooling racks, or unusual size pans, try the mail-order sources we've listed.

BAZAAR DE LA CUISINE, 1003 SECOND AVE., NEW YORK, NY 10022   This marvelous store has a huge array of international cookware and you'll find every conceivable kind of bread-baking accessory in stock. They even sell a Lucite bagel cradle for your home-baked bagels or English muffins. A catalog is available.

BRIDGE COMPANY, 212 E. 52ND ST., NEW YORK, NY 10022   This is a favorite shopping spot for gourmet cooks, professionals, and bread bakers who are looking for unusual and finely crafted utensils. A catalog is available.

H. ROTH AND SON, 1577 FIRST AVE., NEW YORK, NY 10028   Since I live right in New York, I make a visit to H. Roth and Son about four times a year to find the hard-to-get items that I need, including flours, spices, and my favorite bread pans. If I were to choose one single perfect source, this one would be it. A catalog is, of course, available.

STONE HEARTH INC., 40 PARK ST., BROOKLYN, NY 11206   They make exquisite handcrafted black steel and tin-dipped baking utensils—bread pans, loaf pans, French bread pans, cookie sheets, muffin pans, popover pans, and bread pots. They're not cheap by any means, but you may just want to try them for yourself to see if, indeed, the crusts get crustier and the crumb of the bread has a better texture. Stone Hearth has area representatives all over the country and, if you write, they'll send the name of the person you can contact. They also have a catalog.

WILLIAMS-SONOMA (MAIL-ORDER DEPT.), P.O. BOX 3792, SAN FRANCISCO, CA 94119   For many readers, it may be easy to visit one of their six stores: San Francisco, Beverly Hills, Palo Alto, and Costa Mesa in California; Dallas and Houston in Texas. For those of you who need the mail-order service, a catalog is available.   TELEPHONE: (415) 658-7845

These are items which will take a little more time to consider, should you decide to grind your own flour. First of all, unlike the pots, pans, and cookie sheets, mills and mixers can be really expensive. With the trend toward natural foods expanding every day, more and more people are grinding the grains right in their own homes. As a result, more and more mills and mixers are appearing on the market—some of them good, many of them not-so-good.

If you do decide to investigate, you should be thinking of several prerequisites before you buy:

- What is the size of your family and your baking needs? Does it pay to invest a large amount of money if you use only a few pounds of flour each month? Price becomes a factor then.

- Is the machine easy to operate and clean? How much flour can you grind per minute?

- Does the mill slice the grain first, then grind it? Mills that do not slice first have a tendency to build up heat, destroying some of the nutritive value of the grain. Other mills use a fan to cool them, and you may find the grain "blowing in the wind."

For the past year, I've been reading as many brochures and ads on grinders and mixers as I've been able to find and, of the many machines that I've seen, the ones below seem to meet most of the qualifications. I must add that I have not yet succumbed to grinding my own flour, and that's probably because I can find every kind of grain I need right here in New York. But—I have been tempted from time to time.

BLAKESLEE UNI-MIXER—GROVER COMPANY, 2111 S. IN-DUSTRIAL PARK AVE., TEMPE, AZ 85282 The Uni-Mixer features a 600-watt motor with a very sturdy base, all metal construction and it has 14 accessories available in addition to the dough hook attachment. The five-quart model can mix four loaves at one time and the price at this writing is $239. The seven-quart model can mix enough for six loaves and the price is $259. You can get brochures and further information from the Grover Company or from G.S. BLAKESLEE AND CO., 1844 S. LARAMIE AVE., CHICAGO, IL 60650 TELEPHONE TOLL-FREE: (800) 528-1406

Electric
Stone Mills
and Mixers

BOSCH BREAD MIXER—HOWARD AND AGNES ARNS (AUTHORIZED DEALER), 104 S. 200 EAST, CEDAR CITY, UT 84720 Five loaves of bread dough can be mixed in a single batch and 20 additional accessories are available in addition to the dough hook attachment. It comes with a standard plastic bowl, but a larger stainless steel bowl is available for larger jobs. At this writing, the five-loaf model is priced at $270.

MAGIC MILL HOME WHEAT GRINDER, 1135 PAYNE AVE., ST. PAUL, MN 55101 It comes in a wood cabinet, is 18¼ inches deep × 15¾ inches high × 11¼ inches wide. The stainless steel flour holder has a capacity of 26 cups and it is priced at about $275, as of this writing.   TELEPHONE: (612) 774-0955

MARATHON UNI-MILL—GROVER COMPANY, 2111 S. IN-DUSTRIAL PARK AVE., TEMPE, AZ 85282 The Uni-Mill features shear-slice action for cooler grinding and it grinds one pound of flour per minute. It also has a good adjustable grinding range from ultra-fine to coarse and it can grind cereal, beans, oily seeds and hard corn. It is 16½ inches deep × 13¾ inches high × 10¾ inches wide and the price at the time of this writing is close to that of the Magic Mill, about $280. Literature is available. TELEPHONE TOLL-FREE: (800) 528-1406

Photograph Credits

Carl Doney	iii, 1, 33, 34, 67, 68, 101, 102, 135, 136, 169, 170, 203, 204, 237, 238, 271, 272
Mitchell T. Mandel	v, xv, 4, 7, 10, 20, 27, 29, 30, 31, 35, 36, 41, 42, 43, 45, 46 (left), 48, 49 (left), 54, 58, 63, 71, 83, 87, 93, 94, 106, 108, 116, 159, 160, 164, 178, 179 (right), 193, 197, 202, 212, 242, 245, 251, 275, 278, 288, 299, 311, 319, 321, 330, 334
Fred Smith Associates	44, 46 (right), 49 (right), 176, 179 (left), 188, 189, 201, 209, 211, 291, 292
Ed Rath *Omaha World Herald*	56, 57
Mason Valley News **(Yerington, Nevada)**	59
Elise Whitney Lynch	72
Mel London	77, 79, 107, 149, 152, 153, 280, 281, 283
G. Guibor	81 (top three)

INDEX

Italicized page numbers refer to color illustrations.

Favorite Recipes

Favorite Recipes

Favorite Recipes